Chelsea School Research Centre Editon
Volume 5

Maurice Roche (ed.)

Sport, Popular Culture and Identity

in collaboration with the ICCR
(Interdisciplinary Centre for Comparative Research
in the Social Sciences, Vienna)

Meyer & Meyer Verlag

Die Deutsche Bibliothek – CIP-Einheitsaufnahme

Sport, popular culture and identity /
Maurice Roche (ed.).
– Aachen : Meyer und Meyer, 1998
(Chelsea School Research Centre Edition ; Vol. 5)
ISBN 3-89124-468-1

© 1998 by Meyer & Meyer Verlag, Aachen
Cover design: Walter J. Neumann, N & N Design-Studio, Aachen
Cover exposure: frw, Reiner Wahlen, Aachen
Typesetting: Myrene L. McFee
Printed by Firma Mennicken, Aachen
Printed in Germany
ISBN 3-89124-468-1

PREFACE

Most of the chapters in this book have been developed from papers which were originally invited for and/or presented at an international workshop on 'Social Identity and Popular Culture'. This was held as part of a Euroconference on 'Collective Identity and Symbolic Representation' held at the Fondation Nationale des Sciences Politiques in Paris, July 1996, with support from the European Commission. The three main organisers of the conference were the Centre d'Etudes et des Recherches Internationale (CERI), the European Association for the Advancement of Social Sciences (EAASS) and the Interdisciplinary Centre for Comparative Research in the Social Sciences (ICCR, Vienna).

The local conference organizer, John Crowley of CERI and EAASS, helped to make the meeting in general a great success, and helped substantially in the preparation of our workshop. The ICCR was the main sponsor of the event, and its Director Ronald Pohoryles, Vice-Director Liana Giorgi, and Administrator Roman Tronner gave valuable assistance and encouragement both at the meeting and also subsequently in relation to the production of this book. Alan Tomlinson of Brighton University's Chelsea School Research Centre (CSRC), who participated in the workshop, encouraged the development of the papers in the form of a book project in this CSRC Editions series. The ICCR and the CSRC together share the credit for making this book possible.

Myrene McFee played a major role in turning the idea for this book from a possibility into a reality. In particular I would like to thank her for her intellectual and artistic contribution to the editorial work involved in this book, and also for the energy and painstaking professionalism she brought to the design and production of our manuscript.

Finally I would also like to thank Jim McGuigan, Ian Henry and Phil Dine, and my Sheffield University colleagues Nick Stevenson, Jackie Harrison and Ning Wang for their contributions both to our Paris workshop and also to making the experience of the conference as a whole a memorable and enjoyable one.

Maurice Roche
Sheffield, July 1997

Contents

ABOUT THE AUTHORS

John Arundel is a Research Assistant in the Department of Sociology and Department of Journalism Studies, Sheffield University. His general research interests are in the relationship between sport and media. He has researched social and historical aspects of the relationship between sport and radio in Britain and has published on this theme. He also has interests in television's representation of violence. He has contributed to a major BBC funded study and published work related to this theme. He is currently researching contextual, content and production dimensions of sport programming and sport journalism on British television, particularly in relation to soccer and rugby. His contribution to the chapter in this book is the first of a planned series of publications on this theme.

Neil Blain is Senior Lecturer in Communication and Mass Media at Glasgow Caledonian University where he teaches cultural theory, textual analysis and semiotics. Publications have included work on issues of broadcasting control and consumption in Scotland and Europe; on media discourse in the domains of collective identity and national sovereignty; and on comparative questions of European identity (with Hugh O'Donnell). Additionally he has produced during the 1990s several policy-related research consultancy reports for the Scottish broadcasting industry. As well as the foregoing, he has research interests in intersections of cultural theory, and theoretical work in politics and geography; and is currently working with a variety of collaborators on articles on the question of 'nationality' in the British press; on the theorization of collective identity in the social sciences; and on questions of royalty, power and citizenship in Europe.

Philip Dine is a Lecturer in French, Department of European Studies, Loughborough University. The main focus of his research activity to date has been the cultural implications of the economic, political, and social restructuring of France since 1945. This work has centred on three specific poles: decolonization; sport and leisure; popular culture. His principal project at the present time is the production of a single-authored social and cultural history of French rugby football, on the basis of archival research funded in part by the Nuffield Foundation. Publications include *Images of the Algerian War: French Fiction and Film, 1954-1992* (Clarendon Press/OUP, 1994); 'La France du tiercé: horse-racing and popular gambling since 1954', in R. Chapman and N. Hewitt (eds) *Popular Culture and Mass Communication in Twentieth-Century France* (Edwin Mellen Press, 1992: pp. 181-206); 'The Tradition of Violence in French Sport' in R. Günther, and J. Windebank (eds) *Violence and Conflict in Modern French Culture* (Sheffield Academic Press, 1995: pp. 245-260); 'Sport, imperial expansion and colonial consolidation: A comparison of the French and British experiences', in Floris van der Merwe (ed) *Sport as Symbol, Symbols in Sport* (Academia Verlag, 1996: pp. 63-69).

Alan France is a Research Fellow in the Sociology Department, Warwick University. His main general areas of research are the sociology of youth (youth lifestyles, youth work and youth policy); the sociology of citizenship; and empowerment aspects of research methodologies. Within these areas he is currently researching young people's attitudes to issues of health, masculinity and risk-taking. His research has been supported by the UK government's Home Office and he has published widely in British youth and policy journals on issues such as youth work and youth policy. His contribution to the chapter in this book derives from a research project for which he was awarded his doctorate from Sheffield University in 1995. He plans further publications based on this study.

Steve Greenfield and Guy Osborn are co-directors of the Centre for the Study of Law, Society and Popular Culture, University of Westminster, London, UK. Steve is a graduate of the Universities of Middlesex and London (LSE) and Guy was educated at the Universities of Leeds and Leicester. Their work is located within the broad field of law and popular culture and embraces music, sport, film and the media. Forthcoming work includes *Contractual Control in the Entertainment Industry* (Dartmouth, 1997) and an extended study on sport, race and ethnicity; work on cricketers' terms and conditions and issues of policing in football, *The Absolute Game: Commercialisation and Commodification in Football* (1997 Pluto Press). Both are keen sport enthusiasts although their own affiliations show signs of fractured identity!

Michael Hall is a Professor in the Centre for Tourism, University of Otago, Dunedin, New Zealand. He was formerly at the Centre for Tourism and Leisure Policy Research, University of Canberra, Australia, with which he maintains a relationship as an Associate. He has published widely on tourism and heritage issues, including several works on event tourism and the social and political impacts of mega-events. Current research includes the nature of tourism development in deregulated economic environments and small-scale wine and horticultural developments in the South Island of New Zealand. He is author of *Hallmark Tourist Events*, (Bellhaven Press, 1992) and *Tourism and Public Policy* (with J. Jenkins) (Routledge, 1995).

Ian Henry is Reader in European Leisure Policy, and Director of Studies in Recreation Management, at Loughborough University in the Department of Physical Education, Sports Science and Recreation Management. His principal research interests are in leisure policy in European cities, European nation states, and in the European Union. He is author of *The Politics of Leisure Policy* (Macmillan) and with Peter Bramham, Hans Mommaas and Hugo van der Poel he is co-editor of a series of books on leisure in European contexts, *Leisure and Urban Processes* (Routledge), *Leisure Policies in Europe*, and *Leisure Research in Europe: Methods and Traditions* (both CAB International).

Julie Hodges is a Lecturer in the Centre for Tourism and Leisure Policy Research, University of Canberra, Australia. She had previously worked in a number of academic and industry positions in Brazil, Finland and Scotland. Her current research interests include event and festival management, particularly with respect to the role of volunteers.

Hugh O'Donnell is Reader in Language and Media at Glasgow Caledonian University. He has researched widely in the field of mediated sport, analysing the 1990 World Cup, the Wimbledon tournaments of 1991 and 1992, the Barcelona Olympics and the European Championship of 1992, the 1994 Lillehammer Winter Olympics and the 1996 European Championships. Major publications in this field include *Sport and National Identity in the European Media* (with Neil Blain and Raymond Boyle, Leicester University Press, 1993), 'Mapping the mythical: a geopolitics of national sporting stereotypes' (in *Discourse and Society*, Vol. 5, No. 3), and two contributions in Roel Puijk (ed) *Global spotlight on Lillehammer* (John Libbey, 1997). He has also analysed representations of monarchy in Spain and the UK (with Neil Blain), and is currently finishing *Good times, bad times: The new soap operas in Western Europe* (Leicester University Press, 1997), a study of over fifty domestic soap operas and telenovelas in fourteen European countries.

Maurice Roche is Senior Lecturer, Sociology Department, Sheffield University, Sheffield, UK. His current research centres on the political sociology of popular culture (media, sport, tourism, and mega-events in particular); the political sociology of citizenship (social, cultural and European in particular). He is author of *Rethinking Citizenship: Ideology, Welfare and Change in Modern Society* (Polity Press, 1992) and *Mega-Events and Modernity: Olympics, World's Fairs and the Construction of Public Culture* (Routledge, 1998)); co-editor of *European Citizenship and Social Exclusion* (with Rik van Berkel) (Avebury Press, 1997), and author of many chapters and articles on these and related topics.

John Sugden is Reader in the Sociology of Sport at the University of Brighton. Before moving to the University of Brighton he worked for fourteen years at the University of Ulster. He studied politics and sociology at the University of Essex, and took his master's and his doctorate degrees at the University of Connecticut. His books include *Sport, Sectarianism and Society in a Divided Ireland* (with Alan Bairner, Leicester University Press, 1993); *Boxing: An International Analysis* (Manchester University Press, 1996); and *Sport in Divided Societies* (edited with Alan Bairner, Meyer & Meyer, 1997). His work has been published in many edited books and journals, including *The International Journal of the History of Sport, Sociology of Sport Journal*, and *Managing Leisure*. His current research interests are in FIFA and world football, sport in divided cities, and investigative sociology. He is co-editor (with Alan Tomlinson) of *Hosts and Champions: Soccer Cultures, National Identities and the USA World Cup* (Arena/Ashgate, 1994), and their study *Who Rules the People's Game? FIFA and the Contest for World Football* will be published by Polity Press in early 1998.

Alan Tomlinson is Professor, Sport and Leisure Cultures, at the University of Brighton. He studied Humanities, before joint-majoring in English and Sociology, at the University of Kent. He read for his MA degree, and took his doctorate in, sociological studies at the University of Sussex. He has edited many books and volumes, including (with Garry Whannel) *Five Ring Circus — Money, Power and Politics at the Olympic Games* (Pluto Press, 1984) and *Off the Ball: The football World Cup* (Pluto Press, 1986); *Sport, Leisure and Social Relations* (with John Horne and David Jary, Routledge and Kegan Paul, 1987); *Consumption, Identity and Style: Markets, Meanings and the Packaging of*

Pleasure (Routledge, 1990); *Sociology of Leisure: A Reader* (with Chas Critcher and Peter Bramham, E & FN Spon, 1995). He has recently completed a co-authored textbook, *Understanding Sport* (with John Horne and Garry Whannel), to be published by E & FN Spon; and a collection of essays, *The Game's Up: Essays in the Cultural Analysis of Sport and Leisure* (to be published by Arena/ Ashgate). His work has been published in numerous books, and in journals such as *Sociology of Sport Journal*; *Media, Culture and Society*; *Journal of Sport and Social Issues*; and *Innovations*. He is currently researching into FIFA and world football, cultural dimensions of sport and leisure, and investigative method. He is co-editor (with John Sugden) of *Hosts and Champions: Soccer Cultures, National Identities and the USA World Cup* (Arena/Ashgate, 1994), and their study *Who Rules the People's Game? FIFA and the Contest for World Football* will be published by Polity Press in early 1998.

Garry Whannel is Reader in Sport and Culture, and Co-Director of the Centre for Sport Development Research, Roehampton Institute, London. He is currently researching the images of sport stars in the print media for a book he is writing for Routledge on stars, masculinities and moralities, and is part of an international team analysing images of national identities in media sport, coordinated by the Deutsche Sporthochschule, Köln, Germany. He is author of *Fields in Vision: Television Sport and Cultural Transformation* (Routledge, 1992) and *Blowing the Whistle: The Politics of Sport* (Pluto Press, 1983) and co-author (with Alan Tomlinson and John Horne) of *Understanding Sport* (E & FN Spon, forthcoming) With Alan Tomlinson, he co-edited *Five Ring Circus: Money, Power and Politics at the Oympic Games* (Pluto press, 1984) and *Off the Ball: Football's World Cup* (Pluto Press, 1986). He also co-edited (with Andrew Goodwin) *Understanding Television* (Routledge 1990) and (with Graham McFee and Wilf Murphy) *Leisure Cultures: Values, Genders, Lifestyles* (Leisure Studies Association, 1995).

SPORT, POPULAR CULTURE AND IDENTITY: AN INTRODUCTION

Maurice Roche

Sheffield University

In this Introduction the aims and structure of the book are first outlined, then some of the main themes which provide its background and rationale are considered, and finally the contents of the book are outlined.

Aims, structure and overview

This book aims to explore sport as an important form of popular culture which (i) has great significance for collective and personal identity formation and change in the modern world, and (ii) involves processes of power, politics and policy-making at a number of levels at, above and below the national level. The general approaches taken in the book are a combination of interdisciplinary and political sociological perspectives on popular culture, and on sport participation and spectatorship as an important forms and institutions of popular culture, the contributors to this book. In their various different ways the contributors explore two main substantive and interconnected dimensions of contemporary sport culture, its media-event dimension and its event-site dimension. Firstly, then, there is the theme of the increasing importance of the media, both press and television, within contemporary sport culture. The media constructs national and international spectator spheres within which sport culture is both communicated in general and within which it exercises its various influences, particularly on national-level identities. Secondly there is the theme of the increasing importance of sport event locations, particularly cities, within contemporary sport culture. Cities also provide spectator spheres within which sport culture is practised and within which it exercises its various influences, particularly on local/urban-level identities.

These two dimensions, and the two spectator spheres, are evidently also increasingly connected in many ways in contemporary sport culture. For instance, on the one hand television sport needs the drama of events and thereby needs event locations, which are the stages on which the dramas are played out. On the other hand, cities and event locations need the national and international exposure, demand and related income which television can provide. Also the two themes, both separately and in their interconnections, register the no doubt continuing but also declining relevance of the nation state and of national collective identity in the contemporary world. The development and spread of sport since the late 19th century in the West and across the world was once profoundly bound up with processes of nation-building and modernization. The spectator spheres addressed by sport organisations and sport events throughout much of the 20th century, including those constructed by nationally oriented press, radio and early mass television, were predominantly built on a local-national axis. As such they fostered both local and national collective identities (e.g. Arundel and Roche, Chapter 3 below). However, in the late 20th century, — because of the increasingly rapid international spread of both sport culture and media technologies — dynamic sport spectator spheres are being constructed on additional axes running from the local to various transnational levels, such as the European level and the global level. Arguably, these processes encourage the development of additional levels and forms of collective identification, such as European identity (Roche, 1996: ch. 8; Roche, 1998b) and cosmopolitanism (Arundel and Roche, Chapter 3; Tomlinson and Sugden, Chapter 7).

This book explores, in three main Parts, sport culture and the spectator spheres within which collective identities can be developed and displayed. Each Part consists of three chapters which, between them, provide a set of concrete case studies and some relevant theoretical analysis and debate. The studies come from a number of disciplinary backgrounds and are not intended to be comprehensive. However, they do represent active lines in contemporary social research on the themes, and they are suggestive about the developing research agenda in this area.

We will consider the contents of the book in more detail later, but a brief overview is useful at this stage. Part One addresses the first of the two dimensions of sport culture indicated above. Thus it views sport culture as 'media culture' and considers the relation between, on the one hand, the 'media sport' versions of soccer and rugby (looking at both press representations and television coverage) and, on the other hand, collective identities at local, national and European levels. Material from Britain and a range of European countries is considered in this section. Part Two addresses the second of the two dimensions of sport culture indicated above, viewing sport events and local sport policy-making as increasingly important aspects of urban political culture. It considers the relationship between, on the one hand, official sport-oriented urban policies and, on the other hand, local level collective identities. These relationships are illustrated from contemporary studies of the cities of Sydney, Lyon and Sheffield. These studies in particular concern the urban politics of the promotion of major sport events such as the World Student Games 1991 and the Olympics 2000, together with their implications for city images, the civic community and local identities.

Finally in Part Three the aim is to illustrate something of the range of different perspectives which can be usefully applied to analysing the relationship between sport and collective identity. Three perspectives are illustrated in this section, namely those of critical sociology, legal studies and socio-cultural history. Substantive accounts are presented of community identification with soccer in Northern Ireland and South Africa, the changing legal regulation of British soccer and cricket (particularly in terms of its implications for changing sport 'place identities'), and the historical development of rugby in France in relation to changing French regional and national identities.

Background themes and perspectives

This book arose out of contributions to an international workshop concerned with 'popular culture and social identity'[1]. The workshop discussed various forms and institutions of contemporary popular and public culture in modern society, principally sport, but also including other forms such as television and tourism, together with their implications for the construction, reproduction and change of collective identities in modern society. Its aim was to begin to bring a range of disciplinary perspectives and areas, generally concerned with popular culture, but too often seen as disconnected specialisms — i.e. sport studies, media studies, leisure studies, tourism studies etc. — into contact and exchange with each other through comparative studies and multi-factor case studies.

The workshop was also concerned with general interconnecting sociological themes of power and politics in the formation and change of popular and public culture in modernity, and it included contributions on contemporary debates in social and cultural theory[2]. This book generally reflects the sorts of political sociological and theoretical interests convened at the workshop. However, unlike the rest of the workshop, it aims to be substantive and empirically informative about notable cases and ways in which the sport-identity relationship has been problematised and reconstructed in the contemporary period. So it should be emphasised that while the studies in the book are variously theoretically informed (for instance by theoretical interests in globalisation, in citizenship and the public sphere, in post-Fordism, and so on) the book as a whole does not aim to be a collection of theoretical discussions.

Given this, it is worth briefly elaborating on the underlying theoretical points of reference and common concerns both for the workshop in general and this book in particular. Both share concerns for what can be called problems of de-contextualisation and/or over-simplified contextualisation in fashionable versions of cultural and related political analysis. For instance, on the one hand 'post-modern' cultural studies too often is open to the charge that it abstracts cultural processes from their political and economic contexts. Or, relatedly, it assumes that these contexts (e.g. the power, production and reception contexts of contemporary 'cultural industries' broadly understood[3]), can be speculatively and simplistically 'read off' from the texts and meanings of cultural phenomena. On the other hand, 'identity politics' studies can too often either abstract such cultural politics from the broader processes and flows of power and inequality within and between contemporary societies. Or, relatedly, they can assume that these contexts can be speculatively and simplistically 'read off' from identity ideology perspectives. There have been some recent attempts to combine these two sorts of perspective, but they are unconvincing and in what follows, for the sake of discussion and of clarity, they will be considered as polar opposites[4]. Our contributors' varied understandings of the relevance of sport for identity are not polarised in this way and they locate themselves at different points along the centreground between these extremes.

We are mainly concerned with sport as an expression and symbol of collective identity in this book. In a moment we will consider some general problems in the postmodern and identity-political versions of such expressive relations. However first it is worth noting briefly that sport can be argued to play a formative rather than simply an expressive role in relation to human identity at the personal and collective levels. Also this formative role can be interpreted in normative as well as explanatory terms: that is, as helping to provide criteria for evaluating the

progressive and humanistic character of modern culture and society as well as
helping to explain features of modernity. Thus, for example, at the individual
level, in the classic social psychological studies of Jean Piaget, participation in
games and play is understood to be crucial for the 'moral development of the
child' and the formation of autonomous personhood (Piaget, 1977). Relatedly, for
example, at the societal level, the classic cultural historical studies of Johan
Huizinga suggest that collective forms of sport and play should be seen as having
played a foundational, yet too often overlooked, role in the formation and
historical development of Western culture and society (Huizinga, 1970). While
none of them works at these kinds of psychological or historical levels of
abstraction, nonetheless the contributions to this book contain studies which
share something of their spirit. That is, most of them refer to formative as well
as expressive relationships between sport and collective identity. In addition
some of them interpret sport as having at least a potentially progressive and
humanistic role to play in the reconstruction of collective identities in the
contemporary period (in particular, chapters by Henry, Tomlinson and Sugden).

   In terms of the expressive rather than the formative relationship between sport
and identity, understandings of both personal identity ('I') and collective identity
('We') can be formulated in many ways. These include formulating them, as was
suggested earlier, on the one hand in the post-modern and anti-essentialist
language of complexity, fragmentation and becoming ('I/We can be many
things', 'I/We can change' etc.) or, on the other hand, in the essentialist language
of absolutes and nature ('I am/We are black/Chinese etc', 'I am/We are gay/
heterosexual male/female etc.', 'I am/We are Christian/Muslim etc.'). Identity,
understood in these and other ways, can then be analysed as being expressed and
symbolised in popular cultural practices, including participation and/or spectatorship in relation to particular sports, games and forms of 'body culture' (Brownell,
1996). To simplify for the sake of discussion, the anti-essentialist perspective is
compatible with voluntarism, for instance in the formulation: 'I/We play/watch
a sport because I/we I choose to do so'. Against this the essentialist perspective
is compatible with various forms of determinism, including cultural determinism,
as in the formulation: 'I/We play/watch this sport because I/we must, after all,
I am/we are (X), and this is what I/we do'. The contributions to this book explore
both expressive and formative relationships between sport and a range of
contemporary examples of mainly collective forms of identity. They do so
without going to the extremes of these two polar positions. Before we outline the

contents of the book in a little more detail we can first consider these polar positions in the field of the sociology of popular culture, sport and identity, a little further, beginning with essentialism.

Put simplistically, it could be said that identity politics and postmodernism are like mirror images and opposites of each other, each the inarticulate critic that the other deserves. Identity politics, on its side, tends merely to categorically re-assert the sort of 'essentialist' ideas which post-modernism, equally categorically, on its side, merely denies. Essentialist identity politics and theory involves asserting the immutable reality and relevance of gender, ethnic and 'racial' identities and differences. This was once deemed, in political and social scientific circles, to be both mistaken and reactionary rather than insightful and pro-gressive. In the various forms it took, such as claims of male, or imperialist or white (e.g. Aryan or Afrikaaner) supremacy, such 'first wave' 19th century and early 20th century essentialism has been properly criticised and dismissed throughout the mid- and late-20th century in post-colonial and post-war social science. However in some sectors of contemporary social science, forms of gender and race essentialism — together with religious fundamentalism and ethnic 'purity' ideologies, and the various version of identity politics related to these — have come to have a certain allegedly 'radical' currency, and a willingness to recognise such claims has become part of what is deemed to be 'politically correct'.

This allegedly radical 'second wave' essentialism sometimes involves the promotion of divisive and separatist forms of politics (see Note 4). Comparably the recognisably reactionary versions of 'first wave' identity politics and essentialist theory also had their own versions of separatism. And their theories and ideologies of sport were important parts of the cultural aspect of these separatist and exclusionary political programmes. These cultural and exclusion-ary dimensions of essentialist identities and their politics ranged from the patronising sexism and class-ism of the British Empire and its use of sport in the imperialist version of the politics of British identity, to the aggressive racism of the Nazi's use of sport in their authoritarian version of the politics of German identity (Hoberman, 1984; Guttman, 1994; Roche, 1998a: ch. 2 and 5). However, in the post-war period we have lived to see not only the collapse of these ideologies but also the collapse of apartheid and white racism in South Africa, a liberation which is now being celebrated in part through sport, as Tomlinson and Sugden describe in Chapter 7. This celebration is evidently appropriate, since in the long struggle against apartheid sport was a visibly important arena both for the expression of white racist collective identity and also for the fight against it (Archer and Bouillon, 1982; Payne, 1993). The kind of mainstream critical social science perspectives represented in this book, which have long been connected with the struggle against 'first wave' reactionary versions of essentialism and identity politics, understandably are not noticeably tempted by the contemporary 'second wave' versions.

The avoidance, in this book, of this pole of contemporary identity politics and its 'second wave' essentialism is not a product of the contributors moving to the other extreme, and locating themselves alongside the proponents of post-modernist anti-essentialism. Most chapters in the book acknowledge, in one way or another, that collective identities in modernity, even in a certain sense our own personal identities, are complex and 'socially constructed' in various ways. Furthermore they acknowledge that sport culture has played and continues to play a significant part in the construction and mediation of different dimensions of identity as well as in their expression. This is clear particularly in the chapters on media sport and national and other forms of collective identity in Part One, particularly Whannel in Chapter 1 and Blain and O'Donnell in Chapter 2. Through their studies of press reporting of international sport they show how ideas and images of national identity, far from communicating some sort of ethno-national 'essence', contain contradictions and are constructed and reconstructed within media culture. However, while aware of the cultural complexities generated by late 20th century social forces, most of the contributors to this book do not locate themselves at a post-modernist extreme and a number are explicitly critical of post-modernism (for instance in the chapters by Arundel, France, Roche, Henry, Tomlinson and Sugden, and also see their other writings referenced in these chapters).

Post-modernist philosophical and cultural analysis can tend to indulge the understandable temptation to avoid the realities of the late 20th century human condition by intellectually 'deconstructing' them and celebrating their alleged character as a play of mere images. As some analysts suggest (see Harvey, 1989; Featherstone, 1991; and Real, 1996 for relevant discussions), this scarcely differentiates such academic intellectualising from ordinary consumers' more considered and ironic understandings of the play and significance of images in contemporary media, touristic and retail cultures. In this context the many traditional, constrained and obligated features which exist in sports participation and spectatorship, seen as an expressions of both personal commitments and collective identities, tend to be dissolved in favour of an idealised picture of the alleged voluntarism and fluidity of sport consumerism (see Jarvie and Maguire, 1994: ch. 9; also Hargreaves, 1986 *passim*).

As against extreme postmodern approaches the contributors to this book tend, in their various ways, to work on their empirical case studies with a more sober and critical awareness of the continuing relevance of modernity's realities and problems, and of the expression of these realities and problems in the field of sport. Modernity's realities include its social realities of structural and collective constraints and inequalities, and its moral-ontological realities of human needs and rights[5]. Recognition of the at times tragic disjunctions between modernity's social structures and processes on the one hand, and its visions of humanity's moral and ontological characteristics and potential on the other, has fuelled many influential social visions, analyses and critiques. Influential versions of these disjunctions have been expressed in both Enlightenment philosophy and classical social theory in various ways, from Rousseau's and Kant's late 18th century concerns for the conditions of freedom to Marx and Durkheim's late 19th century concerns respectively for the problems of alienation and anomie. Throughout the modern era major cultural and political movements and institution-building projects such as democratisation, nationalism and socialism have been fuelled by these concerns. It was in the milieu of these 19th century modernist movements and projects, of course, that sports were first developed, institutionalised, popularised and internationalised as vehicles of personal and collective identities.

Throughout the modern era, then, sport has periodically appeared to offer people in different genders, classes, and nations a cultural sphere in which, if only transiently, they could express embodied senses of freedom. In this sphere, in Marxist and Durkheimian terms respectively, people could imagine that they could escape from or struggle against the alienating and anomic conditions of modern life, and in Hegelian terms they could begin to recognize and value the identity and difference of others, and be recognized by others. A number of the chapters in this book echo something of the spirit of these sorts of modernist understandings of the potentially positive and progressive character of sport in relation to the formation and expression of identities. For instance they are present in Tomlinson and Sugden's discussion of the positive role and potential of international football culture, particularly in South Africa and in the World Cup (Chapter 7) and in Henry's discussion of the positive role of sport as part of French urban social and cultural policy (Chapter 5). They are also present in the implications of Arundel, France and Roche's discussions that, at least in principle, transnational media regulatory frameworks and urban sport policies can help to promote citizenship on a number of levels (even if current versions of these frameworks and policies signally fail to do so at present) (Chapters 3 and 6; also Roche, 1992, 1994, 1996, 1998a and 1998b).

This book, then, draws on some of these broad background sociological problematics and perspectives. As was noted earlier, unlike the workshop from which it derives it focuses exclusively on studies of sport and sport cultures and their implications, and it focuses mainly on processes of collective rather than personal identity-formation, expression and change. But in the spirit of the workshop and of its generally critical approach to the problem of de-contextualisation, the book approaches the interconnections between sport, culture and identity *contextually*. That is, it approaches them in terms of broader political and economic factors and forces affecting and running through all dimensions of popular culture and the culture industries in late 20th century society. These late 20th century social factors and forces include, in particular (i) the de-industrialization of cities, (ii) the changing character and influence of the nationstate and nationalism, and also (iii) the powerful intervention of the media, particularly television, into popular culture at all levels from the local and the national to the global. These three sets of social factors and forces are represented in the three Parts of this book and provide contexts and themes for the chapters contained in them. We can now consider the chapter contents in a little more detail.

Media sport and social identity

Part One addresses the first dimension of sport culture indicated earlier, namely the media dimension. Between them, the three chapters in this Part address, first, the three major levels of collective identity formation, media operation and sport organisation — namely the regional (Chapter 3), national (Chapters 1, 2, 3), and the international (Chapters 2 and 3); second, both major media forms — namely press and television; and, third, two of the three major dimensions of media processes —in particular, content and production analysis in some detail, while taking a more speculative approach to effects. Chapters 1 and 2 mainly concentrate on sport coverage in the British and European press and Chapter 3 concentrates on television coverage of sport. Chapters 1 and 2 also focus on

complementary studies of the content of media coverage of the Euro '96 sport
mega-event to illustrate their general arguments, while Chapter 3 concentrates
more on media production contexts and processes.

In Chapter 1 Garry Whannel develops a theme from his major study of
televised sport (Whannel, 1992; ch. 8) concerning the construction and current
role of 'stars' in media sport. He draws on a content analysis of British press
coverage of the sport mega-event 'Euro 96' (the European Nations soccer championship held around Britain in 1996) in particular and his analysis of media
sport as popular culture in general. He addresses four main topics — the ways
in which the construction of collective and national identities in sport culture
involves contradictions and differentiations (individual-group, local community-
peer group, localism-nationalism, nationalism-internationalism); the uncertainties
of United Kingdom national identity in sport culture (given the existence of four
'home nations' in sport and given the dominance among them of the English);
the 'foreignness' and 'otherness' that the English ascribe to Europe (even to
imported European football stars) in sport culture; and the inherent instability and
transient character of sport-based national identities. He concludes that while
sport mega-events and their coverage as media sport operate to provoke, shape
and reproduce the public's apparently deep feelings of national belongingness,
nonetheless it is likely that their effects are temporary and transitory.

In Chapter 2 on European sports journalism and its readers, Hugh O'Donnell
and Neil Blain address the constructions of national identity in the sports and
event-related reporting of the press of the ten European countries involved in the
Euro '96 event. In doing so they drawing on themes from their broader context
of comparative European media, culture and media sport studies (e.g. Blain,
Boyle and O'Donnell, 1993). They analyse the press coverage in terms of the
conception of the reader implied in it. They find that, among other things,
continental press coverage of international sport tends to give due weight to
strategic and tactical aspects, provides relevant contextual information and often
aspires to literary qualities, addressing readers generally as 'citizens' and in
particular as intelligent sport lovers. By contrast, almost uniquely in Europe, the
British press generally tends to address readers as the 'subjects' of a confusing
and monarchical constitution, and, in addition, in the tabloid's coverage of sport,
as subject to the influence of alcohol(!). That is, the typical style of tabloid
address to its sport readership constitutes its image of the reader as a young,
drunk, xenophobic male or, worse, as a mob of people like this.

They analyse the sport-society relationship revealed in the Euro '96 coverage of the different national presses into a number of main types depending on how seriously the fate of their national team is seen to represent that of the nation. Most continental presses treat the relationship as merely symbolic, the English press tends to take it most seriously as part of the real contemporary history of their (quasi-)'nation', while the Scottish press tends to treat it in a light and ironic way. Blain and O'Donnell suggest that these and other differences in press coverage of international sport are related to differences in the degree of political modernization experienced by nations and the degree rigidity of their class structures.

Finally in this Part, in Chapter 3, John Arundel and Maurice Roche consider the relationships between media sport and local sport-based identities. They address the general theme of the degree to which and the way in which contemporary processes of cultural globalisation, particularly in the media, leave room for and/or transform 'the local' and traditional collective identities constructed around versions of locality and place. This is a theme of recurrent social research interest, particularly in respect of the global cultural significance of the televising of the Olympic games and the implications of this for national identities (which from the Olympic perspective, are effectively versions of local identity) (see Larson and Park, 1993; Spa *et al.*, 1996). Arundel and Roche focus on the case of British Rugby League and its recent effective 'take-over' by Rupert Murdoch's Sky TV organisation. In doing so they draw on information from a recent interview-based study of media, management and marketing personnel connected with the game. They review the development of the game from its late 19th century social origins to its post-war role as a media sport, and the relative continuity throughout this period of the association between the game and Northern English working class regionality.

To set the stage for the discussion of the interview material they provide an account of the general role of sport in Murdoch's global corporate strategy, the impact of his TV rights acquisitions on the contemporary world of sport and the weakness of nationally-based broadcasting regulation to defend public access even to nationally significant sports and sports events. Sky's new influence over British Rugby League — however important it may appear to be, not least in terms of its implications for local identities, to fans and others within the game — needs to be seen in this context, as only one small aspect of a much bigger process within the globalising dynamics of the contemporary media industry.

Their general approach and conclusion is that the media industry's interest in 'the local', such as it is, bears comparison with that of another globalizing cultural industry, namely, tourism. As with much of the tourist industry it is likely that, realistically, the main options for 'local place identities' (here sport-based identities) in the emerging global cultural economy are either to be marketed nationally and internationally in artificially reconstructed forms, as soccer has been, or to be erased and be replaced with something else. Which of these two options best characterises the future of Rugby League in Britain as both a carrier of local identities and also as media sport currently remains unclear. In this respect this chapter overlaps somewhat with themes in Dine's Chapter 9 on the uncertain future facing regionally-based French rugby.

Sport policies and urban identities

Part Two explores the second dimension of sport culture which was indicated earlier, namely, the role of the local level in sport culture and its influence on collective identity. The three chapters in this Part each explore aspects of the politics of sport policy at the urban level and various substantive and analytical issues connected with the general theme, through case studies of three cities, namely Sydney, Lyon and Sheffield. In the chapters in Part One concerned with media sport versions of soccer and rugby it is evident that major international events and event cycles, such as the European-level and 'world'-level events and tournaments, have a distinctive presence and importance in contemporary national and global sport culture. So too in this Part, sport mega-events such as the Olympic games are shown to have an equivalent importance and influence on the cities which host them.

In Chapter 4 Michael Hall and Julie Hodges address the theme of the urban politics of place and identity involved in staging sport mega-events such as the Olympic Games. Building on their previous research on 'hallmark events' in tourism policy-making (e.g. Hall, 1989, 1992), they examine the case of the city of Sydney's preparations for its Olympic Games event in 2000. In line with Hall's previous studies they focus on the politics of this process and on the event's likely local impacts, particularly its planned and unplanned social impacts. They demonstrate the role of local growth coalitions and booster-groups of politicians and leaders of business and the media in the creation and promotion of Sydney's original bid for the Olympics and its event preparations.

Global sport events of this kind require new sport facilities to be built along with the new urban transport infrastructures necessary to move and manage masses of people at and between the various event sites and facilities. Hall and Hodge are particularly concerned with the social impact of this new build in terms of its effects on the housing market and land values. These can involve housing relocation because of the compulsory purchase of land for clearance and building. It can also lead to a rise in rents and house prices, and generally to 'gentrification' processes in areas of previously low land values and low rents. Each of these processes, but particularly the latter, can cause serious problems for people living on low incomes in these areas. Hall and Hodges propose a new range of policy strategies which need to be seriously considered by urban politicians and planners if they are to adequately respond to these sorts of often very negative social impacts. These strategies include strengthening tenants' rights, developing relevant forms of rent control and generally developing and committing event organizers to undertaking social impact analysis as part of their approach to the staging of sport mega-events. A related set of issues connected with the social impact of sport mega-events is also taken up by France and Roche in Chapter 6.

In Chapter 5 Ian Henry addresses the wide range of sport-relevant policies, from major spectator events to neighbourhood participation, which typically form an important sector of the policy repertoire in contemporary urban development strategies in Europe and America in particular, and which have planned and unplanned implications for city images and civic identities. Drawing on his established research in this field (e.g. Henry, 1993) he contextualises this growing use of sport in terms of general structural changes in Western social formations involving, among other things, economic restructuring and 'post-modern' cultural fragmentation. Like Hall and Hodges he concentrates his analysis on the urban and regional political processes involved in sport project policy-making. His case study city is France's second city, Lyon (also one of the subjects of Dine's study of regional French rugby in Chapter 9). Henry examines, in particular, the various symbolic uses of sport in urban policy in Lyon to promote such things as the image of the city and region at national and transnational levels, positive images of leading politicians and administrative organisations, and positive role models for young people. He notes that, in spite of economic problems, and like a lot of contemporary cities, Lyon has increased its public expenditures on sport-related policies.

Henry shows that sport culture and sport policy in Lyon tends to be seen across the political spectrum as having positive significance and impacts, and there is thus something of an 'apolitical consensus' character to it in the city. The active promotion of sport is seen to add to the attractiveness of the city to the inward investors and service sector professionals needed for economic growth, and also provides opportunities for cultural inclusion for otherwise relatively socially excluded sectors of the city's community, particularly youth and ethnic minorities. Henry concludes by suggesting that sport culture appears to lend itself to the politics of fragmented post-modern societies by offering electorates gratification rather than addressing their needs, and offering them cultural forms in which both inclusive and also conflictual and differentiated identities can be fashioned and symbolised.

Finally in this Part, in Chapter 6, Alan France and Maurice Roche return from the broad and consensual urban sports policy situation illustrated by Lyon to the more 'single-issue' and conflictual situation, illustrated by Sydney, which tends to be produced by sport mega-events. Drawing on their previous and continuing research on these issues France and Roche address the implications of high profile projects for local identities using the concepts and experiences of 'citizenship' and 'social inclusion' to characterise identity (Roche, 1992, 1994, 1998a, 1998b; France, 1995). They focus in particular on the fraught experience of the traditional industrial city of Sheffield, a city which went through a rapid process of de-industrialization and economic restructuring in the late 1970s and early 1980s and then staged a major multi-sport event — the World Student Games 1991— in an attempt, both directly and symbolically, to turn the fortunes and image of the city around.

Drawing on fieldwork and interviews among working class young people — whose main perception was of exclusion from the policy, from the event and from its alleged benefits — France and Roche illuminate the capacity of such mega-events not only to generate social costs as well as economic benefits, but also to polarise urban communities in terms of whether they feel most affected by the costs or by the benefits. They argue that, as well as whatever empowering and inclusionary impacts may be intended, urban regeneration and re-imaging policies need to weigh carefully the risks mega-events pose — not only in terms of the effects of physical reconstruction on host city communities, but also in terms of unintended disempowering and exclusionary impacts on citizens.

Perspectives on sport and the politics of identity

The aim of Part Three on sport and the politics of identity is to illustrate something of the range of perspectives which can be used to understand the relationship between sport and collective identity. In particular sociological, legal studies, historical and comparative perspectives are illustrated in substantive accounts of soccer, cricket and rugby in various societies.

In Chapter 7, on football cultures and identity, Alan Tomlinson and John Sugden use an empirical sociological study of sport to address some broad issues in contemporary social theory relating to identity. In this they are guided by C. Wright Mills' critique, in his classic work *The Sociological Imagination*, of the often misleading character of 'grand theory' in sociology (Mills, 1970). They take issue with Anthony Giddens' approach to understanding identity (in his *Modernity and Self-Identity*, Giddens, 1991), which assumes that the modern social context, generalised as 'high modernity', tends to prioritise the achievement of individual selfhood and promotes it as a reflexively alterable life 'project'. Tomlinson and Sugden argue that this underplays the continuing importance, within the various and complex social formations which actually make up the contemporary world social order, of the collective level and its, at times, imposing and perceivedly unalterable character in relation to individuals. They illustrate their argument by means of a comparative study of the importance of the collective dimension and of political culture in Northern Ireland and South Africa, and, in particular the use of soccer to mobilise and symbolise collective identities in these societies, respectively a traditionalistic sectarianism and a new progressive nationalism. Along with this they also consider the soccer World Cup 1994 competition in the USA as an arena both for nationalist and also cosmopolitan and consumerist identities.

In Chapter 8, on the legal regulation of soccer and cricket in Britain, Guy Osborn and Steve Greenfield illustrate the importance of understanding the role of law, and of a legal studies approach, in relation to understanding sport and collective identity. Sport, particularly British sport, is often understood, both in its historical origins and contemporary practice, as an expression of a free 'civil society', a sphere of voluntary participation and/or 'fandom' outside of the state. Perhaps it is in civil society that we turn sport 'spaces' into the identity-relevant 'sacred (loved and hated) places' characteristic of the popular culture of sport. Osborn and Greenfield, noting the importance of John Bale's work on this aspect of sport culture (e.g. Bale, 1993), critically weigh the idea that sport might best be understood as a form of civil society by studying the development of its internal self-regulatory dynamics and organisation. However, even where the state is not actively and coercively involved in the organisation and promotion of sport — as it typically is, for instance, in physical education in national school systems — it is invariably influential on sport through what Osborn and Greenfield call the 'external regulation' of 'sporting space'. This consists of the accumulation of, and periodic political transformation of, the complex legal frameworks regulating such things as fire and safety, alcohol consumption, spectator behaviour, and even location in relation to participant and spectator sport. They illustrate the importance of 'external regulation' to the shaping of sport spaces and their potential for becoming identity-relevant sport 'places' in Britain with a review of the development of law in the contemporary period. This development includes law deriving from sport stadium disasters, and it has impinged powerfully on the two British 'national sports' and sport cultures of soccer and cricket. In the course of this discussion they reveal some significant differences in the influence and application of legal regulation between these two sports and their cultures.

Finally, in Chapter 9 Phil Dine discusses the changing significance of the sport of rugby, particularly Rugby Union, for regional and national identity in France. Arguably he illustrates the value of another theme from C. Wright Mills, additional to the one acknowledged by Tomlinson and Sugden in their chapter, namely the importance of historical depth in understanding contemporary society, or as Mills put it: the need to recognise "the intimate relation of history and sociology" (Mills, 1970: p. 163). Dine provides a sociologically rich historical account of the 19th century origins and the 20th century development of the changing French love affair with the game of rugby, a rare example of French cultural borrowing from the English. He addresses its cultural significance both for its 'heartland' of the South Western region, the 'Ovalie', the land of the oval ball, centred on Toulouse, with its distinctive ethnic mix of Catalans, Basques and others, and also for the more marginal South Eastern region, centred on Lyon, *'en marge de l'Ovalie'*. Among other things he illustrates the importance of the connection President de Gaulle helped to make, in the postwar period of national reconstruction, between the success of national French rugby teams and the collective identity of the French nation. He also addresses the issue of the uncertain balance in more recent years in France between rugby seen as part of the nation's cultural identity as against it being mainly seen as being part of a regional identity. In this respect, and also in terms of his comments about the roots of French Rugby League and the current importance of the role of the media in French rugby, his chapter contains points of relevance for and comparison with the situation of British Rugby League discussed in Arundel and Roche's Chapter 3.

Conclusion

As the review of the contents has made clear, this book is both thematically and empirically wide-ranging. In general it aims to explore changing collective identities in modern society through case studies which draw on political sociology perspectives and other interdisciplinary perspectives on contemporary popular culture and sport. In particular it aims to illustrate and indicate a range of fertile new areas of social research and inquiry, particularly in the spheres of i) comparative sport politics and history (Part Three), ii) comparative urban sport policies (Part Two), and iii) transnational media sport (Part One).

Notes

1   For details see Acknowledgements p. v. See also Note 2.
2   See books by Nick Stevenson, 1995 and Jim McGuigan, 1996, and also doctoral theses by Jackie Harrison, 1995 and Ning Wang, 1997 who all contributed to the workshop on the basis of these publications. In addition the workshop also involved presentations from Bennetta-Jules Rossette and Denis-Constant Martin, Joost van Loon and Bella Dicks, Phillippe Thiellet, Martin Munk, Birgitta Orfali, Isabelle Veyrat-Masson and a submitted paper from David Chaney.
3   See McGuigan, 1996 ch. 4.
4   On 'post modernism' in relation to the sociology of sport see Jarvie and Maguire, 1994, ch. 9. For interesting reviews and critiques of 'identity politics' in relation to feminism and black politics see, respectively, Bondi, 1993 and McGuigan, 1996, ch. 7. On early 20th century separatist feminism and contemporary radical separatist feminism in relation to sport see Hargreaves, 1994, ch. 3 and ch. 4. 'Postmodern' cultural studies and 'identity politics' forms of analysis need to be fundamentally distinguished from each other, as suggested in this Introduction. Nonetheless a number of efforts have been made in recent years to square the circle by combining

them in more or less sociologically de-contextualised ways and with variable coherence and success. See for instance Fiske, 1989a, 1989b; Jordan and Weedon, 1995; Nicholson and Seidman, 1995. For a critique of Fiske and of post-modernism from a critical and sociologically-sensitive approach to the analysis of popular culture see McGuigan, 1992 and 1996 respectively. See also Note 5.

5   For discussions of these realities, and also of the disjunctions between modern social conditions and moral-ontological dimensions of the human lifeworld see Doyal and Gough, 1991 and Roche, 1996, also 1973. Post-modernist perspectives often claim to dismiss these sorts of human realities as mere constructs of modernity's 'grand meta-narratives'. However, as most of the contributions to this book imply, such dismissal is an intellectual indulgence which does not well serve the task of understanding social identity problems in late 20th century societies.

References

Archer, R. and Bouillon, A. (1982) *The South African Game: Sport and racism.* London: Zed Press.

Bale, J. (1993) *Sport, space and the city*. London: Routledge.

Blain, N., Boyle, R. and O'Donnell, H. (1994) *Sport and national identity in the European media*. Leicester: Leicester University Press.

Bondi, L. 1993 'Locating identity politics', ch. 5 in Keith, M. and Pile, S. (eds) *Place and the politics of identity*. London: Routledge.

Brownell, S. (1995) *Training the body for China: Sports in the moral order of the People's Republic*. Chicago: University of Chicago Press.

Doyal, L. and Gough, I. (1991) *A theory of human need*. London: Macmillan.

Featherstone, M. (1991) *Consumer culture and postmodernism*. London; Sage.

Fiske, J. (1989a) *Reading the popular*. Boston: Unwin Hyman.

——— (1989b) *Understanding popular culture*. Boston: Unwin Hyman.

Giddens, A. (1991) *Modernity and self-identity*. Cambridge: Polity Press.

Hall, C. M. (1989) 'The politics of events', in G. Syme *et al.* (eds) *The planning and evaluation of hallmark events*. Aldershot: Avebury.

——— (1992) *Hallmark tourist events: Impacts, management and planning*, Chichester: John Wiley.

Hargreaves, Jennifer (1994) *Sporting females: Critical issues in the history and sociology of women's sports*. London: Routledge.

Hargreaves, John (1986) *Sport, power and culture*. Cambridge: Polity Press

Harrison, J. (1996) 'British Television News in the 1990s'. Sheffield: Unpublished Ph.D. Sociology Department, Sheffield University.

Harvey, D. (1989) *The condition of postmodernity*. Oxford: Blackwell.

Henry, I. (1993) *The politics of leisure policy*. London: Macmillan.

Hoberman, J. (1984) *Sport and political ideology*. London: Heinemann

Huizinga, J. (1971) *Homo ludens: A study of the play element in culture*. London: Paladin.

Jarvie, G. and Maguire, J. (1994) *Sport and leisure in social thought*. London: Routledge.

Jordan, G., and Weedon, C. (1995) *Cultural politics: Class, gender and race in the postmodern world*. Blackwell, Oxford.

Larson, J. and Park, H-S. (1993) *Global television and the politics of the Seoul Olympics*. Oxford: Westview Press.

McGuigan, J. (1992) *Cultural populism*. London: Routledge.

―――― (1996) *Culture and the public sphere*. London: Routledge.

Mills, C. W. (1970) *The sociological imagination*. London: Penguin Books.

Nicholson, L. and Seidman, S. (eds) (1995) *Social postmodernism: Beyond identity politics*. Cambridge: Cambridge University Press.

Payne, A. (1993) 'The Commonwealth and the politics of sporting contacts with South Africa', pp. 129-150 in Binfield, C. and Stevenson, J. (eds) *Sport, culture and politics*. Sheffield: Sheffield Academic Press.

Piaget, J. (1977) *The moral judgement of the child*. London: Penguin.

Real, M. (1996) *Exploring media culture*. London: Sage.

Roche, M. (1973) *Phenomenology, language and the social sciences*. London: Routledge.

―――― (1992) 'Mega-events and micro-modernization', *British Journal of Sociology* Vol. 43, No. 4: pp. 563-600.

―――― (1994) 'Mega-events and urban policy', *Annals of Tourism Research* Vol. 21, No. 1: pp. 1-19.

―――― (1996) *Rethinking citizenship: Welfare, ideology and change in modern society* (Reprint of original 1992 edition). Cambridge: Polity Press.

———— (1998a) (forthcoming) *Mega-events and modernity: Olympics and expos in the construction of public culture*. London: Routledge.

———— (1998b) (forthcoming) 'European citizenship and the cultural dimension', in Stevenson, N. (ed) (forthcoming) *Cultural citizenship*. London: Sage.

Spa, M. de M. (*et al.*) (1996) *Television in the Olympics*. Luton: John Libbey Media.

Wang, N. (1997) 'Tourism, Modernity and Ambivalence'. Sheffield: Unpublished Ph.D. thesis, Sociology Department, Sheffield University.

Whannel, G. (1992) *Fields in vision: Television sport and cultural transformation*. London: Routledge.

I.

MEDIA SPORT
AND SOCIAL IDENTITY

Chapter 1

INDIVIDUAL STARS
AND COLLECTIVE IDENTITIES
IN MEDIA SPORT

Garry Whannel

Roehampton Institute London

Media products emerge from an elaborate process of production which is both economic and cultural. Audiences need to be won and readers attracted. Sport is presented largely in terms of stars and narratives: the media narrativises the events of sport, transforming them into stories with stars and characters; heroes and villains. In this process of construction the audience are characteristically positioned as patriotic partisan subjects. National belonging-ness is inscribed into the discursive practices which seek to mobilise national identities as part of the way in which our attention is engaged with a narrative hermeneutic. We want to know who will win and "we" hope that it will be our "own" competitor (see Whannel, 1992: p. 110).

In the British media, differences are marked through contrast between English/British identities and the construction of images of other nations. Given the centrality of individual stars, this process can be seen at work in the ways in which stars are represented. In this chapter I examine the representation of contrasts in sports coverage. I intend to cover four main themes. Firstly the ways in which the construction of identities takes place around contradictions and differences. Secondly the extent to which national identities of the United Kingdom have to be thought through in terms of the peculiarities of the English. Thirdly, that Europe, from the English perspective, is foreign, different, other. Fourthly, I will suggest that identities, constructed around sport, have an inherent instability.

The contradictions in identities

There are at least four prominent contradictions involved in the construction of a national identity: the relation of an individual and a group; the tension between geographic community and peer group; the tension between localism and nationalism; and the tension between nationalism and internationalism. In addition, constructions of national identities attempt, but rarely succeed, to devise a magical resolution of conflicts around gender, class, race, and generation.

Individual/group

Sport, even team sport, features individual stars, whose style or behaviour is often in conflict with the demands of the group. Sport stars are often written about as role models, people with broader responsibilities, and people who sometimes fail to live up to such responsibilities. The build up to Euro '96 featured highly publicised stories about the behaviour of the England squad — "Men behaving badly", according to a *Sun* (29 May, 1996) headline; whilst the *Daily Mirror* (29 May, 1996) had "Drunken England Stars plane shame". This prompted Sir Alf Ramsey, referring to Gascoigne, to announce: "I will not go to Wembley if this man plays" (headline in the *Daily Mirror*, 1 June, 1996). *The Sun* announced that "Paul Gascoigne will be read the riot act by Terry Venables when England players report this weekend for Euro '96" (*The Sun* 19 May, 1996). Constantly it was suggested that Gascoigne (and, on occasion others) were not fit to play for England — their behaviour was incompatible with the demands of group discipline and national representation.

Frank Keating in the *Guardian* sounded a note of dissent from this line of moral censure. Quoting the Newcastle Chief Constable David Mellish as saying "...all professional sportsmen have a heavy responsibility to behave properly", Keating asked why this should be so — why should sport stars have a responsibility to set an example? Do we, Keating enquired, ask this of other celebrities? (*Guardian* 30 May, 1996) Keating's question though, was very much against the dominant grain in which the notion of sport stars as moral exemplars is very much part of "common-sense". Both journalists and members of the public, in letters to papers, television vox-pops and radio phone-ins constantly refer to 'role models'. There is very little clarity as to what is meant by the term and very little attempt to probe the relation between stars and the audience. There is little reason to assume that young people are not perfectly able to distinguish between Gazza the football genius and Gazza the overweight clown who drinks too much and allegedly beats his wife. However the concept of stars as role models with broader responsibilities is well entrenched, and links up with the related notion of team spirit and representing the country.

The nineteenth century cult of athleticism regarded sport as a form of moral education in which co-operation, discipline and leadership were forged together in team games (Mangan, 1981). Modern sport, however, with its star system and individual focus, provides pressures that mitigate against team spirit. As products of the commercialisation of sport since the Second World War, modern sport stars are young, fit, glamourous and internationally mobile (Bale and Maguire, 1993). The economic structure of elite sport offers greater rewards for individual effort than for representing a country — in tennis, golf, athletics, and even football — individual careers often come before adherence to the traditional view that representing a country was the peak of success. The first loyalty of today's top sports stars is no longer automatically towards their country. Equally, modern sporting mercenaries, who move from country to country pursuing the most lucrative financial rewards, are unlikely to forge close bonds with the teams in which they play a brief transitory role.

Geographic community / peer group

An older, traditional model of local community, always at least partly mythical rather than actual, has increasingly come into tension with other constructions — the black community, the Asian community, the gay community, the youth, old people, ordinary families — all inhabiting, and often contesting, the same geographic space. While one needs to be wary of constructing the past in terms of organic community, it is certainly the case that growing social mobility, the decline of traditional heavy industry, the re-structuring of work, immigration, the growth of multi-culturalism, and the impact of Thatcherism, are all contributory factors in a society perceived as more fragmented than it was in the past. One symptom of this fragmentation can be seen in the ways that inclusive concepts of local community can no longer easily hold together the diverse range of identities in play in most urban areas. In the sporting context, the restructuring of class composition and decline of traditional working class community cohesion served to weaken the intense ties of localism that bound boys and men to the local football team (see Critcher, 1979).

Whilst in many areas such bonds of localism are still important, in patterns of football support the tradition of support for the local team has been challenged by the media-led prominence of major names. Support for Liverpool and Manchester United has a nation-wide character. Such supporters are denounced by others as glory hunters. Fans mock them by singing "we support our local team". There is a tension at work here between a situated localised identity, and a mediated symbolic identity, which lacks any local embeddedness.

Localism / nationalism

Localism and national identification are also in tension — Geordies, scousers, brummies, cockneys, are all constructions of localism that in some articulations will have a greater effectivity in offering subject positions than the appeal to a nationalist identity. The appeal of national representative sport is not always strong — it requires a degree of performance by the team and faith amongst the spectators to mobilise it. Jack Charlton once said that he wasn't English, he was a Geordie. Support for England's football team is not always whole hearted and unequivocal — a degree of commitment, talent and performance is required to generate enthusiasm. Scottish Catholics who support Celtic are likely to have ambivalent feelings about supporting a national side, as long as this involves integration into a predominately Protestant, loyalist and pro-unionist culture (see Boyle, 1994). National belongingness is never natural, it always has to be produced. This production is not a neat unifying performance, but rather a process in which moments of apparent national unity have to be set against the divisions and tensions that may operate between national and local identities.

Nationalism / internationalism

National identities clearly and visibly have considerable prominence in the process of cultural mapping, yet the internationalist impulse is also a factor in the contested process of representation. There was a controversy over BBC's choice of Beethoven's 'Ode to Joy' for their Euro '96 theme. This developed in the context of heightened political tension around the British relation to the European Community, generated by the BSE situation, in which the more jingoistic British papers and politicians managed to divert attention away from our own farming methods by blaming the Germans for banning "our" beef. The BBC's internationalism, in selecting the European anthem, was criticised as un-patriotic, doubly so in that it was by a German composer. As if in response, ITV chose 'Jerusalem', to accompany a set of images of the green and pleasant land, and were able to occupy the patriotic high ground.

Yet, later on in the competition, when the *Daily Mirror*, notoriously, ran a front page proclaiming "Achtung, Surrender: for you Fritz ze Euro '96 is over", the bellicose tone apparently mis-read the popular mood. The public were apparently enjoying the air of festivity and absence of crowd violence that characterised the tournament and there was a hostile and critical reaction to *The Daily Mirror*'s use of war-time imagery in their build-up to the England Germany match. The following day the paper ran a conciliatory shot of the editor presenting German captain Klinsmann with a hamper, with the rather weak "Peas in Our Time" headline, as an attempted apology. Nationalist or patriotic enthusiasm cannot be taken for granted; whilst an inter-nationalist consciousness has rarely been a strong factor in English political and cultural life, there is always a potential internationalism to counterpose against nationalism.

Clearly national identities are constructed upon difference; upon oppositions between "our" qualities and "theirs". British and English images of self in the tabloid press often stress the Bulldog spirit, the willingness to take bruises in the cause of Queen and Country, the love of pageantry and tradition, the honour of playing for the country, and the commitment to fair play.

In a *Daily Mirror* montage during Euro '96, "England Expects", an image assembled to demonstrate the composite British sporting character included the nerve of Nick Faldo, the spirit of Brian Moore, the heart of Ian Botham, the legs of Seb Coe, the brain of Lester Piggott, and the feet of Bobby Charlton. Such representations serve to produce and reproduce "common-sense" assumptions about "our" national character,

The national identities being forged in the English media can be understood in sharper focus by examining the properties and values within national images of other nations in the British press. There are for example, those, usually Latin, who are too temperamental, such as the "French firebrand" with a "typically fiery French temper" (*Daily Mirror* 20 May, 1995) the "temperamental Colombian hitman" (*The Sun* 11 July, 1995), or the Spaniard "going through one of his opinionated periods" (*Guardian* 18 May, 1995). Then there are those, frequently West Indian, who have great "natural" skills, but a too casual attitude to the game. References abound to "often unfulfilled skills", "dreamy" (*Guardian* 18 May, 1995) to simple instincts, shining smiles, to "stumps fly to the tune of the calypso beat". The style of such cricket is "wild cavalier" with "thunderous sixes" (*Daily Telegraph* 17 May, 1995). Then there are those who, by contrast, take it all too seriously "The Americans just don't have any idea of what sportsmanship entails" (*Daily Telegraph* 15 May, 1995).

Such British xenophobia, which in these times of post-modern irony, is occasionally acknowledged by the very tabloid papers that do so much to nurture it — "When it comes to attacking the French, the English are never last in the queue" (*Daily Mirror* 24 March) — was parodied in 'A Song of Patriotic Prejudice' by Flanders and Swann:

> "The English the English, the English are best,
> I wouldn't give tuppence for all of the rest;
> and crossing the channel one cannot say much
> for the French or the Spanish, the Danish or Dutch.
> The Germans are German, the Russians are red
> and the Greeks and Italians eat garlic in bed."

Sometimes the selection of such national signifiers has a self conscious jokiness. The Dutch stereotype evoked in the *Daily Mirror*, built around tulips, clogs, Heineken, Edam, windmills, and Van Gogh has a degree of absurdity, which makes a reading of the representation as comedic more probable. Yet in Holland the smiles might well be rather weary and thin-lipped at this recycling of symbolic simplicities. The Scots stereotypical fan in the *Daily Mirror* — whisky, shortbread, Braveheart video, Kenny Dalglish, Burns poem, Irn Bru — is similarly cast in joke mode. However a reading from within the context of a subordinate (Scottish) culture may, whilst recognising the comedy, resent the reduction of a rich culture down to a few stereotypical signs. It is dangerous to consider such images as independent from the sets of relations between nations that are always cultural, economic and political, and have a history.

More often, sport reporting has a strong element of violent language. Violent and militaristic metaphors are common — "Open warfare", "verbal volley", "bitter rival" (*The Sun* 10 July, 1995). Dutch footballer Ronald Koeman was "Agent Orange" (*Daily Telegraph* 27 March, 1995) There are "foot soldiers" (*Daily Telegraph* March, 1995), "Aussie hardmen", "battling Scots". People are "raging for revenge", and have a "smouldering rage". The modes of sports reporting are, then, a little more complex in this oscillation between crude jokiness, and confrontational violence. The construction of national identities can have a dangerous potency.

The peculiarities of the British

The United Kingdom is a product of the process of establishing English dominance. The very name of the British state is a source of confusions: British/

English, Great Britain/Great Britain and Northern Ireland, United Kingdom/
British Isles — few seem to understand clearly the distinction between these
terms. Whilst the British are not unique in having this blurred and confused
identity, the particular role of the British in the development of world sport
reproduced these confusions onto the world stage. The Celtic nations, Wales,
Scotland and Northern Ireland are not independent states, yet do, in many sports,
have their own representative teams (see Whannel, 1995).

   Their relation with England is not one of equality, but of dominance and
subordination; a process constantly underlined by the sports reporting of the
media. The ITV title sequence, with its images of the white cliffs of Dover, was
amended for Scottish audiences, but for the most part the Scots are constantly
told, of England's performances, that the whole nation is rejoicing or, alternatively, mourning.

   The peculiarities of the British are, firstly, that we have a state that does not
have a real identity — how many regard themselves as United Kingdom-ers?
Secondly, we have four nations that are not states, but have strong identities.
Thirdly, whilst one of these is dominant, the others are subordinate. Fourthly, we
have a national broadcasting system that on some occasions tries to weld all four
component parts together, whilst on others, such as some sport coverage, offers
separate regional programming. Fifthly, our representative sport is inconsistent
— some sports compete as the UK, others as four separate nations. In the midst
of this confusion, if there is one factor that has tended to act as a unifier it is
Europe and our strong tendency to see ourselves as separate from it.

Europe from the British perspective

Nations are, in Benedict Anderson's phrase, imagined communities (Anderson,
1983). They are the product, not simply of wars, or of linguistic communities,
but also of symbolic practices — mapping, flag design, emblem construction and
so on. Such is also the case with Europe. In such symbolic practices national
media systems are part of the constant marking remarking of difference. As Blain
et al. (1993) suggest, "Television and the press need a variety of Europes".
French, German and Italian media will construct Europe differently.

   There is no single simple or essential Europe — it is an area which has had
shifting geographic divisions (note that the last time the Germans and the Czech
Republic met in a football final, it was WEST Germany versus Czecho-
SLOVAKIA). It has, in different discourses, distinct internal divisions — the cold

war distinction between west and east, the Nazi distinction between Latin and Aryan. Nordic mythology constructs north western Europe as a distinct area. Countries like Russia and Turkey contain strong tensions between European-ness and Asian-ness.

The historical legacies — wars between England and France, Napoleon, the rise of Germany, the World Wars, — have a continuing resonance. The threat from outside — from USSR, from USA, from the Third World, have all featured in the construction of a commonality of interest. In promoting European unity, in discursive terms, the need for a strong Europe to counter threats from outside is a significant element. The tendency to conceptualise Europe in defensive terms has been labelled by some critics as "fortress Europe". So European identity is a complex combination of historical, geographical, economic, and political legacies.

From a British perspective, part of this process of constructing a European identity has been cultural — Eurovision, the Eurovision link, European Sport, The European Cup, Jeux Sans Frontieres, and even the Eurovision Song Contest — have all featured (see, for example, Whannel, 1982). The growth of holidays abroad, and the exporting of football hooliganism (in all directions — it should be remembered that in the fifties hooliganism was seen in Britain as a continental problem) have also played a role.

Of these cultural forms, it is, perhaps, The Ryder Cup that is one of the few forms within sport that does construct a united Europe with some success. And this is precisely related to that factor in identity construction that always serves to forge internal unities — a threat from outside. In this case the might of US golf that could no longer be overcome, ever, by Britain alone. Europe, however has proved capable of giving the USA a good match and as a result, media coverage of the tournament successfully works as a hailing device calling the patriotic subject to identification. In this case, possibly uniquely, it is a European patriotic subject that is being produced. Yet, in England, the notion of Europe as "other" is still remarkably strong, reinforced by a legacy of war imagery. Even the liberal *Observer* drew on this and commented at the commencement of Euro '96, "Will it be VE Day on 30 June?" (*Observer* 2 May, 1996).

From a British perspective, of course, the English Channel always intervenes as a factor in our imaginary landscape, producing a difference between island and mainland. British teams win and "get into Europe". It is deeply inscribed into our sporting language that we are *not* in Europe, that we have to win our way *into* Europe, that we go there, that it is a foreign place, alien. We go there on a trip, as football supporters, like an invading army. You can get 'knocked out' of Europe, and then you have to try and 'get back in' next year.

Yet it would of course be a mistake to think that from this perspective there is only one Europe. Europe from the UK does not necessarily look the same when viewed from a male or a female perspective. Black British citizens, or those descended from mainland European origins may well not experience the division as sharply. In symbolic communication there are many Europes. There is the Europe of British holidays, in which class is writ large. Among the versions of Europe produced in representations, and in cultural practices, we might include: 'The Costa del Lager', English bars, fish and chips, the disco and the beach, scoring, 18-30; France with its gîtes, fine cheese and wine, French cigarettes, elegant fashions; Italy and the Tuscan idyll of the English middle class intelligentsia; the Munich Beer festival; Amsterdam, dope and sex tourism; Paris and romance; Calais and the cheap day trip to stock up with cheap beer or wine. Each version of Europe has its own characteristic images constructing very different concepts of 'the continental'. Then there is also the Europe of business: Brussels, Strasbourg, bureaucrats, suited businessmen, wine bars, expense account meals, fatness and corruption.

The Europe of sport is not a unified one either: the athletics circuit — strawberries in Oslo, Golden Miles, Grand Prix meetings in Zurich, Brussels, Cologne; the tennis circuit — Monte Carlo, Paris and the French Open; the motor racing circuit — Spa, Nurburgring, and above all Monte Carlo with its rich-chic exclusivity; and of course the football world with its own particular passions and shrines — San Siro, Bernabeu, the Stadium of Light.

But what they have in common is that Europe, from a British perspective is seen as different: it's abroad, it's foreign. And this symbolic structure marks out Britain as having a very different perspective on Europe than France, Italy, Spain and Germany, who are already "there", and for whom there is not the same sense of a difference, marked physically and symbolically by the Channel.

It would be hard to over-estimate the impact of this sense of other-ness in sporting discourse. The 1953 trauma of defeat by the Hungarians established a contrast between continental skill and British work rate that has never quite gone away. Football writer Brian Glanville tells the story of "British Soccer and the foreign challenge" (Glanville, 1955). His book *Soccer Nemesis* describes the "insularity, conservatism and obstinacy" of British football. The story of British football and the foreign challenge, Glanville asserts, "is the story of a vast superiority, sacrificed through stupidity, short-sightedness and wanton insularity" (Glanville, 1955: p. 1) He asserts that "foreign football has indeed grown into a strong-man during the past fifty years, but the fact that British football has long since lost its supremacy is as much through its own failings as through foreign improvement" (Glanville, 1955: p. 2).

Such language bears a striking similarity to the bitter accounts of loss of Empire produced by conservative historians and politicians. The first line of Kenneth Wolstenholme's *Young England* (Wolstenholme, 1959) is "We British are an insular race". In the wake of the defeat by Hungary, he writes "we were left wondering what the game we played week after week was called. Certainly it was not Association football, compared to what the Hungarians showed us" (Wolstenholme, 1959: p. 10).

According to historian Percy Young, the Hungarians "combined the individual skills characteristic of the best continental tradition with the enterprise and initiative hitherto thought to characterise the British style" (Young, 1973: p. 263). Young links the Hungarian success to a rediscovery, in the face of adversity, of identity, "the post-war Hungarians, seeking a new sense of cohesion.... An artistic nation, they imbued football with a sense of artistry, but did not cancel either its virility or its chivalry" (Young, 1973: p. 264).

In short, foreign football stars offered a magical resolution of artistry and virility — both qualities admired by British crowds, and supposedly rarely captured in the same body. This might help account for the ambiguity of responses to foreign performers in England like Eric Cantona and Jurgen Klinsmann. Both have consummate artistry, both have a degree of combativeness. However both are also frequently represented as failing to live up to the tenets of fair play. Many English players could be accused of the same, but foreigners are, of course, not permitted the same leeway.

Jurgen Klinsmann arrived at Spurs with the reputation of a diver. Early on, he artfully undermined his negative image. Playing sparkling football, he scored and celebrated by mocking his image, diving full length, an effort imitated by his team-mates. As well as defusing the diver image, he also counteracted the British stereotype that Germans have no sense of humour. For a while he became a popular figure in the British press, and amongst British football fans.

Later however, he began once again to acquire a negative image. In various press reports he was described as "Horizontal Klinsmann" (*Sun* 25 March, 1995); "diver Klinsmann", "he was looking for it all night", "Klinsmann of old",

"Klinsmann the diver"; "Klinn hell" (*Sun* 23 March, 1995); "Jurgen still a con-man", "he was out of order", "the usual horizontal Klinsmann" (*Daily Mirror* 23 March, 1995).

When Cantona arrived in England he was represented as an enigma — French, different, Gallic, moody and temperamental, with great skills but violent temper. His Kung Fu kick at a racist Crystal Palace supporter was seen as confirming the over-shadowing of his talents by his dark side. Yet in the subsequent season, through superb play and immaculate behaviour he earned redemption, whilst remaining an enigma, remaining foreign and other.

Foreign elements can be grafted onto the British game — indeed in the 1996/97 season Zola, Juninho, and Ravanelli, among others, had a spectacular impact — but this is distinct from a process of acceptance or absorption. They remain precisely foreign bodies — fascinating but scary.

Identity and instability

Clearly, in cultural practices and in representations, extensive ideological work is performed producing the construction of the unified patriotic collectivity. Before the quarter final against Spain, the *Daily Mirror* front page proclaimed "Adios Amigos: Make a Noise for our Boys" (22 June, 1996). Inside the paper it exhorted us to "Set your watches for 3pm Wembley time! That's when you can strike a mighty blow for England. This morning the *Daily Mirror* is handing out 200,000 free whistles nationwide. And as the England-Spain Euro '96 show-down kicks off this afternoon we want one minute's noise for our boys" (22 June, 1996).

A whole variety of strategies are produced to demonstrate that "we" are all in this together. Ordinary people are invited to fax in their comments, poems and song lyrics to urge "our" boys on. Features list the stars who will all be watching and cheering along with us. In one *Daily Mirror* feature Liam Gallagher, Julia Carling, Damon Albarn, Anthea Turner all profess their commitment to the England cause.

Yet, I want to suggest, national identities are inherently unstable. To borrow from Laclau (1977), elements of identity have no necessary national belonging-ness, it is only in articulation that they are sutured together into a composite national image. The nation is not a stable category. Football may polarise English/Scottish identities, whilst athletics success may produce a British identity, especially around the success of an Allan Wells or a Liz McColgan.

Englishman Jack Charlton became a hero in Ireland, whilst the Irish journalist and ex footballer Eamonn Dunphy became such a villain in denouncing the ugly and unaesthetic approach of Charlton's Irish team that people in a Dublin pub could be heard chanting "If you hate fuckin Dunphy clap your hands" (see Whannel, 1995). The great irony here is that the substance of the issue of Irish footballing style is one of aesthetics — Dunphy berates the quality of Irish football from a purist perspective — a position one might expect the Irish to espouse. The popularity of football amongst the young in Ireland parallels a decline in the hold of Gaelic sports and Gaelic culture over the young, especially in Dublin (see Boyle, 1992). So an apparent rise in patriotism (focused around an English football manager) may mask a loosening of the ties of cultural nationalism.

The popular press may briefly succeed in establishing a patriotic British subject position around major events, but for the most part sporting cultural practices still have a degree of class specificity. Football, rugby, tennis, athletics and boxing are all sports that for the most part have very different class profiles. The apparent unity forged around World Cups, Olympics, and World boxing fights may be a strictly temporary phenomenon.

Sporting practices polarise the genders — most sport is still largely dominated by men, whether in terms of participation, spectatorship, media image, or officialdom. The discursive structure of media coverage of big events recognises this, indeed makes much play of the contrast in the genre appeal of sport and soap opera to men and women. Men are portrayed as rooted to the television sport, whilst women fume at being deprived of their favourite soaps in their normal slots. A recent edition of *Woman* asked, "Should soaps make way for football?", and featured stories such as: "Colin taught our baby to chant Ooh aah Cantona" (*Woman* June, 1996); and "I'm going to learn to drive so that I can escape soccer on TV" (*Woman* June, 1996).

In the *Sun*, journalist Jane Moore announced a campaign to "have a mis-leading description removed from the English language — football season.... It's one long turgid cycle of league matches, championships, friendlies and foreign never-heard-of-them games" (*The Sun* 29 May, 1996). The resentment is doubtless fuelled by the construction of women as providers whose role is to feed their men folk and their guests. Safeway arranged displays of interesting TV nibbles: Pringles crisps, Phileas Fogg tortilla chips, and assorted dips. Sainsbury's issued a leaflet: 'Good food and drink for Great Football', all linked to sponsorships: Mars, Snickers, Coke and Carlsberg. Women are here hailed as providers and nurturers, whose job is to cater for the comforts of menfolk who will be glued to the television for the duration of the competition.

Women were not the only dissenters from the domination of the airwaves by Euro '96. Commentators in up-market newspapers sometimes struck a dissonant note, and the terms of the discourse were similar. In *The Guardian*, Adam Sweeting berated the tournament for being "another excuse for a round-the-clock orgy of comment, analysis, name dropping, beer drinking and statistic swapping" (29 May, 1996). This of course pre-supposed that men needed an excuse for their indulgence in television football viewing. In the *Evening Standard*, Simon Jenkins wrote, "Euro '96 fills me with dread. Soccer in summer is madness.... As we sweep up the broken glass, cart drunks by the wagon-load to jail and return the old movies to the video shop, we can plead for the rhythm of the seasons to be restored" (31 May, 1996). Ironically, the good behaviour of fans, the relatively peaceful and harmonious relations between them and the general atmosphere of festivity that surrounded them were subsequently widely regarded as one of the successes of the tournament.

The media construction of major events also features a process of winning over — women begin "taking an interest", "get swept along". Dissenting males become fascinated — even if only as commentators from outside on the phenomenon. Commentary from eminent women is enlisted — Germaine Greer wrote in the *Independent* and A. S. Byatt in the *Observer*. For the *Evening Standard*, Nicola Jeal went to her first match and found that soccer chaps are a terribly nice bunch of chaps. In *Woman*, one feature was headed "Julie planned our wedding around the fixtures". The tendency of major sporting events to permeate all areas of the media gives them a great momentum and they tend to become the topic that demands comment from anyone involved in social commentary.

To sum up: identities are constructed around contradictions. The national identities of the United Kingdom are rendered particularly complex because of the existence of three subordinate nations within the British state. Europe, from the English perspective, remains foreign, different, other. Identities have an inherent instability — there is nothing natural or given about national-belongingness -it is a subject position that has constantly to be worked over to be produced and reproduced. Major sporting events offer one of the more fertile grounds for this process. However even in the case of Euro '96, the form of fervent patriotic unity that appeared to sweep England recently may be both illusory and temporary. Illusory because many may have been untouched by it, or alienated by it. Temporary because the following week "we" all want Henman to win, and the next week there will be something else to be concerned with, and it may be nothing to do with sport or the nation.

References

Bale, J. and J. Maguire (1993) *The global arena: Sports talent migration in an interdependent world*. Leicester: Leicester University Press.

Blain, N., R. Boyle and H. O'Donnell (1993) *Sport and national identity in the European media*. Leicester: Leicester University Press.

Boyle, R. (1992) 'From our Gaelic fields: Radio, sport and nation in post-partition Ireland', *Media Culture and Society* Vol. 14, No. 4 (London: Sage).

——— (1994) 'We are Celtic supporters... Celtic F.C., Celtic supporters and questions of identity in modern Scotland', in R. Guilianotti and J. Williams (eds) *Game without frontiers: Football, identity and modernity*. Aldershot: Arena.

Critcher, C. (1979) 'Football since the War', in J. Clarke, C. Critcher and R. Johnson (eds) *Working class culture*. London: Hutchinson.

Glanville, B. (1955) *Soccer nemesis*. London: Secker and Warburg.

Laclau, E. (1977) *Politics and ideology in Marxist theory*. London: New Left Books.

Mangan, J. A. (1981) *Athleticism in the Victorian and Edwardian Public School*. London: Cambridge UP

Whannel, G. (1982) 'It's a knock-out: Constructing communities', in Block No. 6, London: Middlesex Polytechnic.

——— (1992) *Fields in vision: Television sport and cultural transformation*. London: Routledge.

——— (1995) 'Sport, national identities and the case of Big Jack', in *Critical Survey*, Vol. 7, No. 2: pp. 158–164.

Wolstenholme, K. (1959) *Young England*. London: Stanley Paul.

Young, P. (1973) *A history of English Football*. London: Stanley Paul.

Chapter 2

EUROPEAN SPORTS JOURNALISM AND ITS READERS DURING EURO '96: 'LIVING WITHOUT THE SUN'

Neil Blain and Hugh O'Donnell

Glasgow Caledonian University

Theoretical context

This chapter further develops themes addressed in various previous publications on aspects of collective identity such as sport and royalty and citizenship, handled comparatively in the European context, with a particular focus on the national dimension. Interest has concentrated on a group of interrelated phenomena associated with constructions of collective identity, and previous research has generally tried to relate media constructions of the national dimension to other aspects of political culture in both the UK and other European countries which have been considered. The theoretical terrain within which this comparative work has been produced has become increasingly complex. Two aspects of this terrain require clarification here: one relates to modernity, the other to postmodernity.

Modernity

Jean Baudrillard, asked if he had ever envisaged writing something about Great Britain, replied afterwards in a letter that "I do not want to venture into giving my opinions about Great Britain. It strikes me as being a very strange country. Five hundred years after the discovery of America we now have to discover England" (Gane, 1993: p. 208). The problematic of Britain as a 'European' country is especially dynamic in the late 1990s, but for the purposes of this chapter it may be useful to couple the mutual sense of separateness between Britain and Europe specifically with the concept of political modernity and its putative failure to fully develop in the former. There is space here only to note the influence on our thinking of views proposed in often contentious work by Tom Nairn and Perry Anderson, dating back to a series of *New Left Review* articles of the 1960s, and later reworked in texts such as Nairn's *Enchanted Glass* and Anderson's *English Questions*, which point to indications that Britain cannot adequately be characterised as a modern state, but rather a state in which modern and pre-modern elements commingle. Our own work, especially on European accounts of national identity emerging from mediated international sport, and on royalty and citizenship, has only strengthened our conviction that Britain occupies a highly problematic position with regard to the idea of political modernity. It seems difficult to see Britain as a modern culture and society in the sense that France, Germany or Italy are, but as far as this chapter goes we can do no more than suggest this as a serious problem.

We have also insisted in our work on European sport that Britain is quite singular in European terms in its social class structure and the impact of that structure upon a wide variety of areas of culture (Blain *et al.*, 1993). If we look beyond the UK, we find not only that the tabloid press as understood in the UK is missing from most European countries (Germany's *Bild* notwithstanding), but that its equivalent readership is also missing, since the breadth and rigidity of British class distinctions is very much a *sui generis* phenomenon. In particular, the existence of very large culturally and politically disenfranchised working classes or underclasses simply is not replicated in the EC formation: nor elsewhere in the west of Europe. Therefore, to understand the language of the *Sun*, we require to understand the socio-historical conditions of possibility for the *Sun*, and also their national specificity (Blain *et al.*, 1993).

This impinges on notions of citizenship, both national and European, which lie behind our framing of media cultural differences below. We have noted elsewhere (Blain and O'Donnell, 1995) that the concept of 'European citizenship' when framed in France or in the Netherlands, Denmark, Belgium, Germany or Italy is problematic primarily because of the power of national formations — because, say, of the primacy of ideas such as 'French citizenship' over any alternative identity. In Britain there is the at least equal problem that it is hard to find evidence of political 'citizenship' in the European sense at all (Anderson, 1992: pp.302-353). The collective subject defensively invoked by British 'Euro-sceptics' in the late 1990s is generally nostalgic, in fact a fabricated historical subject, what has been termed in another context "a transhistorical national identity going by the name of 'we'" (Wright, 1985: p. 163). That such a tactic may be necessitated by the absence of a collective subject who is a modern political citizen is as good an explanation as any for such defensive behaviour.

To this proposition must be added the possibility that the British, like their citizen counterparts in other developed countries, have to an extent experienced an intensified subjection as consumers during the accelerated period of commodification of culture since the 1970s (the postmodernisation of cultures, which in the British case may or may not have originally been fully modernised). Were we to construct a British *subject-reader* as against a European *citizen-reader* as the protagonist of the transactions below that would be a simplification of the facts, but perhaps not an entirely pointless one, were it read as proposing a relative difference.

Postmodernity

Strong elements of whimsy, pastiche, historicisation, nostalgia and enhanced commodification, among other factors, are at work in the construction of media accounts of sport. These and other factors encourage the rethinking of aspects of late modern sport culture with, at least, an openness to postmodernism theory. It has been characteristic of much work in the field of culture either to sit entirely within a modern, materialist paradigm (this former position has continued to characterise much British work) or, alternatively, to operate entirely within a postmodern paradigm in which concepts such as ideology become, sometimes fatuously, constructed as superseded.

But a more agile conception of late modernity has been available since the 1970s in Charles Jencks's notion of *double-coding* (Jencks, 1991: p. 12), developed to explain how buildings at certain historical periods have accommodated plural readings by architects and users. Elsewhere Jencks's handling of the term 'double-coding' locates it beyond architecture solely, using it in the field of culture generally: "I term Post-Modernism that paradoxical dualism, or double-coding, which its hybrid name entails: the continuation of Modernism and its transcendence" (1989: p. 10). It is possible, appropriating this concept and adapting it for use in the analysis of political culture, to conceive of societies which have been partly postmodernised while retaining late modern features (Blain and O'Donnell, 1994b). In our adaptation of Jencks's idea, we remain neutral as to the general properties of the modern/late modern and the postmodern, preferring to make evaluation only on local instances.

Our primary concern in this theoretical process is to retain the modern concept of ideology while accommodating a postmodern concept of the consumer, placed within a dynamic of material forces, as shown in the following model.

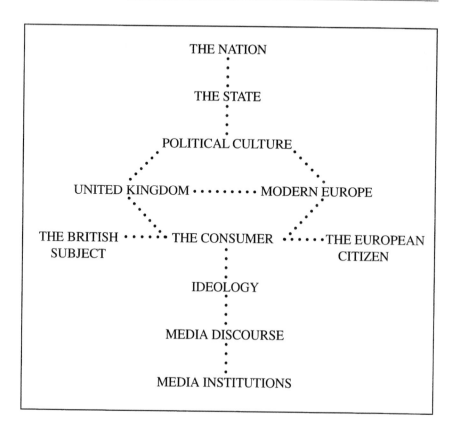

THE NATION

THE STATE

POLITICAL CULTURE

UNITED KINGDOM · · · · · · · · MODERN EUROPE

THE BRITISH · · · · · · THE CONSUMER · · · · · · THE EUROPEAN
SUBJECT   CITIZEN

IDEOLOGY

MEDIA DISCOURSE

MEDIA INSTITUTIONS

In this configuration the postmodern consumer operates not as a transcendence of modern, materialist debates but as an aspect of their development.

Sport and the media

Signification

We further hypothesize that the semiological relationship between sport and culture is different in the UK from the equivalent continental European relationships. We think that while sport operates in a chiefly symbolic fashion in countries like France, Germany and Spain, in the UK it is made to bear, more precisely, an indexical relationship: it is metonymic rather than metaphorical.

Britishness, Englishness and Scottishness, to name but three possible categories of identity from the UK, are peculiarly related to myths, ideologies and discourses of sport in a fashion which we do not think is replicated elsewhere. In Europe there is obsession with sport too, but it is with sport that the fascination consists. In Britain, in the international context, it seems rather to be an obsession with corporate national self, to which sport is virtually incidental (although in Scotland it may be a classically Baudrillardian instance of a replacement of self by simulacrum: this ominous possibility is addressed below, as are these other issues of signification).

The Model Reader

In the following analysis we will make use of the concept of what Umberto Eco calls the Model Reader (1981) — and what other analysts have called the Implied Reader (Chatman, 1978: p. 77) — constructed by sports reports in the mass-consumption newspapers of the UK and a range of Continental European countries. The Model Reader is the theoretical 'average reader' both constructed and addressed by the reporting as a whole, in terms of its content, its mode of address, its style and so on. The Model Reader cannot, of course, coincide with any actual reader: in fact the Model Reader can never be more than a partial extrapolation of any actual reader, and experience shows that many actual readers are capable of identifying, at least partly, with two or more rather different Model Readers (in Germany, for example, it is not so unusual to read both *Bild* and a more up-market quality newspaper). It is even possible for actual readers to have a playful relationship with an ironically projected Model Reader (O'Donnell, 1997). None the less, the Model Reader is as much an economic reality as a theoretical projection, and newspapers can pay dearly for mistakes in this area, as the case of the *Sun* and the Hillsborough disaster graphically illustrates. An analysis of the Model Readers constructed by different newspapers can, therefore, say a great deal about their view of the society within which they operate, and of their target readership within it.

The sample

The following analysis is based on a study of sports reports relating to the Euro '96 Football Championship in those Western European countries whose national teams took part: Denmark, England, France, Germany, Holland, Italy, Portugal, Scotland, Spain and Switzerland. In each case, we chose where possible to

concentrate on those newspapers whose sports reports achieved the greatest
penetration in terms of readership within the country in question, occasionally
contrasting this with reports from more 'up-market' publications. The newspapers included in the study are given in the table below.

	Mass readership newspapers	Dedicated sport newspapers	Quality newspapers
England	Sun Star Mirror		Telegraph Independent
Scotland	Daily Record		Herald Scotland on Sunday
Denmark	Extra Bladet		Jyllands Posten Politiken
Germany	Bild Express Hamburger Morgen- post		Süddeutsche Zeitung Die Welt
Holland	De Telegraaf		De Volkskrant
Switzerland	Blick		Tages Anzeiger
France	France-Soir	L'Equipe	Le Monde
Italy		Gazzetta dello Sport Corriere dello Sport	
Portugal		A Bola	
Spain	El Periódico de Catalunya	As Marca El Mundo Deportivo	ABC El País La Vanguardia

It is clear from this table that we are not in fact comparing like with like across
the different countries. The mass-consumption sports dailies are a phenomenon
of Southern Europe and France, while, although there are tabloid-esque
newspapers in a number of European countries — for example *Bild*, *Blick* and
Extra Bladet in the table above — none are quite like the English tabloids. It is
in fact part of our argument that we are unable to compare like with like.

The English tabloids and Euro '96

Representation

The term 'representation' needs particular attention in the context of sport. When the *Mirror* newspaper runs its infamous "Achtung! Surrender" headline (24 June, 1996) on the imminent England-Germany Euro '96 Wembley clash, this not only 'represents' the English and Germans as soccer combatants in an endless replay of World War 2, but also in a different fashion represents certain very important aspects of English society, culture, and media culture. There is hardly any important sense in which the media in the UK merely use sport as a metaphor. The English media in particular, and most of all in the context of international football, often consign sport itself to a subordinate role. Sport in Britain seems to be made to carry a different sort of relationship to other forms of cultural life, essentially an indexical relationship, in which (say) a German football performance is felt to be truly an aspect of a wider German identity which has to do with organization, energy, commitment and aggression. Sport operates through the media within culture as a way of discussing characteristics of which it is assumed to present direct evidence. In a field like gender this may be true of much of Europe, but where the national dimension is concerned this is a very British phenomenon — and not only in the tabloids.

Scotland on Sunday, with a very high ABC1 readership, ran a leader during Euro '96 which claimed that "with Europhobia filling the political debate day after day, it is crucial that Scotland emerges from the championship without damage to its credentials for internationalism. It is better by far to lose a football match than to gain a reputation on the continent for thuggery and xenophobia. Ask England. There is little shame in a small nation losing a football match; there is in street battles and hooliganism..." (9 June, 1996).

Here is as good an example as any of the assumption that football, politics, and culture generally are continuous and deeply interlocked. Without, in the limited space here, paying any attention to the specifically Scottish aspects of the grandiose claims made in this piece, it will suffice to note that the tabloids operate within a wider context of sport's centrality in British discussion of national character. Television does this too. When England and Scotland play each other at Wembley on 15 June 1996, BBC2 television's flagship current affairs programme *Newsnight* runs an item the night before on the fate of British identity, interviewing Scotland and England supporters on their national allegiances. And when England beat the Netherlands three days later, *Newsnight*'s next edition draws a comparison between the ease of England's victory over its European partner on the soccer pitch — as distinct from its major difficulties with its European Union partners over the ban on British beef products, in the wake of the BSE controversy.

England: the disturbed and nostalgic subject

It would be distressing to dwell too long on the details of the English tabloids' coverage of Euro '96: we choose two of the most revealing front pages from the *Star* and the *Mirror*, in order to emphasize that we use the *Sun* only generically in the title of this chapter. And intertextuality (for the tabloids provide much of their own frame of reference) is a major feature of the signification within these papers of a bizarre ideological cocktail of jingoism, xenophobia and wartime nostalgia — sometimes, especially in the *Star*, complicated by sexism — none of which have much to do with sport. (The quantity of technical coverage applied to the games themselves is limited, indeed very much so by European comparisons, in the English tabloids.)

Ahead of the big England–Germany confrontation, the *Daily Star* leads with "Herr We Go: Krauts gun for Tel" (24 June, 1996) and presents its readers with a front page which is a complex amalgam of male and English chauvinism and a simultaneously xenophobic but also salacious interest in Germanness. In a provocative pose and wearing the skimpiest of bras and shorts, Claudia Schiffer occupies much of the left-hand side of the page. Under the heading "Ooh, ja Claudia" the *Star* notes that "Curvy Claudia Schiffer is one German striker we don't mind being great up front. Her wunder-bra's giving lots of support. Here's hoping that's the breast that they can do." The right-hand side of the page has the headline printed over a photograph of Terry Venables dressed as a military recruiting officer in a Kitchener-style 'your country needs you' shot, over a subheading which reads "Jerry Venables: The England boss will be down and Kraut if the Germans have their way on Wednesday". Such has become the obsession with punning in the tabloids that the incoherence of "Jerry Venables" seems to have been lost on the writer — unless, that is, we instead give credit to the *Star* for producing genuine textual innovation here in a new form of tabloid art. "Jubilant Jerry fans yesterday blasted a Euro '96 warning to England as their heroes marched into the Semi Finals. The German blitzkrieg trampled through Croatia and now their stormtroopers aim to blast Terry Venables' men out of the tournament" (June 24, 1996). This representation, originally a metaphor but perhaps in Britain understood by sections of the tabloid readership metonymically, has a long history (Blain *et al.*, 1993: pp. 55-87; Blain and O'Donnell, 1994: p. 262) and at Euro '96 is ubiquitous. It is both with the style and mode of address that we are most concerned here.

The addressee is primarily masculine and working class but the British tabloids are yet more specific. Their extreme language, studied insensitivity, delight in shocking the sensibilities of others and in constantly pushing the boundaries of taste to the limits also indicates the assumed corporate character of an adolescent ("Girls can't get enough of it! Watching the Euro '96 macho men, that is!", *Star*, 24 June 1996) or a drunk ("They're going home"; "Germany's going home" is the refrain of the same day's *Mirror* in a graphic placed as a kind of obsessive physical border round its first four pages). This is a voice liberated from the constraints of civilized society and indeed civic society. And it is a mob voice, the voice of a gang of drunken football supporters on the rampage, within which the reader is placed.

We should not generalize too much: the modes of address discoverable inside the UK tabloids are in fact remarkably variable as the reader scans front pages, features and leaders in any one edition. But in frequently recurring examples, specifically at times of international conflict, the language becomes very restricted, adolescently masculine, and idiomatic, often deploying spoken modes and mixing them with what have now become codified tabloid habits. Among other features these involve a staccato syntactical simplicity: "But other adjectives are appropriate, etched in red, white and blue. In the win over Spain, this team of Terry Venables showed grit, courage and commitment. Good, old-fashioned 'bottle', if you like. It was there for Wembley to rejoice in" (*Mirror*, 24 June, 1996). There is also an avoidance of figurative language, by and large, other than the most commonly deployed, and a tortuous and juvenile wordplay: "Jurg a Gonner" insists the *Star* (24 June, 1996) as Klinsmann's injury rules him out. It is tempting to conclude that were we to reconstruct the likely reader of the UK tabloids' sports pages he, and it would be he, would be a lager-swilling youth of low intelligence and unprepossessing outlook. However that would also be a mistake: the demographic complexities of the tabloid audience need a much more sophisticated analysis, and indeed the complexities of address in these newspapers suggest some as yet unsolved mysteries about (say) older and female readers.

Although this young male addressee haunts the pages, the constant wartime references suggest that he may be better thought of as one (regrettable) mental component of many of the readers rather than as an actual demographic specimen. It is instructive to note semiological similarities between the nostalgic construction of young British soldiers on the front page of the *Sun* during the Gulf War and their rendition on the infamous "*Mirror* declares football war on Germany" edition's front page during Euro '96, where they have become Gazza and his colleague 'Psycho' Pearce. Both examples, along with others, seem anxious to utilize a World War 2 iconography which constantly suggests, though not intentionally, that British greatness can only be conceived retrospectively. Sometimes it seems possible that English identity is only finally realisable through sport and war, and that these in the last analysis are inseparable. Both social forms certainly privilege masculinity and they still tend to be conceived of as white wherever possible (but here perhaps sport is more dynamic than war).

We return extensively in the conclusion to the question of how far the concept of representation will stretch to cover the relationship between the British tabloids and the world. In the meantime we note characteristics which might point us elsewhere: play and whimsy, pastiche, historicisation, nostalgia, intertextuality, enhanced commodification. And however we imagine the reader or readers for these texts, he or she is a strikingly different demographic construction from the reader envisaged by *L'Equipe* or *Gazzetta*. No such reader as the *Sun*'s, *Star*'s or *Mirror*'s is constructed in continental Europe.

The Continental press

Football as a sport

A number of differences spring immediately to view in any comparison of sports reporting in the British/English vis-à-vis the European press. The most striking of these is the amount of attention actually given to *football per se* in European sports reporting. The large sports dailies such as *Gazzetta* or *A Bola* offer detailed and sophisticated analyses of each game, complete with charts of all kinds, graphic representations of different tactical formations, lengthy discussions of strategy and tactics, and even analyses of the performances of the referees and linesmen. In the case of *Marca* these analyses are usually entitled 'Technical Analysis'. Such articles can often be 1,000 or 1,500 words in length, vastly in excess of anything to be found in the UK tabloids. While non-specialist newspapers such as *De Telegraaf* or *El Periódico de Catalunya* are less detailed in their analysis, the analysis is none the less present and relatively sustained. Even the much maligned *Bild* has, in each major match report, a section entitled 'Analysis' — highly dramatic and expressionistic, in *Bild*'s inimitable style — but even so an attempt to present the game as an actual game of football. During Euro '96 it also drafted in such footballing greats as Günther Netzer and Franz Beckenbauer to provide detailed analysis of the tournament as a whole.

This kind of analysis is conspicuous by its absence in sport reporting in the British tabloids. This is in no sense coincidental. Our now lengthy study of football in the UK shows that, in its dominant presentation, it has nothing to do with tactics or strategy, which are seen as irrelevant Continental elaboration. Football in the UK is, in the popular press, essentially about courage, hard work, effort, commitment, staying power (Blain *et al.*, 1993; O'Donnell, 1994; 1996). It is emphatically non-technical and non-cerebral. Strategy and tactics are presented as 'European', un-British, unnecessarily complicated and irrelevant.

Background information

Allied to the above is what appears to be a genuine interest in many European countries in the broader social and political context within which the football matches take place. When Scotland met England a number of papers not only explained the background to that particular fixture, but also gave at times quite detailed accounts of the relationship between Scotland and England over the centuries (with frequent references to the film 'Braveheart'). There were articles on the class origins of sport in England, on certain uses of the English language in relation to sport, on the styles of different groups of fans and so on. Several articles in a number of countries speculated on the significance of a possible English victory for John Major and his beleaguered Conservative Party. This was all basically very respectful. This contrasts with either a total lack of interest in other countries among the English tabloids, or their often aggressive and insulting treatment of both footballers and fans from other countries, to which we shall return below.

Style

The mass-consumption daily sports newspapers of Southern Europe in particular are often written in a style which would be impossible in the British tabloids. Quotes from literary classics are sometimes used as titles for articles, references to literature or literary figures sometimes appear within the articles themselves, there are references to Greek mythology, to leading figures from art and music and so on. Quite apart from that, figures of literary note often contribute to these publications. Umberto Eco has been known to write for the *Gazzetta dello Sport*. In Spain Manuel Vázquez Montalbán continues to write in *Marca*. A few examples will suffice to give a flavour of this approach.

For example, when the Czech goalkeeper Kouba saved a shot from Ravanelli in a 2–1 defeat which was eventually to send Italy out of the tournament, *Gazzetta dello Sport* (16 June) reported on the incident as follows:

> Poor Ravanelli, generous and unprepared, poor Ravanelli who wanted to scale mountains wearing ballet shoes, poor Ravanelli who takes out of an empty game the only thing left to him, strength, strength to persist blindly with a ball lost and won back, lost again and miraculously slipped through to the magic foot of Chiesa: a thunderous shot, but the spirit of Kouba extends beyond his outstretched hands, and the save of saves cancels out at a stroke his only "plus", a semi-assist on Fabrizio's goal.

Meanwhile, *A Bola*'s reporter Afonso de Melo described his first encounters with London as follows (10 June):

> London — around St. Pancras and Kings Cross the city takes on the sombre tones of a poverty which induces unease. There is the humid heat of approaching thunderstorms, sultry and unbreathable, and the clammy smells of the night bring back to my memory the Indian dog-days of New Delhi and Bombay. The dark faces of the teenagers lean against the metal railings separating the pavements from the roadways which seem like absurd prisons or inadequate obstacles to imminent suicides. The air is heavy, almost unbearable.

And when Garry McAllister missed his penalty against England, he put this down later to the fact that the ball had moved slightly before he struck it. *L'Equipe*'s explanation the following day was that "Æolus had breathed unfavourably on the Scots": Æolus, as any reader of the *Sun* will automatically know, was the Greek god of the wind.

We are not suggesting that sports reporting with certain literary qualities is not available in the UK: it can indeed be found in a number of the broadsheets, though not even here is there prose of quite this degree of literary adventurousness. It is not, certainly, to be found in the mass-consumption newspapers. Contrasted with the language of European mass sports reporting, the language of the British tabloids is restricted and repetitive. It lacks neither colour nor invention, of course, but it implies no knowledge of or access to a more elaborated form of culture nor a familiarity with or interest in literary styles.

Back to parochialism and xenophobia

The most striking difference between sports reporting in the UK tabloid press and that of the mass-consumption newspapers of (most) Continental countries is the undisguised parochialism and xenophobia of the former. This is nothing new. Our study of coverage of the 1991 Wimbledon tournament revealed extensive xenophobia in the English press at the time (Blain *et al.*, 1993), to such an extent that the English press itself became a subject of much reporting in the presses of other European countries. This trend has continued and if anything intensified in the coverage of Euro '96, with the English tabloids again becoming the object of a great deal of generally horrified coverage in the European media (television as well as the press).

We have no wish to appear unnecessarily solemn on this account. Some of the stunts pulled by the English tabloids are in fact imaginative, amusing and enjoyable. As the semi-final against Germany approached, for example, the *Sun* signed up a lion from Chester Zoo to roar along with the fans. This is quite within the normal parameters of good-natured football fandom. However, even the title of this particular article indicated the more aggressive underside to such 'fun': "Herr we go, Herr we go. *Sun* signs up Jake the Lion to maul Germans. Let's blitz Fritz".

The first team to feel the brunt of the tabloid onslaught was in fact Scotland. As the Scotland-England match approached, the English tabloids contained many abusive references to 'Jocks' — "Blow their Jocks off England", was one example. The Daily *Mirror*'s headline — in old-fashioned London script — was "Cry God for Gazza, England and Tel" over a photograph featuring Gazza as a Roundhead and Gary McAllister as William Wallace. The subtitle was "Put 'em to the sword". In the run-up to its coverage of this match, the German PSB channel ZDF carried a feature on this reporting, expressing some dismay at a headline which announced that "Even Hitler would have got a warmer welcome" than the Scots. The next country to come in for such treatment was Spain, England's opponent in the quarter finals. Front page headlines included "Your done, Juan" and "Give 'em a Spainking" while articles inside reproduced countless — at times astonishingly crude — anti-Spanish jokes in which virtually no area of Spanish culture or history was left untouched. All the Spanish newspapers analysed in this study noted this with a sense of obvious dismay.

The pairing of England and Germany in the semi-finals lead to even greater excesses of xenophobia, undoubtedly the greatest ever seen in the English press so far. Chamberlain's speech was rewritten to refer to football instead of World War, and the wave of highly offensive jokes — many relating to farting — continued. Again, all the German newspapers reacted to this with a sense of shock. When Germany eventually won Euro '96, *Bild*'s front page headline was as low-key as it had been in 1990. Then it had proclaimed "Yes! World Champions!". This year's version was "European Champions! 2-1 Golden Bierhoffer".

The only other country in whose sports reporting we have found anything at all similar to this English phenomenon — though far from identical and not at all on the same scale — is Portugal. For example, when England defeated Holland, *A Bola*'s article on the match (20 June), entitled "Rule Britannia", began as follows:

> England's crushing victory over Holland produced hours of joy and a new atmosphere of confidence. For our part we want to say this: any victory over the Dutch gives us pleasure — they were the vultures who planned and executed the destruction of the Portuguese in the Far East, in Africa, in India. And they also tried to drive us out of Brazil. The emergence of the British Empire in History, with more capital and greater military power, brought them to a halt.
>
> Of course, the struggles between empires, some being built up and others already in decline, belong to the past. But the stains remain, as do the feelings of peoples.

(It has to be admitted that by British standards, this is an educated sort of chauvinism.) Portugal's game against Turkey was described by the same newspaper (15 June) as a battle "against the Ottoman Empire". The message — explicitly stated — was that "the Turks deserve to go home"; the argument — less explicit, but fairly clear none the less — being that they weren't really European. We shall return to this below.

Football: sport, life, or hyperreality?

On the basis of our analysis to date, we would like to suggest the following three kinds of relationship between football and society as mediated by the presses of their respective countries:

$$
\text{Football}
\begin{cases}
\text{(1) } \textit{is a sign of} \\
\text{(2) } \textit{is an extension of} \\
\text{(3) } \textit{is a simulacrum of}
\end{cases}
\text{the society in question}
$$

We would suggest that the first relationship (*'is a sign of'*) applies in all the Continental European newspapers studied, with the exception of Portugal. The second relationship applies in England and Portugal and to a lesser extent Scotland. The third relationship applies partly to Scotland, which may, not least as a result of anticipated constitutional developments, be in a period of transition.

Our argument is that these relationships are closely linked with the degree of political modernity of the countries in question. In countries where a modernising project has in fact been attempted — with all the limitations and contradictions which such a project must necessarily involve — sport has developed into one of many possible symbolic signs of the society in question: as *El Mundo Deportivo* put it, "it is one way of being part of Spain". In the bulk of European countries a successful national football team is an object of pride, but is not synonymous with national success: a country can fail in football and still have faith in itself. For example, *Bild* talks insistently of "Fußball-Deutschland", which is clearly not to be taken as synonymous with "Deutschland", while *Ekstra Bladet* also talks of "fodbold-Danmark" in the same vein. The Spanish and Italian newspapers talk of the 'footballing history' of their countries, which is not synonymous with their history in general. It is even possible for supporters in these countries, as a result of principled disagreement with the national coach, not to support the national team, giving rise to the phenomenon of the 'tifosi-contro' in Italy, for example. Since the relationship between team and society is symbolic — in other words entirely conventional — it therefore follows, quite logically, that a national team can fail without the society itself being deemed to have failed. What has happened is that the team has failed to live up to the society. In other words, this is a *footballing* failure: it is painful, of course, and disappointing — both the pressures and the desire to identify with the team are often intense — but it has clear limits. Such an analysis is absolutely clear in the lengthy post-mortems on Italy's early exit from the Championship, in the Spanish analyses of Spain's defeat by England, in similar approaches in Holland, Denmark and France: *De Telegraaf*'s headline "The laughing-stock of Europe" following Holland's heavy defeat by England refers to the Dutch football team, not to the country itself. Headlines and articles show disappointment, but are reasonable and even rational.

The second relationship (*'is an extension of'*) is in our experience restricted to England and Portugal, and is still detectable but appears to be on the decline in Scotland. In semiotic terms the relationship here is indexical: the sign has an existential relationship with the object, as smoke — to use Peirce's famous example — is a physical extension of fire. There is again nothing coincidental here. Portugal and Britain/England are without any doubt the two European countries with the worst post-imperialist hangovers in Europe, and the ones where political and economic modernity — for quite different reasons — are least well developed. The most striking aspect of this relationship is an almost total failure to dissociate Football and History. For the mass-consumption newspapers of these two societies football *is* history. In England, meetings between England and Germany are a prolongation of the Second World War. The infamous *Sun* headline of 1990 was no joke: "We beat them in 45, we beat them in 66, now the battle of 90". This was even clearer in 1996. As the match between Portugal and Turkey approached, *A Bola* (15 June) hearkened back to one of the great battles of Portuguese history when the country won its independence from Spain: "but history tells us that at the battle of Aljubarrota not even the cannons of the Spaniards could save them". Similar sentiments were highly visible during Portuguese coverage of the Barcelona Olympics (Blain *et al.*, 1993). In cases such as this a failure of the football team is synonymous with a failure of the society itself. This not only explains the ferocity of the attacks on the English players following their 1–1 defeat by Switzerland — attacks whose ferocity was mirrored nowhere else in Europe, not even in the case of what were seen as particularly calamitous defeats, such as Denmark's 3-0 drubbing by Croatia or Italy's 2–1 collapse to the Czech Republic — but the astonishing adulation they subsequently received when things started going their way. Only defeat by a 'credible' opponent is acceptable within such a framework (and Switzerland, from England's point of view, is not a credible opponent).

The third relationship (*'is a simulacrum of'*) is one in which the national football team is at least partly presented as referring only to itself, and as lacking any real referent beyond that. This has been increasingly the case in Scotland over recent years, where victories and defeats have been met by the Tartan Army with equal enthusiasm. The travelling Scottish fans have become, as Giulianotti (1993) rightly puts it, "post fans", blissfully aware of the pointlessness of it all, but determined to have fun anyway. This is, rather fascinatingly, a fan-led transformation. It is a cause of some confusion for the Scottish quality press, which resists this move strongly and would in fact wish to return to the kind of symbolic relationship outlined above. There is even some resistance in the tabloids — most notably the Scottish *Sun*, which would prefer the kind of indexical relationship dominant in England. Many Scots remember countless references to Bannockburn and Culloden in popular sports reporting in the past (Blain and Boyle, 1993: pp. 125–139), however this is a frame of reference which popular sports journalists are finding more and more difficult to maintain. Scotland's leading tabloid, the *Daily Record*, reflects this increasing schizo-phrenia, caught between attempts at serious sports reporting and self-mockery. This move to post-fandom is no doubt linked in the case of Scotland with the country's increasing political and cultural dislocation from England, and its consequent disengagement from the dominant discourses and practices of Empire and post-imperial blues.

Conclusion

Britain: post-tabloids?

A catalogue of putative 'postmodern' characteristics has been discovered in UK tabloid coverage: play and whimsy, pastiche, historicisation, nostalgia, intertextuality, enhanced commodification. It seems unlikely that a satisfactory account of what is happening here will use only 'modern' terms of reference. Support was canvassed above for Jencks's 'double-coding' model of post-modernity. It seems likely that the transactions between press and readers as accounted for here do present evidence of actual political realities and relationships in Britain. These include the continuing stratification of British life in social class terms, a fear and defensiveness when confronted with foreignness, and a number of indicators from the domain of 'taste' which correspond to definite material features of the society and culture. And perhaps the nostalgia is real?

Certainly, returning to the plural sense in which the term 'representation' was deployed above, the tabloid coverage represents real relationships of power involving British political culture, state and nation, and readers. The conservative position of British tabloid newspapers (irrespective of some party political repositioning during the 1997 General Election) over existing relations of dominance is related, to put it no more strongly, to the maintenance of an unacculturated and potentially reactionary element in British society. The language of the popular press, with its mockery of radical politics and its sneers at cultivation and culture, is above all a political phenomenon, affecting areas such as gender and race as much as class.

But something else has happened in the UK tabloids, as it has elsewhere in culture (though — should we adopt a cross-cultural perspective — not evenly, because it is not present at all in the European Continental newspapers which have been examined). The sign/object relationship has itself altered and the signifier can alternatively be seen as having emptied itself and/or become self-referential. The UK tabloid press accounts are now as much about the manner of their own signification as about any actual European culture or relationship. Relentless puns are more about their own awfulness than an attempt to spark relationships in the object-world into existence.The photographs of Gazza and 'Psycho' are themselves primarily references to other iconographic instances. The readership is likewise constructed in the familiar postmodern form of the knowing bricoleur/euse, the regular tabloid reader initiated into the sign-games whose welcome familiarity ensures the repetition of consumption.

We should not need to choose between the 'late modern' British reader and the 'postmodern' reader: the operation of forces characteristic of both phases of culture have been amply evidenced here. This replacement of actual symbolic activity by consumer-play has itself to be understood in comparison to a European press which does not seem to have taken on these characteristics. What this might demonstrate about British culture is too large a fact to develop in this chapter, but it is probably of a piece with those other observations which we have made about its distinctness.

Britain, sport and Europe

The first half of the 1990s saw the development of a more sports-centred, technical interest in sport on the part of the British quality press, which has increasingly inclined toward producing sports sections more easily comparable with the serious European sports publications like *L'Equipe* and *Gazzetta dello Sport*, though we do not find the linguistic qualities of literary sports journalism in Europe replicated in the UK quality press. Measured by readership, the majority of UK sports print journalism readers are being addressed in a strikingly different manner from their European counterparts.

The signs at present are that British culture as a whole cannot adequately be characterized in its relationship to Europe: there are contradictory signs involving both hostile signals and some pro-European affirmations, and the General Election of May 1997 showed only that displays of disapproval of Europe were no more of a vote-winner with the British electorate than expressions of favour toward it. Certainly, British society has seemed more polarized in its approach to Europe in the mid- and late-1990s, and to the extent that the tabloids themselves provide an index of British culture, the evidence is that small signs of Europeanisation in some quarters of British life may still be substantially offset by chauvinistic and xenophobic tendencies elsewhere. However representative the tabloids may be, these tendencies certainly operate in a mainstream area of media culture which has traditionally displayed formidable agenda-setting ability. Given similar if less crude and absurd anti-European agendas throughout most of the rest of the British media, certainly up until the 1997 General Election, this would seem likely to help perpetuate the sense of difference from the rest of Europe circulating so pervasively in British culture, and likewise its recognition on the continental mainland.

References

Anderson, P. (1992) *English questions*. London: Verso.

Blain, N., R. Boyle, and H. O'Donnell (1993) *Sport and national identity in the European media*. Leicester, London and New York: Leicester University Press.

Blain, N., and R. Boyle (1994) 'Battling along the boundaries: Scottish identity marking in sports journalism', in G. Jarvie and G. Walker (eds) *Ninety-minute patriots: Scottish sport in the making of a nation*. Leicester, London and New York: Leicester University Press, pp. 125–141.

Blain, N. and H. O'Donnell (1994a) 'The stars and the flags: individuality, collective identitities and the national dimension in Italia '90 and Wimbledon '91 and '92', in Richard Giulianotti and John Williams (eds) *Game without frontiers: Football, identity and modernity*. Aldershot: Arena, pp. 245–272.

Blain, N. and H. O'Donnell (1994b) 'Royalty, modernity and postmodernity: monarchy in the British and Spanish presses', *Acis: Journal of the Association for Contemporary Iberian Studies*, Vol. 7, No. 1: pp. 38–49.

Blain, N. and O'Donnell, H. (1995) 'Monarchy and citizenry: The old and the new', paper presented at the *Political Linguistics* Conference of the Belgian Linguistics Association, University of Antwerp (UFSIA), December 7–9, in collaboration with the International Pragmatics Association (IPrA) and the Interfaculty Center for Applied Linguistics (ICTL-UFSIA).

Chatman, S. (1978) *Story and discourse: Narrative structure in film and fiction.* Ithaca and London: Cornell University Press.

Eco, U. (1981) *The role of the reader: Explorations in the semiotics of texts.* London: Hutchinson.

Gane, M. (1993) *Baudrillard live: Selected interviews.* London: Routledge.

Giulianotti, R. (1993) 'A model of the carnivalesque? Scottish football fans at the 1992 European Championship Finals in Sweden'. Working Paper, Manchester Institute for Popular Culture, Manchester Metropolitan University.

Jencks, C. (1991) *The language of post-modern architecture.* London: Academy.

———— (1989) *What is post-modernism?.* London: Academy Editions/St. Martin's Press.

Nairn, T. (1988) *The enchanted glass.* London: Radius.

O'Donnell, H. (1994) 'Mapping the mythical: A geopolitics of national sporting stereotypes', *Discourse and Society*, Vol. 5, No. 3: pp. 345–380.

O'Donnell, H. (1996) 'Team Europe?: Stereotypes of national character in European sports reporting', in C. Schäffner and A. Muesolff (eds) *Conceiving of Europe: Diversity in unity.* Aldershot: Dartmouth Publishing.

O'Donnell, H. (1997) 'Yes, we love this land that looms: The Lillehammer Winter Olympics in the Scottish Press', in R. Puijk (ed) *The Lillehammer Winter Olympics* [provisional title]. London: John Libbey.

Wright, P. (1985) *On living in an old country.* London: Verso.

Chapter 3

MEDIA SPORT AND LOCAL IDENTITY: BRITISH RUGBY LEAGUE AND SKY TV

John Arundel and Maurice Roche

Sheffield University

Introduction

This chapter explores the development of British Rugby League as a media sport, specifically as a television sport. Its main aims are to illuminate the changing nature of sport-based local identity both in terms of British sport culture in general and also in terms of contemporary media-driven processes of cultural globalization in general. There are three main sections to the chapter. In the first, we review the changing character of Rugby League from its social origins to its postwar role as a media sport. In the second, to set the scene for the discussion of Rugby League and Sky TV which follows, we outline the role and power of the media, in particular Rupert Murdoch's organisations in contemporary sport. Finally, in the third main section, we discuss the new relationship which now exists between Murdoch's BSkyB satellite company and British Rugby League outlining some of the main implications for changes of identity and perspectives on the changes gathered from interviews with personnel involved in Rugby League, and in media sport roles related to the game. However, before beginning on these topics it is first necessary to introduce the chapter by indicating its general themes, some relevant aspects of the particular case of Rugby League, and some relevant general features of contemporary media sport.

General themes

This chapter is animated generally by an interest in the dynamics of collective identity in the context of contemporary processes of cultural and other forms of globalisation. As is evident in other chapters in this book (Chapters 4, 5 and 6) contemporary social changes connected with globalization, while they may

57

involve a certain degree of cultural homogenisation (connected with some standardized consumer products and some media products, including widely played sports such as athletics and soccer), do not necessarily always or generally result in such homogenisation. As a reference point for our discussion an argument by the cultural sociologist Mike Featherstone is helpful here. Featherstone offers a rather optimistic version of this 'other-side-to-globalization' view in his argument that: "one of the paradoxical consequences of globaliza-tion... is not to produce homogeneity but to familiarize us with greater diversity, the extensive range of local cultures", and "the process of globalization leads to an increasing sensitivity to differences" (Featherstone, 1991a: p. 43). Further-more, he suggests, the 'postmodern' culture of cultural fragmentation and collage, which is associated with globalization, also provides new room for local culture: "with postmodernism ... there is a return to local cultures" (*ibid*., p. 53).

In the course of this argument (unlike elsewhere, e.g. Featherstone, 1991b), Featherstone does not much reference the role of cultural industries. Nonetheless some aspects of their contemporary development support his general position. For instance the tourism industry, a leading promoter of global cultural change, and for a long period a vehicle of cultural homogenisation, now attaches increasing market value to the 'unique' features of places including local cultural traditions and heritage (Urry, 1990). Comparably the media-sport industry's longstanding high valuation of 'unique' dramatic and spectacular sport events — 'mega-events' such as the Olympic games, the World Cup soccer — is increas-ingly used by event producers to attach a temporary uniqueness to the local places, usually the cities, in which the event is staged (France and Roche, Chapter 6 below)[1]. This was most interestingly the case in the 1992 Barcelona Olympics seen as a media-event, where — instead of the usual use of a city to present the image of the host nation to the watching world — the city presented both itself and also the particularity of its (quasi-national) region, Catalonia, to the world (Spa *et al.*, 1996; Hargreaves, 1996).

However, in the context of contemporary globalisation, processes of cultural homogenisation and standardization evidently continue to develop in parallel with these potentials for renewed 'localisation', and arguably they tend to outweigh them. This has long been so in the sphere of international sport where the diffusion of standardized games began back in the late 19th century in the context of various competing versions of imperialism, most importantly that of the British and their Empire (Guttman, 1994; Roche, 1998a: ch. 3). This process has been taken to a new level in recent decades by the mass diffusion of television since the 1960s and of TV-based media sport since the 1980s (Bale and McGuire, 1994; Donnelly, 1996; Rowe, 1996). The view taken in this chapter is not so much that television erases the pre-television era identities and traditions of particular sports and local clubs. Rather it is more that, whatever particularity and local identity they may continue to operate with, in the television era these identities are becoming increasingly subject to and dependent upon the power of the media industry. As we will see in the case of British Rugby League, the particularity of their identities increasingly risks being taken over, constructed in, and transformed by television.

The case of Rugby League

In this chapter these general themes will be illustrated by a discussion of the particular case of the British Rugby League and what could be said to be its take-over, in 1995, by Sky television, an arm of the global media industry complex controlled by Rupert Murdoch. The third section of the chapter in particular is based on the interview component of a larger research project studying this topic (Arundel, 1998)[2]. British Rugby League, unlike soccer, has not been the subject of much sociological and cultural studies research, and what there is makes little reference to television and to the game as media sport (e.g. Dunning and Sheard, 1979). In addition studies of British media sport also tend to make little more than passing reference to Rugby League in this context (e.g. Barnett, 1990; Whannel, 1992). So the chapter explores a topic of intrinsic sociological interest on which there is currently a significant gap in the sociology of sport and cultural studies research literature.

The culture of British Rugby League carries a significant weight of collective identities connected with local communities and the general regional 'locality' of the North of England. But, unlike other sports, the sport plays a marginal role in carrying and representing the collective cultural identity of 'the nation'. Since its creation in the late 19th century it has been, and it largely remains at present, a 'local' rather than a 'national' sport. In principle Rugby League has as much potential to provide a vehicle for national identity as has Rugby Union. Rugby Union provides Wales, New Zealand, South Africa and Western Samoa with their most important 'national' sports, and with the international recognition which comes from this. Rugby Union also provides very significant opportunities for national identification and differentiation to England, France, Australia, Ireland,

Scotland and other countries. In the British context, in comparison with Rugby Union's national-level role (and also to a certain extent in the French context: see Dine, Chapter 9 below) Rugby League has tended to play a much more secondary, regional and local role in identity formation and expression. In Britain this secondary role is part of a wider and deeper 'poor relation' position which has existed between the two rugby codes since their split in the late 19th century, and it will be a recurring theme in our discussion. The game of Rugby League, then, as both a spectator sport and as a media sport is thus intrinsically interesting to explore in terms of the sociology of British collective identities, in addition to the wider more theoretical themes of globalization noted earlier.

Sport and the media

'Media sport' as a cultural form, and 'television sport' as a particular TV programming genre (e.g. Goldlust, 1987; Wenner, 1989a; Whannel, 1992 and Chapter 1 above; Real, 1996; Rowe, 1996), have long been seen as important to national cultural identity (e.g. Chandler, 1988; Hargreaves, 1986; Blain, *et al.*, 1993), and thus as requiring full access by national publics. This access has traditionally been provided, in America and Europe in the post-war period, through different mixes of commercial and state-based broadcasting. The importance of the TV sport genre to the health, indeed the very survival of commercial TV networks has been particularly clear in the USA. Since the 1960s the competition between the big three networks for the TV rights to sport events seen as of national significance, such as major league baseball, American football and the Olympic games, has been increasingly intense over the years[3]. It has been less well appreciated in European countries with state-based TV stations, such as the BBC in Britain, which have traditionally had relatively inexpensive and uncontested access to the broadcasting of such sports and events, and also where public access to 'key' sport events via TV may also have been protected in law (as in the case of Britain's 'listed events')[4].

With the advent of satellite and cable TV in Europe since the 1980s and with the simultaneous weakening of the previously central role of state-based broadcasting there has been a greater recognition of the importance of TV sport. On the one hand commercial TV recognises the capacity of media sport to 'capture' massive and/or committed audiences with class and consumption profiles attractive to advertisers and sponsors. On the other hand public service TV recognises the capacity of media sport to provide opportunities for cultural inclusion and for bringing national and international publics together in the sharing of calendars of common events, and of sharable experiences in a common (mediated) space and time — a common and recurrent national and international public culture in an increasingly fragmented and changing world (Dayan and Katz, 1992; Roche, 1998a: ch. 5). State-based and commercially-based versions of wide-access terrestrial 'free to view' TV were competitive with each other, but they could also be compatible. They could even be complementary, in terms of sharing the broadcasting of a given year's major sport events. However the advent of satellite and cable TV systems in the 1980s and their market penetration and growth in the 1990s has begun to shift the balance decisively and inexorably in favour of commercial television. This has raised major regulatory problems in relation to public access for all forms of programming, but in particular for sport TV (see Notes 4 and 6).

These systems, and the further technological development they promise through digitalisation in the late 1990s, have enabled, and will increasingly enable, commercial TV to make profits by processes of 'intensification' of products and markets in ways notably different from, and additional to, the processes of 'extensification' involved in traditional 'broadcasting' to a wide audience. The process of extending mass market penetration in the British and European market, of course, continues in parallel with intensification, as satellite TV in particular attempts to use its buying power to control exclusive rights to attractive major sport events in order to sell receiver dishes. However, in the new-generation digitalised systems, profitability is made viable — to a greater extent than ever before — by attracting special-interest audiences. These audiences are willing to pay for access to channels specialising in intensive single-genre programming (pay-TV), and indeed willing to go further and to pay additional fees for one-off events, so-called 'pay-per-view' (PPV). It is estimated that there is a very strong latent demand for PPV in Britain and Europe more generally. In Britain this latent demand is estimated to be a massive extra £2.5 billion annually in potential consumer expenditure across all programming genres but particularly on sport programming (Gratton, 1997). In Europe generally it is estimated to be of the order of $23 billion by the year 2000 (Short, 1997). To feed the bottomless programming needs of these systems , and in order to reap the profits that are available through both extension and also intensification processes, TV companies (Murdoch's in particular as we will discuss later) have risked taking on heavy debt exposure in order buy up exclusive rights to the transmission of many key national and world level sport events, because of their strategic importance and profitability. This has a number of destabilising effects in relation to the organization and identities of nationally or regionally based sports, and the communities from which they traditionally drew their support (see also Rowe, 1996).

On the one hand the intervention of TV on this scale destabilises traditional relationships between organizers, players and fans within sports. Important new flows of income are injected into sport governing bodies and their clubs, rendering them dependent on TV income rather than gate-receipts from fans and spectators, and leading to inflation and instability in the labour market for players (Bale and McGuire, 1994). On the other hand TV's intervention destabilises the public's access to nationally significant sport events by effectively privatising them. In the late 1990s, particularly in Europe in sports like soccer and rugby, we are seeing the development of complex power struggles over both sorts of issue, involving media companies, representative governments, sport organizations, and fans. These struggles are complicated also by the trans-national character of some of the leading media companies, in particular Rupert Murdoch's stable of companies, and also of the system of governance emerging within the European Union (EU) as a result of the attempt both to create and to regulate the Single Market. In effect these struggles over access to media sport can be said to contribute to the development of new national and 'post-national' conceptions of cultural identity (Morley and Robbins, 1995) and 'cultural citizenship' and the rights of such citizenship in the contemporary period (Rowe, 1996; Roche, 1998b).

British Rugby League: from community sport to media sport

The social origins and development of British Rugby League
As is well known the modern versions of the sport(s) of football were developed in the mid-19th century, in the new and renewed institutions of the elite public schools and the elite universities of Oxford and Cambridge. Football became the exclusive preserve of middle- and upper-class males who codified and organized what were previously relatively unstructured and localised folk and working-class games (e.g. Dunning and Sheard, 1979; Mason, 1980). Along with other

sports created in this period by these groups, such as modern athletics, football was played according to the 'amateur' ethos, and it was developed into the two distinctive forms of the mainly kicking game of soccer and the mainly handling game of rugby. Two separate governing bodies were created for these forms, respectively the Football Association in 1863 and the Rugby Union in 1871. The games were diffused regionally and nationally, and, eventually, also in terms of cross-class participation and spectatorship, all of which occurred rapidly in the 1880s and 1890s. The massive growth of working-class participation as players and as paying spectators in this period necessarily involved the growth of professionalization in these sports. This growth was handled in soccer, following other sports such as cricket, by the toleration of mixtures of amateurs and professionals within and between teams (Mason, 1980), particularly so after the formation of the professionally oriented Football League organisation in 1889. In rugby the growth was handled very differently, with the Rugby Football Union (RFU) attempting to hold to the exclusively amateur line also taken by athletics and the Olympic movement in this period (see Lovesey, 1979; and Killanin and Rodda, 1976 respectively). This led to a breakaway by northern English clubs to form a Northern Union in 1895 (Dunning and Sheard, 1979, chs. 8 and 10). While still aspiring to amateur values, the Northern Union (which became the Rugby Football League [RFL] in 1922) was prepared both to tolerate professionalism and also to make changes to the Rugby Union game to increase its pace and openness in order to increase its attractiveness as a spectacle for a paying public. These changes were codified in new rules defining the nature and character of the game in the early years following the split (e.g. in 1898 and 1904: see Delaney, 1986 and Moorhouse, 1996).

Since its foundation in 1895, professional RL in Britain has predominantly been a game played almost exclusively in the North of England, in the counties of Yorkshire, Lancashire and Cumbria — strongly identified with, and reciprocally a strong cultural identifier of, the North of England and its industrial working-class communities. Unlike the governing bodies of most British sports, the game's organizational headquarters is also based in the region, in the city of Leeds in Yorkshire. A number of clubs have been formed outside of this region, but, with the current exception of London, they have failed to sustain themselves for any significant length of time. This spatial and cultural identity — particularly the game's association with the areas of the British industrial revolution, with the industrial working class, and with working-class masculinity — has had important consequences for its media representation, particularly its traditional representation on television since the 1950s, as we will discuss further later.

However at this point it is worth making two observations about the social context of the game. Firstly the working-class character and roots of the game, while undoubtedly very important in terms of both contributing players and spectators, can be over-emphasised. This is particularly so if it leads to the assumption that the working class were significantly responsible for the creation and organisation of the game, and that in this respect the game was some kind of exception from the general rule of the attempt by the upper and middle classes to exert social control of the working class's increasing non-work time and leisure interests and activities through sport and in general through various related 'rational recreation' movements and cultural institutions (e.g. Bailey, 1978; Cunningham, 1980). In Dunning and Sheard's classic account of the social origins of the game it is argued that it was men from a certain section of the new British middle class — particularly those not educated through the public school system which so influenced every other sport in the mid-late 19th century — men who ran 'gate-taking' rugby clubs and who were involved in business and industry in their locality, who took the lead in the 'break-away' from the RFU. These middle-class men, although more lightly touched by it that their southern counterparts, nonetheless retained a high respect for the amateur ethos. So initially they insisted that their players should be fully employed at something other than rugby. However they were realistic enough willing to compromise on 'broken time' payments to players (i.e. payments in compensation for time off from work). In the South of England the middle class base for Rugby Union was extensive, the working class were effectively excluded from the game, and in any case were attracted to professional soccer. By contrast in the industrial North it was necessary for rugby clubs to be able to stage dramatic and commercially viable sporting events to counter the attraction of professional soccer. Having taken the step into the business of paying players and maximising paying spectators there could be no way back, in the early 20th century, into the class-divided but more nationally significant sport culture of Southern England. The professional, regional and class identity of Rugby League thus had its origins in the different socio-economic contexts and class dynamics of North and South England in the late 19th century, rather than in some direct cultural expression of the British working class. However it is also true to say that the Northern working class, even if they did not create or own the sport, effectively 'took over' its popular culture and identity from this period onwards.

Secondly, while nominally a commercially-run sport, because it was regionally confined and overshadowed by soccer and rugby union, Rugby League was never very successful commercially, in spite of attracting substantial crowds in the early and mid-20th century. This situation was hardly altered, in the post-war period, by the advent of television and coverage of Rugby League games in the 1950s and 1960s. Since at least the 1970s the game has had problems attracting and holding spectator numbers and has been in recurrent financial crisis. Interestingly, as we will return to in a moment, some commentators blamed TV coverage for this. However this view was not convincing even in the 1970s (e.g. see Dunning and Sheard's rejection of it: 1979, p. 235), and it is even less so in the 1990s. It ignores the massive socio-economic and associated cultural and political changes which have been underway in British society since the mid-1970s, particularly the de-industrialization of traditional industrial cities and regions and the undermining of traditional working-class communities in the North of England. By the 1990s the sport was in long-term slow decline and had no clear future, in spite of having had some continuous exposure in media sport in Britain for a number of decades. The situation was ripe for change, and the intervention of the Murdoch media in 1995 certainly provided that. Before we look at the current situation in a little more detail it is first necessary to provide an outline of Rugby League's relationship with TV in the pre-Murdoch period.

Rugby League as media sport

For much of its history as a televised sport in Britain, Rugby League was presented to the national audience as a distinctively regional and 'Northern' game (Clayton and Steele, 1993). As we saw in the previous sub-section, by comparison with Rugby League, Rugby Union has traditionally had a very strong Southern, middle class and capital city presence and identity. It has also tended to have a strong 'national' image as a televised sport. On the one hand, as compared with Rugby League, town and city club-level Rugby Union games have traditionally had little TV visibility. But, on the other hand — and far outweighing this — television has traditionally gravitated to the high status and nationally attractive events offered by Rugby Union's national and international dimensions. So it has focused on the games and competitions of teams representing the three (quasi-)'nations' contained within the nation of the United Kingdom, namely England, Scotland and Wales (in the Home Nations Cup), plus the two nations of Ireland and France (in the Five Nations Cup), and also periodic events involving the powerful Southern hemisphere teams of Australia, New Zealand and South Africa. The international, indeed global, character of Rugby Union in general and televised Rugby Union in particular has been qualitatively enhanced in recent years by the creation, under the influence of the media industry (Murdoch in particular), of the Rugby Union World Cup and various world regional competitions in the two hemispheres.

Although there are and have been some national and international dimensions to Rugby League as a media sport in Britain, particularly in terms of British games against visiting Australia and New Zealand sides, this has been very limited and there is no real comparison between Rugby League and Rugby Union in this respect. Also these dimensions have not been significant within the organization and presentation of televised Rugby League in Britain which has tended to be mainly be of town and city-based club-level games and competitions. In these respects televised Rugby League, with its mainly local and regional character and image, has suffered by comparison with televised Rugby Union with its mainly national and international character and image. As a corollary of this situation, generally speaking in the pre-Sky period, as compared with the televising of Rugby Union, the televising of Rugby League rarely contained complete live games, few highlights programmes, and no real magazine programmes.

The first Rugby League game to be televised in Britain, in 1951, was the international between Great Britain and New Zealand. In this year also the BBC first began to show league club matches. In 1952 BBC covered the Challenge Cup final, but did not do so again until until 1958 (Moorhouse, 1996). In the 1950s ITV staged the Rediffusion Trophy an 8-team competition under floodlights and based in London — but ironically Northern viewers were not able to view this because the ITV network had not been extended fully to the North at the time (Moorhouse, 1996). From the 1960s to the 1980s Rugby League as media sport had two main BBC TV showcases. On the one hand there was BBC1's multi-sport Saturday flagship programme 'Grandstand' which would often show at least a second half of a game live. On the other hand there was BBC2's 'Floodlit Trophy' which ran from 1965-80, a knock-out tournament, run and screened on Tuesday evenings, in which there was highlights coverage of the first half and live coverage of the second half of the selected match. While the floodlit and knock-out elements of the latter helped to construct reasonably dramatic TV programming, it was never able to attract an impressively large viewing audience.

Commentary is a key aspect of the television sport genre, linking the viewer to game in a variety of important ways (Whannel, 1992: pp. 26-32). One central aspect of BBC TV's presentation of Rugby League in this period was its reliance on one main commentator, a crucial mediating personality, who effectively became 'the voice of Rugby League' for most sports TV viewers. Eddie Waring, a successful ex-Rugby League manager, dominated the presentation and image of the game on TV throughout the 1970s until he retired in 1981. He had an entertaining personality and, with his identifiably Yorkshire regional accent and mannerisms, became something of a celebrity on British television as a result of his commentator role. He had been impressed by American TV's presentation of American Football and he brought some of those values to his commentating. He summed up his approach to his role as follows: 'I'm out for the entertainment of the game. Technicalities I certainly explain where I've got to. But I like the picture to do the story. I feel I'm selling a game which is known to only about 60, 000 people. I'm selling it to six or seven million people' (BBC, 1997).

However, whatever Waring's positive image outside of the sport, within the game views were more divided, some seeing his entertainment orientation as selling the game short and as presenting a thoughtless and down-market mage of the game. This was combined with general criticism of the limitations of the game's exposure and presentation by the BBC which, as an organisation, was seen to be run by people raised, via the public schools and Oxbridge connection, on Rugby Union and thus both ignorant about and biased against Rugby League, the permanently 'poor relation' of the Union version of the game. It was also combined with criticisms of the impact of TV coverage on attendances at games (and thus on income from gate receipts), which were poor and declining throughout the 1970s and beyond. These criticisms, although arguable, as has been indicated earlier, were nonetheless given some credibility by a report commissioned by the RFL (the Caine Report 1971, cited Delaney, 1986: p. 42) and circulated to clubs. Prophetically this report also suggested that the sport needed to rid itself of its 'slag heap and drizzle' image (*ibid.*, Delaney).

The critical and suspicious attitude of the sport to television can be indicated by the fact that leading RLFC clubs such as Wigan attempted to prohibit TV from getting access to their games in the mid 1960s. There was a general view in the game that, for much of its period of control of Rugby League's television coverage, as Simon Kellner puts it, the BBC "did not take the game seriously" (Kellner, 1996: p. 81). Our interviewees generally concurred with this[5]. From Waring's light commentaries, which had become parodied by national comedians, to camera-work which often conveyed little more than "bodies rolling around in mud" (Rugby League journalist A), there was a felt sense that the BBC "didn't take it seriously.... I was playing at the time and I found it disturbing that this was the image that was being portrayed" (Rugby League administrator A). The interviewees generally believed that, from fans to players and administrators, people in the game saw the BBC's coverage as poor, with little background information being given, and that they tended to use it to fill dead time in their main Grandstand programme. In addition the main commercial sponsors attracted to support competitions and clubs and advertise through them tended to be 'beer and cigarettes' companies, using the game as a marketing vehicle to address lower working-class male consumer markets. Such advertising (for instance ground advertising which is visible and identifiable in BBC broadcasts), in the view of some in the game, particularly in RFL circles, only served to reinforce and propagate negative, stereotypical and limited popular images of the sport.

However from the mid-1980s the situation began to change notably. In spite of the high regard which people within the British game may have had for the quality of their game the visit of the Australian team in 1982 revealed that playing standards in fact had either declined or at least had stagnated in the post-war period. Modern coaching and training methods had appeared to pass them by. The Great Britain and other British teams which played the Australians during their visit were comprehensively outplayed by a team playing at an entirely different level of skill, strength and fitness. The British game learned hard lessons from this humiliation, and learned some more during another comprehensive defeat by the visiting Australians in 1986. Consequently major improvements in playing standards were introduced during the 1980s (Moorhouse, 1996). Australian stars were recruited and the success of the improvements was evident when the Australian team suffered its first home defeat against Great Britain for over 15 years when they were beaten in one of their games by a visiting Lions side in 1988. From the point of view of Rugby League as British media sport the 1980s upswing received a huge boost in the 1985 Wigan v. Hull Cup Final at Wembley. This made a big impression on the viewing audience with the high quality, pace, power and skill of the game, and began a long period of Wigan domination in the contemporary British game (Moorhouse, 1996).

Also in 1985, the regional commercial company Yorkshire TV broadcast a number of Australian TV programmes covering Australian Rugby League matches. These revealed that a very different and more upbeat and attractively designed television presentation style was possible for the sport than anything the BBC had used up to that point. The late but fitful renaissance of British Rugby League as a potentially attractive spectator sport and media sport for the contemporary period coincided with the arrival of satellite TV in 1988, specifically Rupert Murdoch's Sky TV organisation with its dedicated sports programming needs, although the full impact of Sky on the game was not felt until the mid 1990s.

Before we consider this impact in some detail we first need to put it into context by reviewing Murdoch's widespread media sport interests and operations more generally. It is important to establish the fact that, however significant the fate of British Rugby League is to communities, to fans and even to commercially-oriented interests within the game it is only a very minor piece in Murdoch's 'sport media empire'. While it may be transformed from a 'local' to a 'global' sport by Sky it may also ultimately find that it has traded one version of marginality — a cultural version which at least was associated with independence and self-regulation, for another version of marginality — a financial one involving dependence and vulnerability as a small operational unit within a global media corporation.

Media sport and cultural power: the Murdoch media

Rupert Murdoch has always seen media sport as a key element in his corporate strategies and increasingly so in recent years as his companies have begun to create an international media network with truly global reach. For him they have always been a leading programming genre, along with films (from his USA Fox company's [ex-'20th century Fox']) archives and current production, and from partners like the Disney corporation) and live news (currently only from his USA Fox News and European Sky News operations, having failed in his bid to buy up the global cable TV news market leader company CNN in 1994). These three genres, with media sport prominent among them, are of great value to Murdoch in his efforts to enter and dominate national, international and global press and TV markets. Media sport in particular allows him to create profitable new synergies within his media complex between his press and TV companies, and more broadly between his media companies in general on the one hand, and the wider global corporate market-place of advertising and sport sponsorship on the other.

Before we map out some of the main sport-related aspects of Murdoch's operation, his 'media sport empire', it is worth pointing out that, appearances to the contrary notwithstanding, we do not aim to portray him as an omniscient and omnipotent monopolist destined to rule all of world TV sport into the 21st century. His commercial judgments are fallible and he nearly wrecked his set of companies by overborrowing in 1990 (Shawcross, 1992). Also, while his network of companies constitutes a major and growing force in the global media industry, it is not the biggest fish in the sea. A small number of companies directly concerned with TV programming are as big or bigger — for instance America's General Electric/NBC, Disney Corporation, and Time-Warner corporation, and Germany's Bertelsmann corporation. So too are a number of companies in related audiovisual and information technology sectors such as Sony, Microsoft, and IBM (see for instance Morley and Robbins, 1995). While the priority Murdoch gives to the acquisition of TV sport is currently one of the distinguishing characteristics of Murdoch's global media 'empire' it is not inconceivable that companies such as these other global media operators could decide to enter this market, or to establish a bigger presence in it than they currently may have. It is possible that, when the renewal dates come up for many of his various current sport TV contracts around the turn of the century, he might face the kind of competition in this field at a global level that NBC, CBS and ABC already provide him with in the USA in relation to American sports, and that Kerry Packer's TV organisation provides him with in Australia. On the other hand it is also true that he thrives on competition (Shawcross, 1992).

Murdoch's sport-led corporate strategies have been evident over a number of decades in his various media operations around the world — since the 1970s in Australia and Britain, since the 1980s in the USA, and in the 1990s in continental Europe and Asia (Shawcross, 1992; Tunstall and Palmer, 1991).

Within Murdoch's complex global network of press, TV and other types of media companies his specifically television-oriented companies and interests, which have been most involved in developing his media sports-led global corporate strategy, include the following: Fox TV in the USA, Star TV in Asia and China, Channel 7 in Australia, well as BSkyB in Britain and Europe; and, in Germany, the Vox and Kirsch media companies in which he has a large stake.

Murdoch has had considerable success, particularly in the 1990s, in buying up many significant sports and sport events for his companies around the world (Barnett, 1996). In Australia, for instance, his Channel 7 will be the home broadcaster for the Sydney 2000 Olympics and for the summer and winter Olympic games to be held in the 2002 to 2008 period. In addition he controls TV rights for Australian rules football, the Australian Open tournaments in golf and in tennis, and much of Rugby Union, including the 1999 World Cup. In the USA, his Fox TV network controls the National Hockey League competition and has alternate seasons control of the baseball World Series. In addition, and at the huge cost of around £1billion he has acquired a 50% stake in one of the two major American Football leagues, the NFL. Through this Murdoch has a stake in America's biggest and most lucrative media sport TV events, the SuperBowl, for the period 1995-1999.

Murdoch has a long-proven ability to read and play media-cultural markets, and to take risks in order to dominate them (Shawcross, 1992). Currently, for instance, the revolutionary new digital generation of massive capacity multi-channel and interactive TV systems, in both satellite and terrestrial versions, is being introduced in Britain and more broadly in Europe. The British terrestrial version of digital TV, in which it is likely that Murdoch will have a significant stake, will begin running 30 channels from 1997 while Murdoch's own satellite version of digital TV will begin running 200 channels to Britain and Europe in 1998. This in turn will provide for a much greater development of PPV in sport than already exists, for instance through single club-based channels, and also in other TV programme areas. It is indicative of his entrepreneurial abilities that Murdoch is currently on the verge of becoming the main supplier of the decoding systems necessary to allow the digital media revolution to proceed in Britain and continental Europe into the 21st Century.

However, at this point it is worth noting that, at least in principle, there are certain constraints on Murdoch's room for manouevre in relation to British and European sport. On the one hand there are regulatory constraints. These include the UK's 'listed events' legislation which requires key national and international level sport events deemed to be of national significance to be available on a free and widely available basis in the UK via traditional terrestrial broadcasters such as the BBC or ITV (see Note 4). This could be said to be a media version of 'sport for all' policy, i.e. 'TV sport spectatorship for all' — a version of the cultural rights of national citizenship, and there is a possibility that the number of these listed events protected for 'free to view' TV may be increased by the Labour government elected in 1997. Some other European countries have similar media regulation, and currently there is some prospect of this kind of legislation being supported and complemented by EU-level media legislation[6].

On the other hand there are also competitive constraints on Sky. Sky, unlike the BBC, is not a member of the European Broadcasting Union (EBU). This alliance of EU nations' 'public service' broadcasters has been very effective in gaining European transmission rights to global mega-events such as the Olympics and soccer World Cups, and also the prestigious European Nations soccer competition. However there is currently some doubt about its 'cartel'-type role in the EU broadcasting sphere given the EU's Single Market project and anti-cartel competition policy, which may give Sky greater room for manouevre in future (Short, 1996; Henderson, 1996). In addition, even with Sky's willingness to pay what often appear to be very high prices for exclusive TV rights sports events, organisers can be prepared to sell the rights for lower prices because they value the mass audiences that terrestrial channels can still deliver, or for other reasons. So, for instance, Sky has not been able dislodge the BBC from its position as prefered TV transmitter for the World Snooker Championships and some key national Rugby Union games.

All of this being said, since it began operation in 1988, and particularly as it has grown in the 1990s, Sky has been enormously successful in buying up the rights to key British sports and their events and international events of keen interest to the British sports fans, and has thus begun to exercise a major and growing influence on the nature and future of British sport. Sky controls the British rights for golf's 'world cup' (i.e. the USA v. Europe Ryder Cup competition), cricket's World Cup, rugby union's 1995 World Cup together with other rugby union and rugby league events which we will come to in a moment. In addition, although Sky may have limited access to the 1998 soccer World Cup in France it has sole rights to the four nation 'warm-up' tournament in France in 1997 involving the 1994 World Cup finalists Brazil and Italy (together with England

and France). As far as future soccer World Cups go, Sky's part-owned German partner (Kirsch) has bought the rights to European transmission of the 2002 and 2006 World Cups and may be able to transmit them to Britain via Sky, by-passing British media regulation and side-lining British terrestrial broadcasters.

However the 'jewel in the crown' for Sky's British media sport strategy has been the acquisition of TV rights to Premier League soccer, which in turn, for good or ill, has effectively revolutionised the professional soccer game in Britain. Since 1992 and the formation of the British Premier League (PL), Sky has paid unprecedented amounts (around £1billion in total, i.e. £304million 1992–7, and £640 million 1997–2001) for exclusive rights to live TV transmission of PL games, with the BBC restricted to subsidiary rights to highlights. This has both directly and indirectly (through sponsorship and other commercial spin-offs) produced unprecedented income flows into the top forty to fifty British soccer clubs, leading to the creation of new stadia, the acquisition of large numbers of foreign 'star' players, and the flotation of clubs as investment-worthy businesses on the London stock exchange. Sky's relationship with Rugby League, which we will come to in a moment, needs to be set into this context of Sky's strategic commitment to the acquisition of major sports and sport event programming both in general and also in the nationally important case of soccer. In addition there is Sky's interest in British rugby.

From 1995 British Rugby, in both its Union and League codes and forms, has been revolutionised by the arrival of Sky to a comparable extent to that to which British soccer has been transformed since 1992. Murdoch's involvement in the historic 1995 RU World Cup in South Africa, his acquisition of the TV rights to the international games of South Africa, New Zealand and Australia, for the 10 year period 1995–2005, and the effective 'professionalization' of the sport which this involvement led to, indicated the scale of his presence and ambitions in world Rugby Union.

In the context of British and European Rugby Union, despite some opposition from various quarters, by 1996/7 Sky had established a firm grip on club rugby (Williams, 1997). This led to the historically significant abolition of amateurism and the explicit professionalisation of the sport in the heartland of the amateur tradition. It also led to the restructuring of clubs internally as businesses and externally into new organisations (e.g. the English Professional Rugby Union Club organisation EPRUC) and new leagues distinct from those controlled by governing body, the Rugby Football Union (RFU). At Rugby

Union club level Sky owns the TV rights to the major English competitions
(e.g. the Courage Cup) and European competitions (the Heineken Cup, involving
French clubs, with the potential involvement also of Italian and Romanian clubs:
Borthwick, 1997).

Sky is also currently exercising a powerful influence on the future of
Rugby Union at national and international level. This is potentially disruptive
of the RFU's traditional 'Home Nations' competition (involving England,
Scotland, Wales and Ireland) and 'Five Nations' competition (involving the
'home nations' plus France). These competitions, as prestigious TV events, have
traditionally been identified with BBC TV which has monopolised them
throughout the post-war period. However the English Rugby Union has been
faced in the mid-1990s, on the one hand with the need to repay huge
debts (c.£70million) for the reconstruction of their stadium at Twickenham, and
on the other hand with the desire to maximise their great earning potential from
the sale of TV rights to England's games. In a 'break-away' move in 1997
the English Rugby Union sold the exclusive rights to all of England's home
matches for the 1997–2002 period — including Home Nation and Five Nation
games staged at Twickenham — to Sky for £87 million. Sky had since
1995 attempted unsuccessfully to buy the rights to the entire Five Nations
tournament. However the three Celtic nations resisted this. Their particular
needs and interests, for instance in the popularisation of their sport in their
countries, are arguably better served by the kind of renegotiation of the
BBC arrangement they achieved in 1997 (a new £40million deal for the
1997–2000 period), a deal which includes TV rights to the Celtic nations' home
games against the powerful southern hemisphere nations as well as against
England and France (Rees, 1997).

However it is by no means certain that this resistance to Sky will necessarily benefit the Celtic nations in the long run. The problem here is that
Sky now has no financial interest in promoting competitions and games
involving Celtic nations at all. It is not just that the Home Nations and Five
Nations competitions could wither by neglect, it is more that they could
be undermined by the creation of alternative and stronger international competitions. Sky's financial interest lies in maximising its current investment in
televising the national games of England, Australia, South Africa and New
Zealand. So the serious possibility now exists that Sky might create a new
world-level 'Five Nations' competition with France invited to join and with

the Celtic nations left on the sidelines, which would overshadow and devalue the traditional competitions (Armstrong, 1997). These problems indicate the general problem of sustaining relevant 'local' collective identities, even when the concept of 'local' refers to nations, in the context of dynamic processes of media-driven internationalisation and globalisation. The problems are likely to be even greater for regionally-based versions of the 'local' such as those operating in culture of British Rugby League.

Rugby League and Sky Television

The main changes

In 1995 — ironically in the centenary year of the original creation of British Rugby League — a declining game in financial difficulties, accepted a 5 year deal with Sky TV Sports which has utterly transformed it (Kellner, 1996). Murdoch offered £87 million .and promised: "We'll make Rugby League look like you've never seen it played before" (quoted in Hadfield, 1995b). The governing body of the RFL, with the support of the leading clubs, accepted this history-making deal with all of its complex consequences, relatively rapidly and unconditionally (Calvin, 1995; Hadfield, 1995a). This reflected the relative weakness of its bargaining position in relation to Sky as well as the scale of its problems and needs. In addition to its problems in holding attendances the sport as it was had little ability to address the major financial problem of implementing the government safety requirements for sports stadia introduced after the Hillsborough and Bradford stadium disasters in the late 1980s. For instance in 1992 such implementation was estimated to cost more than the £20million annual turnover of the game (Lindsay, 1997). A major injection of new resources was evidently desperately needed from somewhere if only to renovate the stadia and keep the sport afloat. Sky's Rugby League Super League competition got under way in Britain in the summer of 1996. These resources were not going to come from the BBC which had never paid the game very much for its transmission rights, and which continued this parsimony during the Sky era. The Sky deal was not completely exclusive and the RFL continued to make the sport's two cup competitions available to the big terrestrial audience through the BBC. However, because of the season change required by Sky (see below) the Challenge Cup, for instance, which was once the game's grand climax, now has less significance, and the Regal Trophy's future is unclear.

In its first season Sky transmitted 45 live games plus highlights and a magazine programme devoted to the sport. This amount (and quality) of coverage is unprecedented: it appears to have enhanced most clubs' attendance figures, and to be attractive to British viewers outside of the Northern region, 50% of Sky Rugby League viewers being in this category (Brady, 1996; Lindsay, 1997). However it is currently being received by only a small proportion (290, 000) of the audience which used to see televised Rugby League on the BBC's Grandstand programme (4 million) and which watched the BBC's coverage of the Challenge Cup in 1996 (2.9 million) (Brady, 1996).

Sky's historic intervention in the game has led the RFL to see itself as a single commercial operation. The RFL's Marketing Manager believing that people in the sport now have "the huge opportunity to ... grow it as a corporate entity rather than lots of little people running around doing their own thing" (quoted in Brady, 1996). However it is a 'corporate entity' which is now largely owned and controlled by Sky TV. What could be called Sky's effective 'takeover' of Rugby League appears to be one of the clearest demonstrations of the power that television can now exercise over sport in the contemporary period. In this section we will first consider some of the main features of the take-over. We can then consider some responses and views about it both from within Rugby League and also from within sport media circles connected with the Rugby League.

The consequences for the sport are massive and far-reaching. In a short-term perspective they relate to the current organization of the clubs' competitions and of their matches. In a longer-term perspective they relate to the identity of the clubs and the game in general. From the more short-term perspective the consequences of Sky's takeover are organizational. Firstly Sky required the restructuring of the clubs into three new divisions, the top division being the new Super League (SL) which included two extra clubs from London and Paris. Secondly Sky has required that the playing seasons be switched from winter to summer. This is in part to compete better in terms of sports programming with the ailing British county cricket programme rather than with the (equally Sky-controlled) audience-pulling power of Premier League soccer and national-level and international Rugby Union. The switch resulted in increased attendances in the first 1996 season (Brady, 1996; Hodgson, 1996). Thirdly a number of changes have been introduced to the game to make for more exciting TV programming. These include the introduction of video play back to assist referees in making decisions and also, in a big screen format, to allow the crowd to observe these decisions more closely and participate in the drama surrounding them. However, since these innovations are only put into practice in televised Super League games there is some concern about different standards being applied in games the other divisions.

In the longer-term perspective there are implications for the identity of the clubs on the one hand and of the sport in general on the other. As has already been outlined, British Rugby League clubs are strongly and traditionally identified with, and are identifiers of, the North of England working-class local communities which support them. The cultural world in which they have traditionally existed has mainly been, at its broadest, an English regional world. The clubs and communities, unlike leading clubs in soccer or other sports, have not seen themselves operating in or recognised by the broad national culture, nor have they seen themselves as being able to represent the nation in international club competitions comparable, for instance, to those in European soccer. However Sky's intervention created strong pressures to change local club identities in a number of ways, some positive, some negative. For instance, firstly some small and weakly supported clubs might have to lose their identity altogether by being merged with others to create units which would have more potential for surviving and succeeding in the Super League competition. Secondly clubs would need to actively publicise and market themselves to Britain as a whole, to new constituencies and in radically new ways if they were to take advantage of the sponsorship and commercial opportunities presented by Sky coverage of their games. Thirdly clubs would need to start seeing themselves as potential participants in international club competitions which would have a 'European' and 'world' significance in their sport.

The prospect of the first change noted above — that is, club mergers and the creation of artificial new units — generated much debate and press coverage in 1995 at the time of the Sky-RFL deal (e.g. Kellner, 1995; Welland, 1995)[7]. Supporters of clubs with a great tradition but currently in a weak financial position, for instance Featherstone Rovers in West Yorkshire, demonstrated against the prospect of merger with their long-standing local rivals (in Featherstone's case the near-by towns of Castleford and Wakefield). Labour Party Members of Parliament representing affected North of England constituencies — no friends of Rupert Murdoch because of what they saw as his powerful influence, through his British press, over Labour's 1992 General Election defeat

— were concerned about the changes and their effects on their local communities. They raised questions in Parliament, particularly critical of this new
deployment of cultural power by Murdoch and his media organisations. They
sought to have the Sky-RFL deal reviewed by the Monopolies and Mergers
Committee (Johnston, 1995). Their concerns continued through to 1996 and
helped to tighten up the clauses in the new 1996 Broadcast Act prohibiting
exclusive rights deals for listed events (in which, however the sport of Rugby
League has never featured). The proposals to merge British clubs met with much
local resistance in 1995 in defence of local identities. As a result they were
shelved, but they have been revived again in 1997. The Chief Executive of the
RFL remains convinced that mergers "are inescapable" (quoted in Ledger, 1997)
(see Note 7).

On the other hand, if the clubs could survive intact, this did not in itself mean
that their identities would survive. In order to address the new national marketing
world opened up by their participation in and media exposure in the Super
League many of the leading North England clubs have attempted to change their
image by changing their traditional names. Thus they have added American and
Australian-style club identities to their traditional names often in bizarre new
mixtures such as 'Leeds Rhinos', 'Bradford Bulls', and 'Warrington Wolves'
(Nevin, 1997). In the 1997 Super League only the St.Helens club retained its
original name. As the RFL's Marketing Manager observes, this renaming and
nickname process "removes the necessity for the name of the town to be
mentioned when speaking about the team" (quoted in Brady, 1996). There is a
suspici on in the game that the name changes are part of a process aimed at the
elimination of place identities in order, in future, to enable Super-League team
locations to be more determined, along American sport business lines, by the
auctioning of franchises rather than by tradition.

Generally in line with this is the attempted re-spatialization of the
clubs' identities towards a national and even international sphere through
the inclusion of clubs from London and Paris in the competition. The indifference of the Super League to the contradictions involved in this 'construction
of locality' is evident in the fact that these teams mainly consist of Australian
players. Finally the Murdoch organisation's attempted construction of a '
world' club competition between northern and southern hemisphere
Super League teams is also consistent with this re-spatialization of British clubs'
traditional identities.

On the latter project one observer has commented: "The entire Super League enterprise, designed to take the game to a new public, is underpinned by the idea of internationalising a sometimes parochial club scene and introducing regular competition against the Australians" (Richards, 1997; also Bose, 1995)). In 1995, in the same process in which the British end of the Super League was created, Murdoch attempted to create an equivalent superleague (ASL) in Australia. This was delayed because the Australian Rugby League (ARL) governing body and its commercial TV partner Kerry Packer went to court to block the move (Rowe 1996). However the court ruled that the development could proceed (Hadfield 1996), and so now two parallel Rugby League club competitions exist in Australia — the 12 team ARL and the 10 team ASL, which includes a New Zealand club. The first 'world'-level tournament between clubs from the two northern and southern hemisphere 'super leagues' will take place in autumn 1997 (Wilson, 1996; Edgar, 1997). The British clubs participating in this will have travelled a long way in terms of identity and image from the local to the global in a very short period of time. Whether they can continue for very much longer to carry much of their traditional local identity with them on their travels in the media world of Super League remains to be seen.

Perspectives on the changes

The wider research on which this Chapter draws, concerning the contemporary world of Rugby League and its television presentation, involved interviewing administrators and managers in Rugby League and TV producers and executives and sports journalists connected with the presentation of the sport on TV (see Notes 1 and 5). It reveals a complex and in some respects contradictory set of views about the costs and benefits of Sky's new leading role in the sport. This is understandable in that the changes, even 'the revolution', brought in by Sky are very recent, and it will inevitably take the clubs — at least those that survive — some years to feel familiar and confident with the new order of things.

Within the world of Rugby League all of the interviewees said that they believed that the televisual presentation of the of the sport's live games by BSkyB represented progress for the game. Interviewees considered that the particular attributes of League, such as its movement, quantity of action, ball handling skills, pace and colour, conveyed themselves to great effect in the transmissions. They also believed that the volume and sophistication of the technology used contributed significantly to improving the sport's image in this context. Sky typically use around 17 cameras at a match and employ high quality editing which allows the game to be shown in a very positive way, offering improved opportunities for viewers to appreciate the skills and action in the sport.

A consistently reproduced observation was that Sky's approach to coverage had forced a re-appraisal and an improvement of the BBC's approach to its continuing terrestrial coverage. For instance, in the 1997 Challenge Cup the BBC made one of the quarter-finals and one of the semi-finals the centrepiece of two editions of its flagship Saturday afternoon multi-sport programme 'Grandstand'. Interviewees observed that Sky coverage improved on traditional BBC coverage in a number of ways. Sky showed more matches, devoted more resources to pre-match build up and post-match analysis, and provided a regular magazine programme for the game — traditional areas of neglect by the BBC. They also observed that the scale of Sky's financial investment in the securing rights to the game gave them a commercial incentive to make a success of their coverage.

Interviewees believed that the variety of angles, perspectives and shots employed made excellent sports television, and that this approach did justice to the speed and intensity of one of the world sport's most demanding high physical contact games. One interviewee observed that: Sky "came along and…shot a cannon through all the rules of television coverage" (Rugby League administrator B). Another believed that: "the one thing that Sky TV has done is to present …Rugby League like we've always wanted it …. What you've got to say about say about Sky is that they really do it well" (Rugby League journalist B).

However some interviewees nonetheless believed that, even in this new television era, the particular skills and attributes of the game remained understated by Sky's coverage. For instance the game requires high concentration from the players and an ability to react quickly to rapid changes in the pace, direction and character of moves and actions during the course of the game, and these aspects were not currently being identified and presented very well. Clubs required their top class players to possess these more analytical abilities in addition to physical power and pace. By passing them over in favour of the more aggressive physical contact and bodily collision aspects Sky was missing an opportunity to present the game as having a serious and technically complex dimension which could illuminate for viewers the planning and strategy involved in play.

This aspect could have been covered in magazine programming devoted to the sport. But interviewees, while welcoming the creation of the single supporting magazine programme ('Boots 'n' All' 1996, 'The World of Super League' 1997) felt that it did not cover this particular aspect well, and in general that the informed sports journalism needed to properly support the coverage of the live games and to inform and educate the public about the game was lacking in quantity and quality on Sky's programmes. Furthermore interviewees expressed a number of reservations and concerns about the degree of control of the coverage and presentation of game which the RFL had conceded to Sky. One observed: "Can I point out the difference between Rugby League and Rugby Union? Rugby Union took the money but insisted that they would have two or three magazine programmes every week regardless, covering different aspects of the game to enhance the interest of the viewer" (Rugby League journalist C). This implies that, by comparison, Rugby League, which perhaps could have attempted to do the same sort of thing, nonetheless was more interested in simply securing the new money and failed to place any such conditions on the deal.

Another interviewee concurred with this view: "I think if it someone comes in with that amount of money you've got to say 'yes'. Then it's a question of how much you can keep control of your own destiny once you've accepted someone's cheque" (Rugby League journalists D). He was critical of the element of hyperbole and oversell in Sky's presentation of the sport: "We know it's hard ... exciting ...physical ... rough. [But] we don't have to have it rammed down our throats all the time." He acknowledged that TV has an imperative need to expand its viewing audience and to reach out to new viewers unfamiliar with the game, and that to do this it is necessary to put the game into some context of meaning. But nonetheless he believed that in Sky's magazine programme: "They don't put it into context. What (they) do is just oversell it and give a layer of importance it just doesn't have." This is consistent with press criticism of the magazine programme, such as Martin Kelner's comment that it "reached hyperbole levels that Goebbels might have rejected" and that it was "little more than a two-hour puff for Sky's coverage" (Kelner, 1997).

Another interviewee, while acknowledging the improved quality if Sky's live coverage, supported this concern with the decontextualisation of the game: "The actual coverage overall you've got to say is very good. They throw resources at it. But it's blinkered to the extent that it's played in isolation. You wouldn't know that anything else went on outside of that [the Super League] and you wouldn't really know that there was much of a history of the game before that" (Rugby League journalist A). Overall, interviewees generally welcomed the new leading financial and presentational role of Sky TV in their sport. Nonetheless most were concerned with the price that the sport had paid for this in its considerable loss of access to a large viewing audience that, whatever its faults, the BBC was more capable of delivering for them than Sky TV. They were aware that the image of Rugby League needed to be promoted on a number of media fronts simultaneously, including the press and broadsheets in particular, and also including the limited access which continues to be available to terrestrial TV.

However, in relation to these points most interviewees also recognised that the clubs themselves were lacking media and public relations skills and needed to develop them rapidly to cope with the organizational and media changes which had overtaken the sport. They felt that the clubs needed to be more informed about the full range of the media's actual and potential interests. They needed to be aware of the possibilities for negative publicity and to develop the ability to prevent or manage and minimise this. They needed to be proactive in relation to the media, for instance by training players and managerial personnel to make clear and effective statements in media interviews. One interviewee observed: "Nobody in League is attuned to selling the game and until they are it won't be as successful as it has the potential to be.... The principle of succeeding in sport is to manipulate the media and the clubs just don't understand that at all" (Rugby League journalist C). The sport as a whole needed to take an intelligent and proactive approach to the platform offered by both terrestrial and satellite television. However, many employed in the game were still learning how the media operates. It is consistent with this that, in 1996, the RFL appointed a Marketing Manager whose view is that "Rugby League has never marketed itself before, in ... a professional manner" (Mark Newton, quoted in Brady, 1996). His offer to provide clubs with this expertise in 1996 met with little response, a fact he regarded as "unbelievable" (quoted in Brady, 1996).

Other interviewees observed the importance of the media for the popularisation and promotion of sport. For instance the development within the sport of 'stars' with a high media profile can allow the sport to reach a wider public than that of existing spectators. Stars can positively influence the popular image and status of a game by their association with it, helping to create new spectators and viewers for the game (see also Whannel, Chapter 1 above). In Britain a number of soccer players (e.g. Paul Gascoigne) and a few RU players (e.g. Will Carling) have this kind of star status and national recognition. H(

from Martin Offiah, Rugby League has so far seem(
equivalent, and equivalently useful, stars.

In addition they noted that most leading sports, an
grammes — such as those connected with Rugby League
dominated. The appeal of sports TV to men can to a certain extent be assumed.
Nevertheless TV companies and advertisers increasingly prefer to prevent these
programmes becoming 'male cultural ghettos', of no real interest to the female
half of the viewing and consuming public. Apart from attempting to attract
female viewers by increasing the visibility of women's sports in TV programming, another media strategy is to attempt to sexualise the male world of sport
by developing sport stars with an appeal to women through their sexuality and
their charismatic presence in the wider popular cultural entertainment and
advertising culture. So the lack of nationally recognized Rugby League stars is
seen both to express and to help create (i) a general problem of lack of national
public awareness for a sport still assumed to be of only regional significance, and
also (ii) a particular problem of the lack of appeal to women as viewers and
consumers by a sport still assumed to be a celebration of 'masculine' (and hence
potentially sexist) values of power and aggression. While there is a significant
degree of female spectatorship at these matches, these points are also consistent
with the view of the RFL's Marketing Manager who believes that: "What we are
trying to do is to get the message across to the female audience and the young
audience… We need to create heroes in the game…" (quoted in Brady, 1996; for
a recent version of such star/hero presentation see Edgar, 1997).

In general the interviewees broadly accepted the changes Sky had brought to
Rugby League and regarded them, or versions of them, as necessary for the
survival and development of the game. Their criticisms tended to be constructive
and forward-looking, aimed at ways of consolidating and improving on the
current position of Rugby League as a media sport. Little nostalgia was
expressed for the past, whether in terms of the inadequacies of previous BBC TV
coverage or the previously low levels of finance in the game, or generally in
terms of the traditionally close relationship between clubs and their industrial
working-class communities. Ordinary fans might well share the former view
with our set of interviewees. Nonetheless, given fans' negative responses to the
original merger proposals (see Note 7), it is unlikely that they agree with our
interviewees' lack of nostalgia for the local identity of clubs.

Conclusion

In this chapter we have discussed the increasingly transformative relationship between media sport and traditional collective identities in sport typically inherited from the pre-television era. In particular we explored the sport-led corporate media strategy of Rupert Murdoch's 'media empire' and its recent impact on British Rugby League. Our general theme has been to consider, within contemporary processes of cultural globalization such as those driven by the media, the new role and fate of the 'local' and locally-based identities. Our discussion of media sport does not support Featherstone's view, outlined in the Introduction, that, with globalization and the postmodern culture connected with this, "there is a return to local cultures" involving "an increasing sensitivity to differences". This is not to say that, on the contrary, the kind of media-driven globalization we have discussed automatically produces some kind simplistic cultural homogenisation. Evidently national, regional and local/city differences can be resymbolised and reproduced through globally organized media sport. This currently holds true for cases such as nationally-based and European-based soccer competitions where the 'place identity' of clubs such as Manchester United, Inter-Milan or Real Madrid evidently remains very strong wherever their matches are broadcast and viewed, whether nationally or internationally. It also seems to hold true currently even for global multi-national sport mega-events such as the Olympic games, where national TV intermediary organisations typically edit and refashion event coverage to focus on and promote the significance and role of their nations and national identities in relation to the event (Spa *et al.*, 1996).

However, as with the tourism industry, the media sport industry, in general — in so far as it sees a value in it — tends to the promote local identities in a way which transforms them from the unreflected 'ways of life' and traditions of local people, into reflexive and organised cultural productions and stagings for outsiders, whether tourists or TV viewers. Where there this process does not threaten the very existence of cultural forms and ways of life, it certainly raises the problem of their 'authenticity' in their new touristic or mediated guise (Urry, 1990; Roche, 1992).

In the case of British Rugby League it would appear that, at best, the sport's traditional local club identities have now been transformed by becoming media-based, being effectively licenced by Sky TV and dependent upon the clubs' relationship with, and success in, Sky's Super League operation. At worst, as we saw, they are seriously threatened by the RFL's and Sky's willingness to "grow [the sport] as a corporate entity", with the possibility of re-spatialising, even de-spatialising club identities into a franchised future. In this scenario the RFL is not only buying into Sky's version of global sport culture, but is also buying into a new financial form of 'localism' as a marginal and dependent small company within Rupert Murdoch's 'sport media empire'. Perhaps British Rugby League has only escaped being the 'poor relation' of one dominant cultural organisation, namely British Rugby Union, to become an admittedly temporarily better-off 'poor relation' of an even more dominant one. Time will tell.

Notes

1   On sport mega-events see Roche 1992, 1994, and 1998.

2   The broader project is based on an historical, production and content analysis using interview, observation and content analytic methods as well as secondary analysis. The social research agenda in this area is still developing and independent studies of Rugby League fans and viewers, beyond the market research conducted by Sky and other interested parties, are needed in particular. See also Note 5.

3   On TV and American football and baseball in relation to US TV networks see Chandler, 1988 and Wenner, 1989b; on the escalation of US network bids for the the Olympics see Larsen and Park, 1993 and Spa *et al.*, 1996.

4   The British legislation dates from 1954 Television Act originally prevented TV companies from securing exclusive rights to a set of 'listed events' deemed to be of national importance (Whannel, 1992: p. 46). This was weakened somewhat by the pro-market and pro-Murdoch Conservative government in the 1990 Broadcasting Act which aimed to provide an encouraging regulatory environment for the development of commercial and satellite TV. The Act merely prohibited the listed events from being transmitted on a pay-per-view basis (DNH, 1990: Part X, para 182). It does not name specific events, rather it governs the general category of 'listed events' and gives responsibility to the Minister of National Heritage to determine in practice what the precise contents of the 'list' might be, which thus, in principle, is subject to review and can change. The traditional and current contents of the list — which it would in practice be politically difficult but not impossible to change without changing the legislation — are the following eight events: the Olympics, soccer's World Cup, the

Wimbledon tennis championships, the English and Scottish soccer FA Cup
Finals, the Derby and the Grand National horse races, and English cricket's
home Test matches. However the legislation was tightened up notably in the
1996 Broadcasting Act which prohibits the rights to transmit listed events
from being acquired on an exclusive basis by any one media organisation
(DNH, 1996b: Part IV, para 99). This tightening up was produced by
the widespread political concerns which developed following Rupert
Murdoch's acquisitions of TV rights for British soccer in 1992 and the two
codes of rugby in 1995, and these concerns featured prominently in debates
in both Houses of Parliament in 1996 during the reading, revision and
passage of the Act. However the 1996 legislation also aims to give some
recognition to the rights and role of governing bodies and/or event owners
to be consulted if it is ever proposed that their event should be included in
the controlled list (DNH, 1996a).

5   The interviews were conducted in the period October 1996 to May 1997
(see also Arundel, 1998) on a guaranteed anonymity basis. The set of
interviewees included the following categories of people connected with
Rugby League as a media sport: (i) Rugby League managers, coaches and
administrators; (ii) Rugby League journalists; (iii) TV sport producers
and executives; (iv) sports broadcasters; and (v) general sports journalists.
The views reported in this Chapter mainly come from some of the interviews with some of the people in the first two categories.

6   In 1996 the European Parliament called on the European Commission: "to
work for the granting of transmission rights for big sports programmes to
free television channels" (EP, 1996). In response the European Union
Commissioner for competition policy, Karel Van Miert, recognised a
responsibility to monitor, and if necessary control, the growth of exclusive
TV rights arrangements in Europe (Short, 1996; Henderson, 1996). For a
general discussion of European cultural identity in relation to the development of global media see Morley and Robins, 1995 (their chapter and their
book in general).

7   The mergers proposed in the original Sky deal in 1995 involved clubs in the
same general geographical area: i.e. Widnes and Warrington (Cheshire);
Oldham and Salford (Manchester); Castleford, Featherstone and Wakefield
(West Yorkshire); Sheffield and Doncaster (South Yorkshire); Hull and Hull
Kingston Rovers (Humberside). These were strongly resisted at the time by
many of the clubs and local communities involved. For some accounts of

the emotions raised by these proposed mergers at the time see Bibliography for 1995 press reports by Crossley (1995), Fitzpatrick (1995b), Hugill (1995), Hodgson (1996), Irvine (1995a, b, c), and Weaver (1995). The list of teams which was finally agreed to comprise the Super League in May 1995 were the 12 teams of Bradford, Castleford, Halifax, Leeds, London, Oldham, Paris, St.Helens, Sheffield, Warrington, Wigan and Workington (Fletcher and Howes, 1995). So far the original Super League merger proposals have not been reactivated, but they may be if, as is possible, the Super League develops towards a club franchise system. There were signs in 1997 that some of the mergers may be back under consideration, particularly given the strong possibility that, by 1998, one of the traditional heartlands of the game, the Castleford/Wakefield/Featherstone area in West Yorkshire, split as it is between three clubs, might have no Super League representation. Mergers were part of the commercial logic of the original Sky-RFL arrangement. In spite of fan resistance, which has delayed the process, since the logic of the situation has not changed it is reasonable to assume that sooner or later the pressure for mergers is likely to prove successful.

References and bibliography

Arundel, J. (1998) (forthcoming) 'British Rugby League, soccer and television'. Postgraduate research thesis, Sociological Studies and Journalism Studies departments, Sheffield University, Sheffield.

Armstrong, R. (1997) 'Elite plot to dump Five Nations', *The Guardian*, 9th May.

Barnett, S. (1990) *Games and sets: the changing face of sport on television*. London: BFI Publishing.

———— (1996) 'Turn on, pay up', *The Guardian*, 26th July.

Bailey, P. (1978) *Leisure and class in Victorian England*. London: Routledge.

Bale, J. and McGuire, J. (1994) 'Sports labour migration in the global arena' in their edited collection *The global sports arena*. London, Frank Cass.

BBC (British Broadcasting Corporation) (1997) 'Voices of sport' BBC Radio 5, 3rd March.

Blain, N., Boyle, R., O'Donnell, H. (eds) (1993) *Sport and national identity in the European media*. Leicester: Leicester University Press.

Borthwick, I. (1997) 'Compromise saves rugby cup', *The European*, 8th May.

Bose, M. (1995) 'Murdoch targets global rugby code', *The Daily Telegraph*, 20th May.

Brady, S. (1996) 'Market mania', *Rugby Leaguer*, 11th November.

Butler, E. (1996) 'Rugby beleaguered banks on Rupert', *The Observer*, 17th November.

Calvin, M. (1995) 'Rugby League interview: Maurice Lindsay, RL chief executive', *The Daily Telegraph*, 27th October.

Chandler, J. (1988) *Television and national sport: the United States and Britain*. Urbana: University of Illinois Press.

Clayton, J. and Steele, M. (1993) *When push comes to shove*. Castleford: Yorkshire Arts Circus.

Crossley, M. (1995) '14 club Super League set to switch RL to summer game', *The Sunday Telegraph*, 9th April.

Cunningham, H. (1980) *Leisure in the industrial revolution*. London: Croom Helm.

Dayan, D. and Katz, E. (1992) *Media events*. London: Harvard University.

Delaney, T. (1986) 'Television', *Code 13*, No. 1 (September): pp. 42–43.

DNH (Department of National Heritage) (1990) *Broadcasting Act 1990*. London: HMSO.

——— (1996a) 'Broadcast sports rights: informing the debate', White Paper, London: Department of National Heritage.

——— (1996b) Broadcasting Act 1996. London: HMSO.

Donnelly, p. (1996) 'The local and the global: globalization in the sociology of sport', *Journal of Sport and Social Issues* Vol. 23: pp. 239-257.

Dunning, E. and Sheard, K. (1979) *Barbarians, gentlemen and players: a sociological study of the development of Rugby Football*. Oxford: Martin Robertson.

Edgar, H. (1997) *The official fans' guide 1997*: Stones Super League. London: Carlton Books.

EP (European Parliament) (1996) 'TV — Challenge to satellite sport monopoly', EP News 4, European Parliament, Brussels.

Featherstone, M. (1991a) 'Global and local cultures', *Vrijetijd en samenleving (Leisure and Society)*, Vol.9, No.3/4: pp. 43-58.

——— (1991b) Consumer culture and postmodernism. London: Sage.

Fitzpatrick, P. (1995a) 'Rugby League; a century of independence', *The Guardian*, 26th August.

——— (1995b) 'Rugby League chairmen braced for supporter backlash', *The Guardian*, 10th April.

Fletcher, R. and Howes, D. (1995) *Rothman's Rugby League yearbook 1995-6*. London: Headline Publishing.

Fox, P. (1995) 'Television sport: Rugby at the crossroads', *The Daily Telegraph*, 1st May.

Goldlust, J. (1987) *Playing for keeps; sport, the media and society*. Melbourne: Longman Cheshire.

Gratton, C. (1997) 'The economic and social significance of sport', unpublished paper, Leisure Industries Research Centre, Sheffield Hallam University, Sheffield.

Guttman, A. (1994) *Games and empire*. New York: Columbia University Press.

Hadfield, D. (1995a) 'Rugby's new world; the gift and the gamble', *The Independent on Sunday*, 20th August.

———(1995b) 'Super Leagers shape up for the small screen', *The Independent*, 8th November.

———(1996) 'Murdoch wins Super League battle in Australia', *The Independent*, 5th October.

Hargreaves, J. (1986) 'Media Sport' ch.7 in *Sport, power and culture*. Cambridge: Polity.

———(1996) 'The Catalanization of the 1992 Olympics' (unpublished conference paper) Euroconference on 'Collective identity and symbolic representation', the European Association and the ICCR, Fondation Nationale des Sciences Politiques, Paris.

Henderson, J. (1996) 'Behind the screen', *The Observer*, 27th November.

Hodgson, G. (1995) 'This sport always belonged to the working man...', *The Independent*, 15th April.

———(1996) 'This sporting life turned upside down', *The Independent*, 25th October.

Hugill, B. (1995) 'How 'Judas' sold town's birthright', *The Observer*, 16th April.

Irvine, C. (1995a) 'Disbelief greets swift creation of Super League', *The Times*, 10th April.

———(1995b) 'Super League hatred rife on the terraces', *The Times*, 18th April.

———(1995c) 'Last post for the smaller clubs', *The Times*, 22nd April.

Johnston, P. (1995) 'Minister seeks inquiry into deal with Murdoch; MPs angered by the end to 100 years of tradition', *The Daily Telegraph*, 27th April.

Kelner, M. (1997) 'Sky present the champions of the hyperleague', *The Guardian* 14th March.

Kelner, S. (1995) 'The betrayal of a heritage', *The Independent on Sunday*, 16th April.

Kelner, S. (1996) *To Jerusalem and back.* London: Methuen.

Killanin, L. and Rodda, J. (eds) (1976) *The Olympic Games.* Macmillan, New York.

Larson, J. and Park, H-S. (1993) *Global television and the politics of the Seoul Olympics.* Oxford: Westview Press.

Ledger, J. (1997) 'Moves afoot for clubs to merge', *The Yorkshire Post*, 15th May.

Lindsay, M. (1997) 'The 'other' game: rugby to follow football?' conference presentation, 'Football and finance' conference, 22nd April (available RFL Leeds).

Lovesey, p. (1979) *The official Centenary History of the AAA.* London: Guinness Superlatives Ltd.

Mason, T. (1980) *Association football and English society, 1863-1915.* Brighton: Harvester Wheatsheaf.

Moorhouse, G. (1996) *A people's game: The centenary history of Rugby League.* London: Hodder & Stoughton.

Morley, D. and Robbins, K. (1995) 'Globalisation as identity crisis', ch.1 in their *Spaces of identity: Global media, electronic landscapes and cultural boundaries.* London: Routledge.

Nevin, C. (1997) 'Once there were warriors', *The Guardian*, 14th March.

Real, M. (1996) *Exploring media culture.* London: Sage.

Rees, P. (1997) 'BBC grabs Five Nations prize', *The Guardian*, 27th February.

Roche, M. (1992) 'Mega-events and micro-modernization', *British Journal of Sociology* Vol.43, No.4: pp. 563-600.

———— (1994) 'Mega-events and urban policy', *Annals of Tourism Research*, Vol. 21, No.1: pp. 1-19.

———— (1998a) (forthcoming) *Mega-events and modernity: Olympics and expos in the construction of public culture.* London: Routledge.

———— (1998b) (forthcoming) 'European citizenship and the cultural dimension', in Stevenson, N. (ed) *Cultural citizenship.* London: Sage.

Rowe, D. (1996) 'The global love-match: sport and television', Media, *Culture and Society* Vol.18: pp. 565-582.

Shawcross, W. (1992) *Rupert Murdoch: Ringmaster of the information circus.* London: Pan Books.

Short, D. (1996) 'TV contenders get a new referee', *The European*, 25th July.

———— (1997) 'Picture changes as digital alliance boxes clever', *The European*, 16th May.

Spa, M. de M. *et al.* (1996) *Television in the Olympics*. Luton: John Libbey Media.

Thompson, L. (1995) 'In a league of their own — but for how long?', *The Independent*, 6th October.

Tunstall, J. and Palmer, M. (1991) *Media moguls*. London: Routledge.

Urry, J. (1990) *The tourist gaze*. London: Sage.

Weaver, p. (1995) 'Satellite war plunges 'Calder' community into identity crisis', *The Sunday Telegraph*, 15th April.

Welland, C. (1995) 'Time for tears, but for realism too', *The Observer*, 23rd April.

Wenner, L. (1989) 'Media, sport and society: the research agenda', in Wenner, L. (ed) *op cit*.

Wenner, L. (ed) (1989) *Media, sports and society*. London: Sage.

Whannel, G. (1992) *Fields in vision: Television sport and cultural transformation*. London: Routledge.

Williams, R. (1997) 'Rugby rides out the revolution', *The Guardian*, 9th May.

Wilson, A. (1996) 'World club competition in the offing', *The Guardian*, 7th October.

II.

SPORT POLICIES
AND URBAN IDENTITIES

THE POLITICS OF PLACE AND IDENTITY IN THE SYDNEY 2000 OLYMPICS: 'SHARING THE SPIRIT OF CORPORATISM'

C. Michael Hall
University of Otago

Julie Hodges
University of Canberra

Selling places: mega-events and cultural capital

'Place marketing' (Madsen, 1992) also sometime described as 'selling places' (Burgess, 1982; Kearns and Philo, 1993), 'geographical marketing' (Ashworth and Voogd, 1988) or 'reimaging strategies' (Roche, 1992; Hall, 1994), is a key feature of contemporary global capitalism. According to Ashworth and Voogd (1988: p. 65) the process of place-marketing is a new paradigm which affects the manner in which cities, regions and places are viewed as a commodity to be promoted and sold. At the heart of the idea of place marketing is the notion that places need to compete for investment, employment and economic growth in the same manner as corporations compete. According to Kotler *et al.* (1993: p. 346), "The globalization of the world's economy and the accelerating pace of technological changes are two forces that require all places to learn how to compete. Places must learn how to think more like businesses, developing products, markets, and customers". However, as Robins (1991: pp. 35–36) observed:

> Whether it is to attract a new car factory or the Olympic Games, they go as supplicants. And, even as supplicants, they go in competition with each other: cities and localities are now fiercely struggling against each other to attract footloose and predatory investors to their particular patch. Of course, some localities are able successfully to 'switch' themselves in to the global networks, but others will remain 'unswitched' or even 'plugged'. And, in a world characterized by the increasing mobility of

and the rapid recycling of space, even those that manage to become connected in to the global system are always vulnerable to the abrupt withdrawal of investment and to [partial] disconnection from the global system.

Culture is intimately connected to place marketing. Whether we are using culture in the sense of being indicative of a "particular way of life, whether of a people, a period, a group, or humanity in general" or "as a reference to the works or practices of intellectual and especially artistic activity" (Williams, 1983: p. 90), culture is becoming commodified and bought and sold in the global marketplace. Cultural policies are used to generate artistic and 'high' cultural activity in order to attract visitors and to make the city an attractive place to live for the middle-class, white collar workers and business that places seek to attract, while wider notions of cultural identity are also being used to attract investment, visitors and employment. The use of cultural images to attract visitors is not new. It has been around for as long as tourism. However, place marketing is new, because the notion of selling places implies not only trying to affect demand through the representation of cultural images, but it also implies the manipulation and management of the supply-side, e.g. those things which makes up a community's life, into a package which can be 'sold'. Such actions clearly have implications not only for how the external consumer sees places but also for how those people who constitute place are able to participate in the making of their collective and individual identity and the structures which sell place.

The Olympic Games have long been associated with culture and politics. Images of the amateur gentleman (Athens 1896), the purity of the German people and the legitimacy of the Third Reich (Berlin 1936), the power of state communism (Moscow 1980), and the glorification of American capitalism and notions of freedom (Los Angeles 1984), have all seen wider cultural visions overlie the Olympics sporting facade. However, more recently, the Olympics role of 'putting a place on the map' has become integrated with the process of place marketing and the conscious use of mega-events, such as World Fairs and Olympic Games, by growth coalitions to achieve economic and political goals, particularly with respect to the promotion of rejuvenated urban places. For example, Hughes (1993: pp. 157, 159) observed that "the Olympics may be of particular significance in relation to the 'inner city' problems that beset many urban areas of Europe and N[orth] America" and noted that Manchester's bid for the 2000 Summer Olympics were "seen as a possible contribution to solving some of' the city's 'inner city problems". Indeed, it is the inherent belief that the Olympics or other mega events will attract tourism and investment because of the improved image and promotion of a place which serves to justify redevelopment, often with large investments of public funds and with the suspension of normal planning practice.

The use of tourism as a mechanism to regenerate urban areas through the creation of desirable middle-class leisure-tourism environments appears almost universal in Western society. Roche (1994) and Hall (1994) have argued that tourism is therefore an integral component of urban reimaging strategies which aim to provide an urban environment which will attract and retain the interest of professionals and white-collar workers, visitors, and investors in order to generate employment and redevelopment. According to Roche and Hall, urban imaging processes are characterised by some or all of the following:

- the development of a critical mass of visitor attractions and facilities, including new buildings/prestige centres such as convention and exhibition centres;

- the hosting of hallmark or mega events;

- the development of urban tourism strategies and policies often associated with new or renewed organisation and development of city marketing; and

- development of leisure and cultural services and projects to support the marketing and tourism effort (Hall, 1994).

The ramifications of reimaging are far reaching. However, while 'selling places' through reimaging and redevelopment strategies may be an effective way by which cities and regions can compete with each other in attracting capital, investment, employment and the tourist dollar. Substantial questions are now being asked as to the manner in which the communities which are sold and affected through reimaging and the hosting of mega-events, are able to parti- cipate in the planning processes which led to the adoption of such strategies and in the promotion of particular representations of culture (Hall, 1992, 1994, 1997a, b; Roche, 1992, 1994; Kearns and Philo, 1993; Hughes, 1994).

Mega-events and reimaging

Although hallmark or mega-events are not themselves a new phenomenon, what is relatively new is the implicit belief of politicians, planners and key industry and real estate players that "such events can provide a significant boost to their economies" (Gittins, 1995: p. 28). This has developed to such an extent that "the motivation for seeking to sponsor such events has less to do with the promotion of sport or culture than with the pursuit of economic advantage" (Gittins, 1995: p. 28) although, of course, sport and culture may be used to justify or compliment such pursuit. Mega-events have therefore assumed a key role in urban and regional tourism marketing and promotion strategies. Their primary function being to provide the host city with an opportunity to secure high prominence in the tourism market place. The hosting of mega-events is now often deliberately exploited in an attempt to 'rejuvenate' or develop urban areas through the construction and development of new infrastructure, including road and rail networks, airports, sewage, and housing. This has been used to revitalise inner-city locations that are regarded by government, municipalities, and business interests as requiring renewal (Hillman, 1986; Olds, 1988; Law, 1993; Hall, 1994, 1997a; Long and Sellars, 1996).

Since the early 1970s the Olympic Games have undergone a dramatic change in their intention and focus, which has shifted away from the athletes and more towards the event and the prestige that it provides the host nation (der Maur, 1976 in Wilkinson, 1994). "The strongest underlying assumption in a nation's hosting of an Olympic Games is the expectation that it will result in vastly increased international exposure and a resulting overall economic gain for the city, even the nation" (Wilkinson, 1994: p. 16). As a result the Olympics have also been utilised to redevelop areas which have been perceived as being 'rundown' and to provide a justification for the development of new infrastructure, such as urban transit systems, highway construction, airport redevelopment, and housing (Hall, 1992). These assumptions clearly characterised the last summer Olympics held in Barcelona in 1992. According to the *Official Report of the Games of the XXV Olympiad* (1992 in Wilkinson, 1994: p. 17), "the Games acted as a catalyst in standing and completing the construction work that Barcelona needed, not only in the organisation of the Games, but also for the modernisation and development of the city". Similarly, with respect to the Atlanta Games to be held in 1996 "Georgia's economic development community has created a program that uses the Atlanta Olympics as a way to attract new corporate investment to the city and the state" (*Atlanta Constitution Journal*, 1994: p. 9).

The redevelopment of the inner city in terms of visitor attractiveness can lead to the transformation of the community-based organisation of local spaces and populations into an individual, or family-based organisation, or what Castells has characterised as the 'disconnection of people from spatial forms' (Castells, 1983). The implications of the transformation of the core of many cities for lower socio-economic groups is amplified by the reallocation of local state resources from social welfare to imaging functions, because at the same time that the inner city is being promoted and developed as a leisure and tourism resource, public spending on social programmes, such as subsidised housing, has also been decreasing (Mommaas and Poel, 1989). Indeed, in examining the hosting of large-scale hallmark events and associated rejuvenation in various Western countries, including Australia (Hall, 1994), concluded that the preponderance of political and economic benefits of the hallmark event to local growth coalitions (a combination of business and real estate interests and politicians) appeared to outweigh the costs to the less politically organised segments of the host community, usually the poor.

Culture, in both its narrower (high culture) and broader definitions (as a way of life and as a signifier), is therefore a vital component of mega-events and reimaging strategies. However, the representations and definitions of culture in the new corporatism of place marketing do not necessarily go uncontested. As Bramham *et al.* (1989: p. 4) observed:

> ... the question arises as to whether or not there should be some form of public life or culture, accessible to all local citizens of the city; and if so, how this can be stimulated by local policies. This last question is particularly relevant in local politics. Is the city a product to be sold on the tourism market and/or as a location in which to invest money? Or is a city a place to live, where people can express themselves, even if it is in terms of resistance to, rather than rejoicing in, the dominant culture?

The Sydney 2000 Games

The success of the Sydney 2000 Olympic bid has been highly regarded by much of the Australian media and certain quarters of government and industry as having the potential to provide a major economic boost to the New South Wales and Sydney economy. The economic impact study undertaken for the New South Wales Government by KPMG Peat Marwick suggested that the net economics impacts as a result of hosting the Games would be between $4,093 million and $4,790 million, and between $3,221 million and $3,747 million for Sydney (KPMG Peat Marwick, 1993).

From its earliest stages the political nature of planning and decision-making associated with the Sydney Olympics was quite clear (political in the sense that politics is about who gets what, where, why and how). Much, if not all, of these planning decisions will have substantial implications for the longer term economic and social development of Sydney and New South Wales. For example, the state government passed legislation in 1995 with respect to the Sydney Olympics to assist in the development and regeneration of projects associated with the Games. This was achieved at the cost of the people of Sydney losing their rights of appeal to initiate a court appeal under environment and planning legislation against the proposed Olympic projects. The location and dealings of the amendment were far from being open and honest. As Mr. Johnston of the Environmental Defenders' Office commented, "this amendment is buried on page 163 of the threatened species legislation ... not a bill where you would find such a change, and you have to wonder why they put it there" (Totaro, 1995: p. 1).

Further legislation passed under the New South Wales Government's *Olympic Co-ordination Authority Act* allows, somewhat ironically given the green image which was an integral part of the Games bid (Sydney Organising Committee for the Olympic Games (SOCOG), 1996), all projects linked with the Games to be suspended from the usual Environmental Impact Statements requirements. These changes are expected to affect all the areas involved with Olympic activities (Totaro, 1995). Unfortunately however, the same reasons which propel cities to stage large scale tourist events (i. e. redevelopment, dramatic urban development) and also to fast-track the planning process, "are also the some of the very factors which result in an adverse affect on residents in cities in which they are held" (Wilkinson, 1994: p. 28).

In the case of the Sydney Olympics at least the need to consider the environmental dimensions of the Games did receive attention. In contrast, the socio-cultural dimensions of the Games were not an issue in the bidding process, except to the extent in which the different cultures of Australia could be used to promote an image which might see the bid attempt succeed. According to the Sydney Olympics 2000 Bid Limited (SOB) (1992: p. 19), "With the dawn of the new millennium, the peoples of the earth will look to the Olympic Movement for renewed inspiration. Sydney's cultural program for the 2000 Olympic Games will celebrate, above all, our shared humanity and the eternal goals of peace, harmony and understanding so sought amongst the peoples of the world". Indeed, one of the objectives of the cultural program is to "foster awareness and international understanding of the world's indigenous cultures, some of which have survived from earliest times, and to promote especially, a knowledge and appreciation of the unique culture of the Australian Aboriginal peoples" (SOB, 1992: p. 19). It is therefore ironic, that at the time in which this chapter is being completed, the Australian federal government is trying to alter native title legislation in order to extinguish some Aboriginal claims to pastoral leases. An action which is already leading to suggestions that some Australian Aboriginal groups may call on some African and South Pacific nations to boycott the Games in order to attempt to improve the human and land rights position of Aborigines (*Sydney 2000 Olympic Games News*, 1997). While this form of cultural contestation is significant — particularly because mega-events provide an opportunity for various groups to gain world attention for their grievances, e.g. the Palestinian attack on the Israeli Olympic team in Munich in 1972 — it is not likely to be the most critical cultural effect of the Games. More significant in terms of the number of people affected is consideration of the broader social impacts of hosting an event of this size.

Social impacts

Until recently, the socio-cultural effects of mega-events on host communities has, apart from several anthropological and sociological studies, received relatively little attention (Olds, 1988; Hall, 1992; Roche, 1992). However, the development of negative reactions towards tourism development in some destination areas has meant that government and private industry are forced increasingly to pay attention to community attitudes towards the hosting of large events (Hall, 1995a). Negative social impacts gaining most attention include such problems as increased crime and social dislocation. A longer-term effect may be a breakdown or loss of an individual's sense of place as his surroundings are transformed to accommodate the hosting of an event (Dovey, 1989). Nevertheless, while the sociological and psychological effects of mega-events are real, research on these areas is not forthcoming, perhaps because it might spoil the typical 'good news' economic and employment stories attached to the hosting of large events. Therefore, attention to the social impacts of mega-events is usually restricted to such as housing (which is a logical topic area given the real estate dimensions of large events) and employment prospects and, to a lesser extent, pre and mid-event, 'feel good' attitudinal studies (Hall, 1992, 1994). This chapter will now pay special attention to the former.

The housing and real estate dimensions of mega-events

Mega-events may have a considerable impact on housing and real estate values (Hall, 1992; Wilkinson, 1994). There have been several instances that have demonstrated that the hosting of large events "have a tendency to displace groups of citizens located in the poorer sections of cities" (Wilkinson, 1994: p. 29). The people who are often most impacted by hallmark events are typically those who are least able to form community groups and protect their interests. At worse, this tends to lead to a situation in which residents are forced to relocate because of their economic circumstances (Hall, 1994).

In a study of the potential impacts of the Sydney Olympics on low-income housing, Cox *et al.* (1994) concluded that previous mega-events often had a detrimental effect on low income people who are disadvantaged by a localised boom in rent and real estate prices, thereby creating dislocation in extreme cases. The same rise in prices is considered beneficial to home owners and developers. Past events have also shown that this has led to public and private lower-cost housing developments being pushed out of preferred areas as a result of increased land and construction costs (Olds, 1988; Cox *et al.*, 1994). In the case of the Barcelona Games "the market price of old and new housing rose between 1986 and 1992 by 240% and 287% respectively" (Brunet, 1993 in Wilkinson, 1994, p. 23). A further 59,000 residents left Barcelona to live else where between the years of 1984 and 1992 (Brunet, 1993 in Cox *et al.*, 1994). In relation to Australia, past mega-events have led to:

- increased rentals;
- increased conversion of boarding houses to tourist accommodation;
- accelerating gentrification of certain suburbs near where major events are held; and
- a tendency for low income renters to be forced out of their homes (Lenngren, 1987; Day, 1988; Cox *et al.*, 1994; Moore, 1994; Hall, 1995a, b, 1997a).

Studies of previous events also indicate that inadequate prevention policies and measures were developed to ameliorate the effects of hosting mega-events on the low-income and poor sectors of the community. The pattern that has occurred from past events therefore has very real and serious implications for the hosting of the 2000 Games.

Housing impacts of the Sydney 2000 Olympics

Despite the increasing concern and attention being given to resulting social impacts caused by hosting mega-events such as the Olympics, and the undertaking of such a study with the previous Melbourne bid to host the 1996 Summer Olympic Games (Hall, 1992), no social impact study was undertaken by the Sydney bid team during the bidding process. This may be considered as somewhat surprising given the potential impact of the Sydney 2000 Olympics and associated site development on housing and real estate values in the Sydney region.

After the bid was won, a comprehensive housing and social impact study was carried out by Cox *et al.* (1994). The housing report also presented a number of recommendations that could be implemented as a positive strategy to ameliorate such impacts in relation to the preparation and hosting of the Sydney Games. However, this study was undertaken for low-income housing interests not the State Government or the Sydney Olympic organisation.

Although the greatest socio-economic effects of the Games will likely occur in the period closest to the event being held and during the event itself, several studies (e.g., Lenngren, 1987; Day, 1988; Olds, 1988; Hall, 1992) indicate that housing and real estate impacts occur from the time that any bid for an event is successful and when associated infrastructure development occurs. Indeed, in some cases real estate speculation may occur on even the possibility of a bid being successful. Even in the case of rental prices it has been noted that the loss of rental stock through conversion into tourist related accommodation or redevelopment as high-quality housing commences early in the redevelopment process (Hall, 1992).

Since the announcement in September, 1993 that Sydney would be the Olympic 2000 host city, an increasing number of developments have either been announced or are underway in the traditional inner west industrial suburbs near the main Games site at Homebush Bay. In the municipalities of Leichhardt, Ashfield, Drummoyne, Burwood, Concord and Strathfield an increasing number of apartment projects are being built in an area known as the 'Olympic corridor' (Chancellor, 1994). The increase of residential activity is having a significant affect on the housing areas located through the Olympic corridor with one of the main outcomes sought by real estate interests being to "raise the profile of this area and create demand for residential accommodation" (Ujdur, 1993: p. 1).

Recent housing developments have indicated a movement towards the 'gentrification' of many of the inner western suburbs of Sydney by white-collar professionals and a move away by lower income earners from the traditional low income areas as higher income households are targeted (Ujdur, 1993). The Olympics will therefore likely greatly accelerate existing socio-economic processes. As a result, the cost of private housing is expected to increase in the inner west region in particular and throughout the metropolitan area in general. The potential for problems to occur is heightened by the fact that many of the tenants in these areas are on Commonwealth (federal government) benefits for unemployment, sickness, disability and aged persons, and more often than not are single people (Coles, 1994). It is these people who will suffer as the prices of houses and rentals increase in their 'traditional' cheaper housing areas forcing them to relocate in extreme cases.

Approximately 20% of Sydney residents rent accommodation, yet Sydney is already facing a 'rental squeeze' as the shortage of rental properties continues to increase along with a rise in rentals. The situation worsened significantly throughout, 1995, and church leaders and welfare groups expect the situation to get more desperate as the Olympics approaches (Russel, 1995a).

David Ramsay, a policy officer with the New South Wales Tenants Union, expressed concern as the rise in rents has started to force residents away from the inner suburbs into the outlying areas, affecting an average of 5% of renters in 1995 (Russel, 1995a). Again, the situation is expected to get worse as the Olympics approach, particularly affecting areas in the 'Olympic corridor' (Ashfield, Auburn, or Concord), where up to 28,000 tenants live. Added to this is the pressure being place on public housing authorities by federal housing policies to move low income people and the aged into outlying areas (Russel, 1995a). The shortage of rental properties has led to substantial rental price increases, rising between average increases of 10–15% during, 1995 (Russel, 1995b). Groups such as sole parents, aboriginals and people on low incomes are finding it increasingly hard to find rental properties in areas of the inner west, eastern suburbs and the inner city (Russel, 1995a, b), areas which presently provide better access to public transport and medical facilities than the outer suburbs.

Although the Sydney Olympics were four years away, by early 1996 housing impacts, such as increasing rental and real estate prices, had clearly begun to emerge in specific areas of Sydney. Indeed, as has been stated in the Sydney media: "As the revitalization of the inner city continues and is hastened by the Olympics, it is expected that the problem of homelessness will be exacer-bated" (Coles, 1994: p. 15). As the redevelopment for the Games continues, the Homeless Centre predicts that "the greatest potential negative impact of the Sydney 2000 Olympics will be those living in low cost accommodation" (Coles, 1994, p. 2).

A number of means are available for protecting and monitoring the effect of the Games on low-income residents (Hall, 1992; Cox *et al.*, 1994). The main options include:

- the establishment of a housing impact monitoring committee;

- development of an Olympics accommodation strategy;

- tougher legislation to protect tenants and prevent arbitrary evictions;

- provision of public housing and emergency accommodation for disabled people; and

- a form of rent control.

The 2000 Olympic Games are still several years away. There is still time enough to prevent, or ameliorate many of the negative impacts associated with the hosting of the Games. However, the successful implementation of such policies relies on back-up, coordination, funding and implementation from the national, state and local governments and assistance from the private sector. However, despite intensive lobbying from housing, welfare and social groups the State and Commonwealth Governments have failed to act on the significant housing and community issues which are emerging. One likely reason for this is the increas-ing concerns within government over delays in getting the Olympic facilities ready and the desire to avoid the transport problems which were observed in the 1996 Atlanta Olympics. Furthermore, a change in government at the federal level from the middle-ground Labor Party to the right-wing Liberal-National Party coalition, has meant that national financial assistance to the New South Wales Government for low-income housing and urban redevelopment and infra-structure projects has all but dried up.

'Share the Spirit. And the Winner is…?' (SOCOG brochure, nd)

The Olympics are an exercise in cultural politics *par excellence*. However, it is not just the politics of cultural representation which are of concern, but the wider 'spirit of corporatism' which the Games have come to represent. The Olympics are not symbolic of public life or of a culture which is accessible to all local citizens. The Sydney Olympics, along with the event and casino-driven economy of the State of Victoria (Hall, 1997a), are representative of the growth of corporatist politics in Australia and the subsequent treatment of a city as a product to be packaged, marketed and sold, and in which opinion polls are a substitute for public participation in the decision-making process.

In the case of the Sydney Olympic bid the former Premier and key member of the bid team, Nick Greiner, argued that 'The secret of the success was undoubtedly the creation of a community of interest, not only in Sydney, but across the nation, unprecedented in our peacetime history' (1994: p. 13). The description of a 'community of interest' is extremely apt, as such a phrase indicates the role of the interests of growth coalitions in mega-event proposals (Hall, 1997a). The Sydney media played a critical role in creating the climate for the bid. As Greiner stated:

> Early in 1991, I invited senior media representatives to the premier's office, told them frankly that a bid could not succeed if the media played their normal 'knocking role' and that I was not prepared to commit the taxpayers' money unless I had their support. Both News Ltd and Fairfax subsequently went out of their way to ensure the bid received fair, perhaps even favourable, treatment. The electronic media also joined in the sense of community purpose. (1994: p. 13)

Greiner's statement begs the question of "which community?". Certainly, the lack of adequate social and housing impact assessment prior to the Games' bid and post 'winning' the Games, indicates the failure of growth coalitions to recognise that there may well be negative impacts on some sections of the community. However, in terms of the real estate constituency of growth coalitions such considerations are not in their economic interest. Those which are most impacted are clearly the one's least able to affect the policy making and planning processes surrounding the Games (Hall, 1997). The 'need' perceived by some interests for the tourism and associated economic developments of hosting an Olympic Games, creates "a political and economic context within which the hallmark event is used as an excuse to overrule planning legislation and participatory planning processes, and to sacrifice local places along the way" (Dovey, 1989: pp. 79–80). The result of focusing on one set of economic and social interests is that other community interests, particularly those of traditional inner-city residents, are increasingly neglected (Hall, 1992; Hall, 1994).

Undoubtedly, there will be some positive benefits arising from the hosting of the Olympics. Any event of an Olympic size with its associated spending on infrastructure must have some trickle-down and flow-on effects. However, broader issues over the most appropriate long-term economic, social, environmental, and tourism strategies have not been adequately considered, while the most effective distribution of costs and benefits through the community is all but ignored. Indeed, a substantial case could be put forward that the Olympics has in fact deflected Sydney's planners and developers away from the longer term to concentrate on the target year 2000 (Hall, 1997a). The irony is that government, which is meant to be serving the public interest, is instead concentrating its interests on entrepreneurial and corporate rather than broader social goals.

The Olympics are not only a sporting celebration but a celebration of culture. However, the culture they celebrate is the culture of corporatist politics which is synonymous with contemporary global capitalism. The celebration of global corporate sponsorship, global television coverage and the imaging of Sydney and the Olympic movement to the world are powerful signifiers of capitalism as culture. Many people of Sydney will not be able to share the spirit, and they will not be the winners.

Acknowledgments

An earlier version of this chapter was presented at the January, 1996 Australian Tourism Research Conference at Coffs Harbour, New South Wales. The authors would also like to gratefully acknowledge the comments of Neil Leiper and Dave Crag on an earlier version of this work. Ms. Hodges' research was supported by a University of Canberra Research Grant. Professor Hall's research was supported by funding from the Australian Research Council.

References

Ashworth, G. J. and Voogd, H. (1988) 'Marketing the city: Concepts, processes and Dutch applications', *Town Planning Review* Vol. 59 No. 1: pp. 65–80.

Atlanta Constitution Journal (1994) 'Economic leaders use Olympics to pitch Atlanta to execs', *Atlanta Constitution Journal, The 1996 Report*, September: p. 9.

Bramham, P., Henry, I., Mommaas, H. and van der Poel, H. (1989) 'Introduction', in P. Bramham, I. Henry, H. Mommaas and H. van der Poel (eds) *Leisure and urban processes: Critical studies of leisure policy in Western European cities.* London: Routledge, pp. 1–13.

Burgess, J. (1982) 'Selling places: Environmental images for the executive', *Regional Studies* Vol. 16: pp. 1–17.

Castells, M. (1983) 'Crisis, planning, and the quality of life: Managing the new historical relationships between space and society', Environment and Planning D, Society and Space Vol. 1: pp. 3–21.

Chancellor, J. (1994) 'Prices up, but caution prevails', *Sydney Morning Herald* 20 September: p. 29.

Coles, S. (1994) *Submission to the preliminary social impact assessment of the Sydney Olympics.* Sydney: The Homeless Persons Information Centre.

Cox, G., Darcy, M. & Bounds, M. (1994) *The Olympics and housing: A study of six international events and analysis of potential impacts.* Sydney: University of Western Sydney.

Day, P. (1988) *The big party syndrome: A study of the impact of special events and inner urban change in Brisbane.* St. Lucia: Department of Social Work, University of Queensland.

Dovey, K. (1989) 'Old Scabs/new scares: The hallmark event and the everyday environment', in G. J. Syme, B. J. Shaw, D. M. Fenton and W. S. Mueller (eds) *The planning and evaluation of hallmark events.* Aldershot: Avebury, pp. 73–88.

Games of the XXV Olympiad (1992) *Official report of the Games of the XXV Olympiad, Barcelona, 1992,* Vol. 11. Barcelona: Games of the XXV Olympiad.

Gittins, R. (1995) 'Measuring gains from the games', *Sydney Morning Herald,* 16 December: p. 28.

Greiner, N. (1994) 'Inside running on Olympic bid', *The Australian,* 19 September: p. 13.

Hall, C. M. (1989) 'The politics of events', in G. J. Syme, B. J. Shaw, D. M. Fenton and W. S. Mueller (eds) *The planning and evaluation of hallmark events.* Aldershot: Avebury, pp. 219–241.

——— (1992) *Hallmark tourist events: Impacts, management and planning.* Chichester: John Wiley.

——— (1994). *Tourism and politics: Policy, power and place.* Chichester: John Wiley.

——— (1995a) *Tourism in Australia: Impacts, planning and development*, 2nd. ed. South Melbourne: Longman Australia.

——— (1995b) 'Urban imaging strategies and hallmark events: An examination of the Sydney 2000 Olympics and the Melbourne Formula One Grand Prix', in B. Gidlow and C. Simpson (eds) *Leisure connexions, proceedings of the second conference of the Australian and New Zealand Association for Leisure Studies*. Lincoln: Department of Parks, Recreation and Tourism, Lincoln University.

——— (1997a). 'Mega-events and their legacies', in P. Murphy (ed) *Quality management in urban tourism*. New York: John Wiley, pp. 75–87.

——— (1997b) 'Geography, marketing and the selling of places', *Journal of Travel and Tourism Marketing* Vol. 6, No. 3/4: in print.

Hillman, S. (1986) 'Special events as a tool for tourism development', *Special Events Report* Vol. 5, No. 16: pp. 4–5.

Hughes, H. L. (1993) 'Olympic tourism and urban regeneration', *Festival Management and Event Tourism* Vol. 1: pp. 157–162.

——— (1994) 'Urban tourism and the performing arts: The constraints of current research on the analysis of the role and significance of the performing arts in urban tourism', in P. E. Murphy (ed) *Quality management in urban tourism: balancing business and environment, conference proceedings*. Victoria: University of Victoria, pp. 224–233.

Kearns, G. and Philo, C. (eds) (1993) *Selling places: The city as cultural capital, past and present*. Oxford: Pergamon Press.

KPMG Peat Marwick (1993) *Sydney Olympics 2000 economic impact study*, 2 vols. Sydney: Sydney Olympics 2000 Bid.

Kotler, P., Haider, D. H. and Rein, I. (1993) *Marketing places: Attracting investment, industry, and tourism to cities, states, and nations*. New York: The Free Press.

Law, C. M. (1993) *Urban tourism: Attracting visitors to large cities*. London: Mansell.

Lenngren, E. (1987) 'The America's Cup — its impact on property values in Fremantle, Western Australia', unpublished M. Sc. in Surveying Research Project. Stockholm: Department of Real Estate Economics, Royal Institute of Technology.

Long, P. and Sellars, A. (1996) 'Tourism, culture, and the arts in the United Kingdom — an overview and research agenda', *Festival Management & Event Tourism* Vol. 3: pp. 149–158.

Madsen, H. (1992) 'Place-marketing in Liverpool: A review', *International Journal of Urban and Regional Research* Vol. 16 No. 4: pp. 633–640.

Mommaas, H. and van der Poel, H. (1989) 'Changes in economy, politics and lifestyles: An essay on the restructuring of urban leisure', in P. Bramham, I. Henry, H. Mommaas and H. van der Poel (eds) *Leisure and urban processes: critical studies of leisure policy in Western European cities.* London and New York: Routledge, pp. 254–276.

Moore, M. (1994) 'Housing winners and losers in games study', *Sydney Morning Herald* 4 October: p. 3.

Olds, K. (1988) 'Planning for the housing impacts of a hallmark event: A case study of Expo 1986', unpublished MA thesis. Vancouver: School of Community and Regional Planning, University of British Columbia.

Robins, K. (1991) 'Tradition and translation: national culture in its global context', in J. Corner and S. Harvey (eds) *Enterprise and heritage: Crosscurrents of national culture.* London and New York: Routledge, pp. 21–44.

Roche, M. (1992) 'Mega-events and micro-modernization: On the sociology of the new urban tourism', *British Journal of Sociology* Vol. 43 No. 4: pp. 563–600.

———— (1994) 'Mega-events and urban policy', *Annals of Tourism Research* Vol. 21, No. 1: pp. 1–19.

Russel, M. (1995a) 'Plea for action as rent squeeze tightens', *Sydney Morning Herald* 20 September: p. 2.

Russel, M. (1995b) 'The city's high life', *Sydney Morning Herald* 6 September, p. 2.

Shannon, T. (1994) 'Is the price right?', *Sydney Morning Herald* 30 March, special supplement: p. 1.

Sydney Morning Herald (1994) 'Editorial. Taken for a ride to the airport', *Sydney Morning Herald* 22 September: p. 14.

Sydney Olympics 2000 Bid Limited (1992) *Fact sheets: A presentation of the bid by the City of Sydney to host the games of the XXVII Olympiad in the year 2000.* Sydney: Sydney Olympics 2000 Bid Limited.

Sydney Organising Committee for the Olympic Games (SOCOG) (1996) *Environmental guidelines.* Sydney: SOCOG.

Sydney Organising Committee for the Olympic Games (nd) *Share the spirit. Building up to the 2000 Olympics. How Sydney's games plan is taking shape* (Brochure). Sydney: SOCOG.

Sydney 2000 Olympic Games News (1997) 'Aboriginal activist Michael Mansell suggests that some nations could boycott the games', *Sydney 2000 Olympic Games News*, 8 February,
http://www. gwb. au/gwb/news/olympic/080927. html

Totaro, P. (1995) 'Olympic opponents denied sporting chance', *Sydney Morning Herald* 16 December: p. 1.

Ujdur, G. (1993) *Sydney: Olympics 2000: Impact on property, Sydney*: Hooker Research Limited.

Wilkinson, J. (1994) *The Olympic Games: Past history and present expectations.* Sydney: NSW Parliamentary Library.

Williams, R. (1983) *Keywords*. London: Fontana.

Chapter 5

SPORT, SYMBOLISM AND URBAN POLICY: SPORT POLICY AND URBAN IDENTITIES IN LYON

Ian Henry

Loughborough University

Introduction: the context of urban sports policy in the 1990s

The flight from Keynesian welfarism has been undertaken in different ways and with varying levels of enthusiasm by governments of differing political complexions across a range of nation states since the beginning of the 1970s. Such shifts are described in policy terms as a move to post-welfare systems (Pierson, 1991), in political economy terms as a shift to post-Fordism (Jessop, 1990) or in cultural terms as a shift to the post-modern (Featherstone, 1991). The description of such changes as structural shifts has been called into question by those who prefer to refer to 'high modernity' (Giddens, 1980), or 'neo-Fordism' (Tomaney, 1994), arguing that new forms of cultural, political and economic organisation have yet to emerge and that the present represents important continuities with the past such that reference to structural shifts are misplaced or exaggerated. However, commentators do nevertheless agree major change (whether it can be regarded as structural or not) has occurred, that such change is widespread, and that it carries with it implications for the role of the state in generic terms and in relation to particular policy areas.

The nature of these changes is bound up with globalisation processes as the growing intensity of the interconnections across time and space of hitherto 'distant' locations is reproduced by accelerating flows of finance, people, technology, values and ideas across the globe (Appadurai, 1990). In this contest the role of the nation-state as conduit and controller of such flows is diminished, and that of sub-national entities (cities and regions) or transnational entities (e.g. the European Union, the International Monetary Fund etc.) are enhanced.

113

These shifting patterns of culture, politics and economics have clear implication for local government policy in general and for local sports policy in
particular. The traditional concerns of the Fordist nation state for economic
development, have been adopted and adapted by cities in the post-Fordist (or
neo-Fordist) context, particularly those faced with problems of industrial
restructuring and the social restructuring which accompanies this phenomenon
(Lash and Urry, 1994). Indeed, given the tendency for such economic change to
foster the development of a two-tier society in which marginal groups are
increasingly distanced in terms of life chances from those benefiting from the
fruits of economic growth, local governments are left with two sets of priorities.
The first of these is economic development, the stimulation of the local economy.
The second priority is that of promoting social integration, the 'binding in' of
marginal groups into the wider community. The significance of sport as a policy
area is enhanced by the fact that it is able to lend itself in particular ways to both
of these priorities.

In economic development terms sport is seen as potentially significant in that
not only does sport represent opportunities for direct profit generation, but it is
also seen as contributing to the kind of cultural infrastructure which may attract
inward investors, particularly service sector capital. Industrial location decisions
for the service industries are not made on the same basis as those of the
traditional industries, by reference to factors such as access to raw materials,
markets or transport infrastructures. Rather they are made in part by reference to
the availability of a professional workforce with appropriate skills. In developed
economies, given available university level education, cities vie with one another
to provide culturally attractive locations capable of attracting and retaining
mobile service sector professionals (Harvey, 1989). Sport clearly has the
potential to play a role in the identity both of places (e.g. cities) and of individuals. As Harvey (1987) points out, Bourdieu's analysis of the construction of
cultural distance / difference between social groups can also be usefully applied
to the construction of cultural distance between spaces (both within and between
cities) and sport can play a significant role in such processes of identity
distanciation (Bourdieu 1984).

Sport has also traditionally been employed in welfare systems as an arena for
providing social benefits. As the crisis of welfare funding emerged in Britain, the
emphasis on 'sport for all' and on sport as a right of citizenship inscribed for
example in the 1975 White Paper on Sport and Recreation (Department of

Environment, 1975) was replaced by an emphasis on schemes specifically targeted rather than universal, often aimed at volatile inner city populations and motivated in part by concern for social disorder in Britain's cities (Henry, 1993). Thus sport, in addition to its economic function, is recognised as a policy tool with potential for promoting social integration.

Although these trends may be generally evident in cities in developed economies, different cities may react in policy terms in different ways, given their peculiarities of history, politics and culture. Thus the research which is reported here represents an analysis of a particular sports policy system at a specific historical juncture. It is a study of policy in the Lyon conurbation, involving all four levels of government from the commune through to the central state.

Analysis of sports policy: the selection of Lyon as a case study

There is a fashionable concern within the social sciences with the concept of globalisation and global-local tensions. Part of the fascination with a study of city policy in a comparative context is consideration of how global forces are responded to in different types of context. France provides a particular interest in this respect in that it contrasts neatly in a number of important ways with the case of Britain. One of the most obvious contrasts is in terms of political control at central government level. While Britain has enjoyed unbroken one party rule by the Conservatives in the period since 1979, French governments have been of both Socialist and Centre Right persuasion, but the period has been one of predominantly Socialist control. A further important difference lies in the implementation of decentralisation legislation in the 1980s which gave rise to a regional tier of government and which widened and to some extent formalised the powers of other levels of local government. The third point of contrast lies in France's traditional reputation for cultural closure, whether this takes the form of the 'policing' of the French language, or the protectionism of the French government in respect of the cultural industries in, for example, the last round of GATT talks (when France, in order to protect its film industry, delayed the signing of the international agreement until the United States conceded that protectionism could be exercised in relation to films and other such cultural products). This begs the question of the extent to which French sporting culture (and for that matter French political culture) is 'open' or 'closed'.

The choice of Lyon for a study of local sports policy was made not because it was in any way necessarily typical, but rather because certain features rendered it an interesting case[2]. It is France's second city, a city with its own considerable cultural resources, seeking to promote its identity beyond the capital, as is evident in its prominence as one of the founder members of the Euro-cities consortium. Thus, it is seeking also to promote itself in the European space. However, it is also a city which has been subject to severe social and economic stresses reflected in the urban disorders of the 1980s and 1990s at Les Min-guettes, Bron and Vaulx-en-Velin.

Methodology

In order to begin to unravel the nature of sports policy in the Lyon conurbation it was necessary to gain an overview from the full range of the bodies responsible for the development of policy. The decentralisation legislation had in fact said very little about responsibility for sport and culture and as a consequence there was involvement at all levels, the région, the département, the commune, and the regional and départemental arm of the central government department of the sécrétaire d'État de la Jeunesse et aux Sports. Thus policy at each of these levels was reviewed.

It was necessary however to be selective in terms of the number of communes to be investigated within the conurbation, and five were ultimately selected for incorporation in the sample to be studied. These were the communes of Lyon, Villeurbanne, Vaulx-en-Velin, St. Priest, and Vénissieux. The selection was made on the basis of four criteria. The first of these was centrality: the Commune of Lyon clearly had to be included in a discussion of the conurbation, but equally the other communes were of major size and cultural and political significance. The second criterion was that of political control: the sample included one centre right controlled authority — Lyon; two Socialist led — Villeurbanne and St. Priest; one Communist led — Vénissieux; and another Communist/Socialist led coalition — Vaulx-en-Velin (see Table 3). The third criterion for selection of communes was that of relative affluence/poverty, with percentage of households in receipt of Revenue Minimum d'Insertion, and average household income being taken as indicators. Finally, communes were selected which were known to have a defined sports policy with an established 'Service des Sports'.

Sources of data for identifying sports policy in each case involved interviews with a key informant located within the strategic apex of each organisation, together with documentary analysis of policy statements, budgetary data, and other policy relevant documents, municipal newspapers, transcripts of speeches by politicians responsible for the direction of sports policy, proceedings of the Conseil Régional and the Conseil Général. Restriction of interviews to a single key informant was clearly a limitation, though one which was unavoidable in the context of a time constrained study, and was mediated to some degree by reference to documentary sources. The selection of interviewees was made on the basis of the centrality of the individuals concerned in the development of policy within their own organisation, as gauged by informed external opinion (an adapted form of reputational grid was adopted). Fieldwork was conducted in two periods of two weeks in July and September 1994.

Interviews were semi-structured, lasting between one and three hours. The symbolic uses of sport in the urban context was only one of a number of research concerns. The principal research issues or questions to be addressed included the following:

- establishing the priorities adopted in sports policy by each of the bodies and how these had developed over time;

- the effects of party control on sports policy;

- the development of relations between the various tiers of government and the other organisational actors in the policy system.

A further set of six subsidiary concerns were also explored.

Tables 1, 2, and 3 following summarise the major themes cited by interviewees in their accounts of sports policy and in policy related documentation. The commentary below does not deal with these in detail case by case, but rather seeks to identify key themes in relation to the symbolic functions of sport in policy, and to evaluate their significance.

Table 1a: Sports Policy and Budgets for the Rhône-Alpes Région

Conseil Régional Major Policy Themes	Regional Budget 1994 (FF)
1) Sporting Equipment for Education Sector —for new facilities, aid to local governments for: • provision of sports halls and gymnasiums; • specialist indoor facilities; • outdoor pitches and tracks —for management of new facilities in exchange for use by lycées	15,000,000
2) Other Sports Provision; elite sport and Contrat Globaux de développement —facilities of regional significance (15% of pre-tax costs) • support for sporting sections of lycées with regional recruitment • support for elite athletes in competitions, training and employment • support for established centres for training and sports coaching • support for sports medicine centres. —contribution to provision in areas under-provided for in the region.	6,500,000
3) Promotion of Regional Sport —aid to the sports movement in the region including • provision for the acquisition of materials and technological support for coaching of athletes and training of administrators; • agreements with the sports movement in the form of contracts with specific objectives; • financial support for sporting organisations working at regional level for the integration of young people (e.g. Centres Régionaux Information Jeunesse). —sports events	8,000,000
4) Miscellaneous Other Categories, e.g.: • promotion of employment of young people in sport • major events • sport and tourism	10,000,000

Table 1b: Sports Policy and Budgets for the Rhône Département

Conseil Général Major Policy Themes	Départmental Budget 1994 (FF)
1) Aid to Sports Clubs and Associations	
—elite club subsidy	7,768,300
—sport for all	1,547,000
2) Funds for Other Sporting Operations	618,500
3) Aid to Departmental Olympic Committee	2,000,000
4) Subsidy on Entry Tickets to major Sporting Events for Special groups	2,600,000
5) Opérations Prévention d'Été	290,000
(Other hidden subsidies:	
—funding of communes for construction and management of facilities	20,000,000
—supply of facilities and transport by collèges for sport)	30,000,000

Sources:
Interviews with administrators at Regional and Départemental levels;
Conseil Régional de Rhône-Alpes (1994) 'La Politique Régionale en Faveur du Sport' internal document, unpublished report, May;
Conseil Général du Rhône (1993) *Travaux de l'Assemblée Départemental*, 'Rapport de M. Michel Mercier, Présentation du Budget 1994, Culture et Sports' (pp. 40-42).

Table 2:   The Principal Sports Policy Themes of the Communes

Major Policy Themes	Lyon	St. Priest
Social integration and prevention of delinquency	• neighbourhood small scale facilities for difficult areas • operations prévention d'été • DSQ scheme	sport and social integration / insertion
City promotion	• high profile events • recruitment of sporting champions to promote sport • upgrading of prestige sports facilities	primarily through top clubs with local players and athletes
Sporting animation	including links between schools and clubs	
Support / subsidy for sport clubs	including elite (professional) clubs and those providing for mass sport	subsidy for top level sporting clubs
Support of sport in education		
Sport for all / leisure services		improving the general level of sporting practice in the town
Facility construction	facility construction to promote geographical equity	
Miscellaneous		promotion of the Service des Sports

Vaulx-en-Velin	Vénissieux	Villeurbanne
• opérations d'été • équipements de proximité • employment of top level sports people as role models	combating unemployment and idleness	• DSQ • équipements de proximité • opérations d'été
• subsidy to clubs • staging of events		high level sports clubs
		sporting animation
mass sports clubs and provision of free high quality facilities	aid to clubs (material and subsidy)	• high level sport • local sports promotion
• in-school teaching • links with clubs and out of school coaching	educational programme of support within and outside formal education	support of sport in formal education system
	leisure sector sport provision for the community	
development of infrastructure to very high standard		

Sources: Interviews with political and administrative personnel in selected communes; 'Ville de Lyon (1994) Pour Une Politique Sportive de Qualité', *C'est 9 à Lyon: Revue Municipale de Lyon*, No. 55, April; Ville de Villeurbanne (1994) *Bilan sur le Sport 1989-1995*; Service Des Sports, Vénissieux (1993) *Tableaux de Bord*

Table 3:   Background Data on the Communes and their 'Service Des Sports' (1993)

	Lyon	St Priest	Vaulx-en-Velin	Vénissieux	Villeurbanne
Size	422,000	41,800	45,000	60,400	120,000
Political Control	Nouvelle Democratie / RPR / UDF	Socialist	Communist / Socialist	Communist	Socialist
No. of graduate level Employees (Cadre A)	3	4	1	3	3
No. of Employees with University Degree in Sports / Physical Education (UFRAPS)	0	4	0	2	1
No. of Employees with Brevet d'État in Sports Field (BEESAN)	26	7	2	6	4
Revenue Budget for Sport as % of Revenue Budget of Commune	1.5% excluding indirect costs and cost of personnel	6% excluding personnel and maintenance costs	6.3%	9.41%	13.2%
Per Capita direct grants to Clubs and Associations	55.60 FF	48.35 FF	61.98 FF	50.60 FF	105.10 FF

Sources: Morel, H and Racouchot, E (1993) *Organigramme des Service des Sports des Communes du Rhône et le Recensement des Piscines du Rhône avec leurs M.N.S. (BEESAN)*, l'UFRAPS, l'Université Claude Bernard, Lyon 1, *Guide Politique de l'Agglomeration de Lyon*, 1994; Interview data , Internal budgetary documents from the Communes selected.

Sports policy in the Lyon conurbation

The financial context

It is worth noting that although the precise responsibilities of each of the levels of government below the level of the central state had not been clearly defined in relation to sport, at each level there was a clear indication of the perceived importance of this policy field given at the local to regional level of government. When the decentralised system of government was introduced in the early 1980s, one of the divisions of responsibility which it failed to make clear was that for sport. Sports policy has thus been treated as a discretionary area by Communes, but more particularly by the Départements and the Régions. With the replacement of criteria-specific grants by a block grant to local government (the Dotation Global de Fonctionnement), together with greater freedom to raise local taxes, there has been increasing room for local manoeuvre, at least in principle, in terms of how local governments spend their money (Keating and Midwinter, 1994).

Each of the communes investigated reported a significant increase in the level of funding for sport, which in some cases was spectacular. In the case of Lyon for example subsidy to sports clubs grew from 3.5 million francs each for recreational sport (sport de masse) and for elite sport in 1989, to 7 million francs each by 1993, and this figure excluded 10 million francs awarded to Olympique Lyonnais the city's professional football team (which also received 4.5 million francs from the Département). Similarly, Villeurbanne's subsidy of sports clubs grew from 5.5. million in 1989 to 13 million francs in 1994, of which approximately 10 million francs went to elite and/or professional clubs (including 6 million francs to ASVEL the commune's basketball club). In all of the communes staff numbers and professional expertise had expanded across the 1980s and 1990s, and this had been accompanied by significant expansion in facilities also.

At the regional and départemental levels also, major growth had occurred. The Région's budget for sport had grown from 6.3 million francs in 1986 to 33.3 million francs in 1992, although it had fallen for the first time in 1993 to 30 million francs. The budget for the Département presents some difficulties of interpretation since the range of budget heads included under sport varies from year to year, but since the establishment of a separate Bureau des Sports in 1992 there have been indications of an increased financial commitment to particular aspects of sports policy, in particular the budget for sports promotion trebled in

1993. The growth reported for the Région and imputed by staff for the Département is typical of the experience of Conseils Généraux et Régionaux throughout
France (Ministère de la Jeunesse et des Sports, 1993).

Thus, while sports provision is, for local and regional authorities, for the
most part, not a statutory obligation but a matter for discretion, budget growth
reflects the general recognition of the importance of this policy domain.
This experience is in marked contrast to that of British local authorities.
Legislation introduced by Conservative governments over the 1980s sought
progressively to reduce the autonomy of local government, to tightly circum-
scribe its powers to raise local revenue, with the overall objective of reducing
public sector spending. By the end of the 1980s the expenditure figures for local
authorities in England and Wales demonstrate that levels of expenditure in
real terms were beginning to tail off and in some years actually fell (Henry,
1993). In effect, whether English local authorities chose to regard sports policy
as important or not, by the beginning of the 1990s their room for manoeuvre was
tightly constrained.

The symbolic functions of sport and sports policy in the Lyon conurbation

Respondents, both politicians and bureaucrats, were clearly aware of the
symbolic value of sport for various purposes. Six major ways in which such
symbolism was consciously employed or evoked are outlined below.

(i) Promotion of the city and the region at transnational level

This was most obvious in the case of the commune of Lyon itself which sought
to attract a range of international events precisely because of the kudos and
exposure such events provide. In 1990 the World Championships in boxing, ice
hockey, and chess were staged; in 1991 World Championships in rock acrobatics,
the Volleyball World Cup, the Davis Cup Final; in 1992 the Lyon Marathon, the
World University Table Tennis Championships, Urban Motocross; in 1993 the
Masters of Rock Acrobatics competition, the Tennis Grand Prix de Lyon. These
represent a selection from 24 such internationally focused events staged over the
three year period 1991–3 (Lyon, ville de, 1994). The city's strategy had been to
provide event organisers with a media management package which alleviates the
tasks facing the organisers of major sporting events, and which allowed the city
to manage the way the event (and through the event, the city) was projected.

The Région has also been involved in the promotion of regional identity. Regional support for the Winter Olympics at Albertville had been substantial and during the fieldwork in September 1994 the President of the Région, M. Millon announced that Rhône-Alpes would actively consider the development of a regional bid to stage the 2004 Summer Olympics. The region, it was argued, contained a network of cities (Lyon, Grenoble, St Etienne) which could stage a world event. The proposal provoked a caustic response from the Adjoint au Maire of Lyon responsible for sport, reflecting, amongst other things, a degree of inter-organisational rivalry:

> I think this bid is more about the Région than it is about sport. It is unrealistic, it is ruled out by the rules of the IOC because it is not a bid by a city, it is unfeasible and undesirable. (Adjoint au maire, Lyon)

(ii) Promotion of the city/commune within the national context

While the symbolic use of sport to promote the place of the city on the international stage is a readily recognisable phenomenon, a well documented aspect of the globalisation of inter-city competition, something which is less recognisable, to British eyes at least, is the promotion of the Commune in a national context. While Lyon promoted itself as a European city, its satellite towns were concerned to use sport to establish their identity, out of the shadow of their bigger neighbour. Vaulx-en-Velin and Vénissieux, in particular suffered from negative images generated by their association with urban disorders of the early 1990s and 1980s respectively.

Although Vaulx had a policy of seeking to attract major events (though of a lesser order than those sought by Lyon) which can be accommodated in its relatively rich infrastructure of facilities, all four of the communes neighbouring Lyon sought to promote their own identities by funding of their major elite sporting clubs. Public sector subsidy of professional sports clubs has been deemed of questionable legality, and is subject to objections from professional clubs of other EU member states:

> The support of professional clubs like this is a specifically French practice. According to the Treaty of Maastricht (sic) these are enterprises, and therefore should not have financial support. If this were the case in France there would be no more sport. Nearly all professional clubs work like that. (Adjoint au maire, Villeurbanne)

At the level of the European Union, there has been some support for exempting professional sports clubs from the application of market rules (Coopers and Lybrand, 1993), but there is still some doubt as to whether a challenge to its legality would be upheld by the European Court.

(iii) Promotion of political entities

In the case of the Département the value of sport in promoting a positive image of the political/ administrative machine of the Conseil Général was recognised. Sport was not only a new area of policy intervention but also one which generally attracted a positive response from the community (or electorate). Thus the distribution of grants to clubs which had been devolved to the Départemental Olympic Committee was subsequently undertaken by the Département's own staff in consultation with representatives from clubs, the Départemental Olympic Committee and from the Offices Municipaux des Sports of the communes. The existence of this consultative body, it was argued, helped to broadcast the Département's support for sport:

> The policy for sport of the Conseil Général is not widely known. For example the Conseil Général distributes money to the Departmental Olympic Committee. Before the Committee did not know that the money came from the Conseil Général. It was important that they be made aware of where the money came from. The Conseil Général needs to show that it is contributing strongly in this field. (Director, Bureau des Sports, Conseil Général)

The use by the Région of sport as a means of popularising a new tier of government had clearly also been grasped by the administration in the early days of its development:

> At first it was not really clear whether the Région had any competence in sport but almost from the beginning it was understood that the Région could demonstrate its vitality by being active in a type of policy which has a popular appeal. (Directeur, Bureau des Sports, Conseil Régional)

(iv) The symbolic function of sports personalities as role models

The subsidy of elite and/or professional sports clubs was often tied to the requirement that members act as coaches or foster participation in other ways. Vaulx-en-Velin went further along this road, employing sporting stars on the permanent staff of the Service des Sports because of their value as role models demonstrating to the young people with whom they work the possibility of success in at least the sporting sphere. This was particularly true in the case of a young boxer, of African origin, who had been a national champion, produced locally and who was clearly seen by the local authority as part of their policy to counter the disaffection of black French 'immigrant' youth. The relationships between, in particular boxing, the internalising of the lessons of discipline and hard work, and the use of sportsmen and women to symbolise the possibility of success, are not limited to the Lyon sub-region, but reflect strategies adopted in other urban contexts (Bozonet, 1991).

(v) The appropriation of symbolism by oppositional groups

This is perhaps the most contentious claim in respect of symbolism and sports policy in this case. Urban social disorder had been sparked off in Vaulx-en-Velin and in Bron (another of the Lyon communes) in 1993 by an incident in which a young joy rider (of North African origin) had been killed by police. In both places, rioters had chosen to express their anger by setting fire to sports halls in the city. In the case of the sports hall in Vaulx, the arsonists had driven a stolen car through a plate glass window into the gymnasium and set alight to it.

Now it is possible to read these events in a range of ways. At one extreme one might provide a relatively crude account of the intentional attack on the symbols of a bread and circuses policy to express derision at authorities who fail to provide for the 'real' needs of young people, particularly from the 'immigrant' population (unemployment in Vaulx-en-Velin stood at 16%, with a very young population: 30% below the age of 20 and with 23% of the population of North African origin). At the other extreme one might argue that the selection of these buildings was a coincidence, or owed more to the fact that access was possible (the buildings were empty at the time) and that no symbolism was intended. However, regardless of the intended meaning or lack of it, it is clear that the acts themselves conveyed a symbolic meaning to the population affected, and the events themselves throw into sharp relief the marginality of sport as a vehicle for combating social and economic exclusion.

(vi) Sporting uses of space and the symbolic (re)appropriation of space

The final dimension along which the symbolic use of sport is identified here, is its use particularly by local governments in reclaiming public spaces which have taken over by 'inappropriate' groups. Perhaps the best example of this in the

Lyon conurbation was represented by the establishing of a huge climbing wall on the outside of a block of flats in Vaulx-en-Velin. In the early 1980s the area had been subject to a high degree of vandalism and graffiti, with a number of flats left empty being broken into and extensively damaged, and with the areas around the buildings colonised by 'problem' youth groups, leaving local people feeling unsafe, particularly in the evenings. In 1990 the Commune opened a climbing wall constructed on the exterior of one such building, and covered the wall with a colourful canvas, allowing all-weather use. Some of the empty flats were converted into offices for local sporting bodies who would make use of the climbing facilities, providing coaching etc. Schools, youth groups and associations were able to make use of the facility during the day, at evenings and at weekends.

The Commune of Vaulx-en-Velin had had a policy of promoting outdoor pursuits in an urban setting (Association-Sports-Ville-Nature-Aventure, 1989), but here this policy was combined with the reclaiming of an area for public use. People were brought into the area on a relatively regular basis, and during a range of times extending into evenings and weekends, thus reversing the previous tendency to abandon these spaces to particular youth groups, and making local people feel safer, and, it was claimed by the Directrice du Service du Sport, reducing the incidence of vandalism and criminal damage. The addition of the sporting use to the way the area was defined for the local population was 'announced' by the construction of the huge pink canvas covered frame, covering the full height of the building (15 storeys). This represented a highly visible symbol of the redefinition of this locality as a public space, dominated by new, 'safer', public authority approved, forms of leisure.

Although this was the most spectacular example of using sport to redefine the nature of public spaces, there were others, such as the introduction of small scale sports facilities into public parks to redefine traditional parks as 'exciting' recreation spaces. In Villeurbanne for example, this included the provision of small scale climbing walls, or artificial boulders, to allow unsupervised bouldering to take place, attracting, in particular, youth into the parks.

Sport and social integration/social insertion

In each of the communes there was a major concern for the use of sport as a tool for combating the alienation generated by the acute social problems experienced in parts of the city. It is not so much lack of employment which is perceived as the problem but lack of hope of employment, in particular on the part of youth of North African extraction. Three initiatives in particular were cited by each of the communes — Opérations d'Été, a scheme initially launched by central government in 1982 in response to the urban disorders at Les Minguettes, a suburb of Vénissieux; Développement Social du Quartier, a central government funded scheme for specifying areas of special need within the city to be in receipt of concentrated funding and social action; équipements de proximité, a third government scheme launched at the beginning of the 1990s as a means of fostering sports participation by those who are unlikely to join formal sporting organisations, which involved the provision of small scale local facilities.

The terminology describing the function of these forms of provision is revealing. They are to combat 'idleness' (désoeuvrement), delinquent behaviour, to promote social integration, or social insertion. Each of these terms was employed by respondents at interview in describing their schemes. They are cited here in roughly the chronological order that one comes across them in the professional literature, from combating the passive (tackling idleness), to the more proactive social insertion:

> The substitution of the term insertion for that of integration appears as the consequence of the displacement of the goal of public action from the search for the society of production to the production of society. (Donzelot and Estèbe, 1994)

The use of sport as a vehicle for social insertion is an ideology firmly embedded in each of the respondents, and evident throughout the interviews:

> Sport is a means of socialisation, of access to citizenship. They [young people] have to train, the hours are fixed, there is the discipline of training and of the match. There is work in courses to become trainers and referees. (Director of Service des Sports, Vaulx-en-Velin)

An interesting and very significant difference between the approach adopted in the Lyon context to social and cultural provision for youth of immigrant communities is that the goal is seen as one of integration into mainstream culture of the French. (This is not integration into mainstream French culture, as a brief glance at the small scale informal street basketball games taking place around Équipements de proximité will illustrate.) As Lionel Arnaud (1993) has noted the goal of cultural integration contrasts with the formal commitment to multi-culturalism in the British context. The promotion in Britain of, for example, Kabbadi as a game by local authorities is a consequence of this multi-culturalist approach.

In addition to the goals of social insertion, the Région sought to promote economic insertion on the part of the young in providing training which could lead to employment in the sports industries.

Sport, equity of access and the market for sport — the role of political values in sports policy

One of the purposes of the study was to explore whether there were differences emerging in sports policy rationales and styles between local governments controlled by left and right. Within the sample of communes only Lyon itself was controlled by a centre right coalition under the heading of Nouvelle Dèmocratie, essentially a coalition of RPR (Rassemblement pour la Rèpublique) and UDF (L'Union Dèmocratique Française) interests organised around the then Mayor Michel Noir. The Region and the Dèpartement were both also controlled by centre right coalitions.

Almost universally the respondents rejected the notion of there being significant differences in the types of policy pursued, though there was some indication of differences in the style of implementation by at least one respondent:

> Take [names political counterpart in Lyon] who is not the same character politically as me at all. He's done the same as me. He has set up Èquipements de proximitè et cetera. The difference is how we have done it. For us we use the Èquipement de proximitè schemes to consult young people, and to organise them into a network. In ... quartier we set up an association managed by the young who also manage the facility and other things concerning membership, or dialogue with the Office Municipal de Sport. (Maire adjoint chargè du sport, Villeurbanne)

This description of a community development approach to provision of sporting opportunities was particularly prevalent in the DSQs where one aspect of the policy philosophy was the development of sustainable community structures. However, as Schmidt (1990) points out, decentralisation of the French government system has not necessarily increased democratic participation. In Lyon which like Paris and Marseille, is large enough to have a separate tier of politicians for each arrondissement, the role of this tier in decision-making in regard to sporting facilities and management was regarded as minimal. As the Maire Adjoint pointed out:

There are Adjoints au sport in the arrondissement, but they are only message bearers...because the money is here at the Town Hall.

To underline the point about the apolitical nature of sports policy, however, the political Maire adjoint in Lyon claimed that when he had been invited by the mayor to consider taking over this portfolio he was not a member of a political party and it was by virtue of his interests and experience in sports administration that he had been approached. In fact Lyon had demonstrated a concern with the lack of equity in provision of facilities since this individual's appointment and had undertaken considerable investment in sporting infrastructure. Between 1989 and 1994 the commune had 22 gymnasia and sports halls built or refurbished, as well as 8 stadia and 11 sports grounds.

Another scheme which illustrated a concern with equity was the use of subsidy for sports tickets to major events. The Département funded a scheme operated by the communes for the distribution of tickets particularly to children and disadvantaged youth. For events such as the Lyon Golf Open, and the tennis Grand Prix, and the Fencing World Championships, tickets were provided to children who immediately after the event were taken to clubs for coaching and introduction to the sport. The benefits of this scheme were thus two fold. The events themselves designed to promote Lyon had the potential to magnify the distance between the affluent and the poor in the city. Providing a spectacle in the city to attract the tourist and media attention, but which much of the city's population could not afford to attend carried potential negative implications. Free or subsidised tickets might help to overcome this. However, in addition to the use of the scheme for external marketing of the city the sports development potential of such events could be realised by building on the enthusiasm of young spectators who might become recruits to the sport. (There is of course a question mark over how enduring an introduction to golf can be when the cost of playing is very high.)

There was little evidence from the interviews of the favouring of collective sports forms on the part of the communes of the left, though in one of the communes Villeurbanne, support for sport was promoted as one of the last bastions of collective life:

The only place where there is collective life is in the life of the associations — the sports club has become a location of change, a place of
solidarity. (Maire adjoint chargé du sport, Villeurbanne)

By contrast the Director of the Service des Sport at Vaulx-en-Velin argued that
recognition of the individualised nature of sporting demands was important:

> People are attracted more now to individual sports and we have tried to
> provide these with things like windsurfing, rock climbing and some new
> sports like roller hockey

Politicisation in this field, and at the local level, should not perhaps be anticipated. Although with decentralisation party politics is much more evident in
local and regional politics, as Schmidt (1990) points out, this is a limited
phenomenon. Party discipline is sustained (with difficulty) only at times of
elections with the drawing up of party lists and agreement of coalition arrangements. Between elections, party discipline is weak with many local parties
pursuing local, rather than nationally decided policy priorities.

Professionalisation

One of the striking features of the policy system was the relative lack of
professionally qualified personnel operating in this field. Graduates (cadre A)
were relatively rare in these, which were among the most developed of the sports
policy organisations in the conurbation. Even rarer were those who had graduate
level qualifications in the field of sport. The situation was not more advanced in
the case of the Département or the Région, both of which employed one
specialist graduate. Cadre B personnel, those with below graduate level
qualifications (the equivalent of two years post-18 training) were restricted to
technical qualifications generally in teaching and coaching.

Professionalising the mode of operation of the Service des Sports, even where
they had been in existence some time, was a relatively new phenomenon.
The communes of Lyon and Villeurbanne had both benefited from the appointment of energetic politicians who had taken over in 1989 and had had significant
impacts on the professional nature of the professionalism of the service. The
Bureau des Sports and the Département had only been established in 1992.

However, notwithstanding the youth of the profession and the lack of
qualified personnel, there was a striking similarity between the organisations in
the development of policy. Two examples can be given of this and these hint

at the sources of this policy uniformity. The first is the development of criteria by which decisions concerning grant aid to sports organisations were to be made. Three of the communes had recently established, or were in the process of establishing, a points system based on criteria such as the number of children as members, the number of qualified coaches etc. In addition the Département had also recently adopted a similar policy in adapted form. Such policy convergence is not of course coincidental, and betrays aspects of ideological corporatism, that is the communication of shared values and shared policy advice throughout a policy community such that even in very different contexts, similar policy outcomes are generated. Indeed this technocratic attempt to reduce essentially political decisions to 'objective', 'technical' criteria is typical of a professionalising strategy.

Conclusion

The decentralisation of government in the French context has resulted in a significant decline in the role of the central state in sports policy vis-à-vis sub-national government (Chazaud, 1989). The case study of the Lyon conurbation illustrates just how much the Région, the Département, and the Communes have taken on in respect of sports policy. Sports expenditure and policy have indeed expanded in importance since decentralisation in most communes throughout France, particularly the larger ones, despite the global recessionary tendencies experienced in the 1980s and 1990s. Why should this be the case? One of the functions of this article (which has focused on only one aspect of sports policy) is to suggest that this is in part because the phenomenon of sport lends itself to the nature of contemporary urban politics in particular ways. Sport may play a significant role in both local economic development and in local social integration, but it may perform such roles at the symbolic level. While in terms of economic development sport may be a direct generator of revenue, it has the potential to play an even more significant role as an image enhancer. An appropriately vibrant image is seen as a prerequisite for the attraction of new service class professionals, and with them the inward investment of service capital (Harvey, 1987). At the level of social integration or insertion, symbolic integration into a 'host culture' is also assumed to be fostered by sport.

  A central concern in this study was the evaluation of political difference between constituencies controlled by different political groupings as reflected in sports policy. In the case study area, political parties may have differed in the detail of policy advocacy, but in practice there were few differences between the seven sub-national governments controlled by different party political groups in terms of their approach to sport. This perhaps is unsurprising in that party discipline in sub-national government in France is said to be weak, and thus party political differences in local government less sustained[3]. However, it also reflects a broadly consensual approach to sports policy which was professed by virtually all respondents[4].

The fact that sport was 'apolitical' in nature enhanced its value as a vehicle for promoting a positive image of the political entities which sponsored it. A positive input by local, départemental, or régional government associated it with success, and the excitement and hedonism of major national or international sporting events, or with the improved quality of life seen to derive from participating in sporting activities. Such a policy had few of the drawbacks of more politicised policy areas such as education, health or housing. At this level at least sport lends itself to post-modern politics.

Post-modern politics reflects the abandonment of modernist political pro-grammes building support on the basis of 'rational' appeal to structurally defined (most often, class based) interests. It appeals to a fragmented electorate through a logic of gratification rather than the meeting of needs (Heller and Fehér, 1991). Sport and sports policy has, therefore, because of its symbolic potential, a signi-ficant role to play in the post-modern construction of political consensus and support, and, as the case of the destruction of gymnasia illustrates, it also has the potential to provide an expression of dissension and conflict. Thus, in a context of flexibilised economic, and fragmented social structures, increasing inter-urban competition, and restructured cultural hierarchies, the significance of sport seems likely to remain an enduring concern of urban politics and urban governance.

Notes

1   This chapter draws substantially on an earlier version of the analysis reported here in 'The politics of sport and symbolism in the city', *Managing Leisure: an International Journal*, Vol. 3, No. 2, April 1997.

2   In addition there were pragmatic reasons for selecting Lyon as a case study, in particular, ease of access through local intermediaries, in the form of staff at the Université Claude Bernard, whose social science and sports management education provision and expertise was a considerable resource for the local sports policy community. Indeed the influence of that team on the policy community was one of the factors to investigate.

3   Except perhaps at election periods (Schmidt, 1990).

4   Indeed the Adjoint au Maire in Lyon had been brought in by the mayor to take responsibility for the sports portfolio even though he had not been a member of the ruling party (though he had subsequently joined Nouvelle Democratie — the local coalition of the right).

References

Appadurai, A (1990) 'Disjuncture and difference in the global cultural economy', in M. Featherstone (ed) *Global culture: nationalism, globalization and modernity*. London: Sage.

Arnaud, L. (1993) *Équipements Sportifs et Politiques d'Intégration Sociales en France et en Grande Bretagne: Analyse Comparé*, Univerité Lyon 1, unpublished mémoire.

Association Sports-Ville-Nature-Aventure (1989) *Expansion de Sports d'Aventure en Ville et Avenir des Équipements de Loisirs*. Vaulx-en-Velin: Vaulx-en-Velin/ École Nationale de Travaux Publics de lÉtat.

Bourdieu, P. (1984) *Distinction: A social critique of the judgement of taste*. London: Routledge.

Bozonet, J.-J. (1991) Extract from Le Monde, 'Ne pas désespérer la banlieue: Sport et musique', in Menanteau, J. (ed.) *Les Banlieues, Éditions Le Monde*. Paris, 1994.

Bramham, P., Haywood, L. and Henry, I. (1982) 'Recreation versus vandalism', *Leisure Management*, Vol. 2, No. 12.

Chazaud, P. (1989) *Le Sport dans la Commune, le Département, et la Région*. Paris: Berger Levrault, Administration Locale.

Coalter, F. (1988) *Sport and anti-social behaviour: A literature review.* (Scottish Sports Council Research Report no. 2) Edinburgh: the Scottish Sports Council.

Conseil Régional de Rhône-Alpes (1994) La Politique Régionale en Faveur du Sport. Unpublished report, May.

Coopers and Lybrand (1995) *The impact of the activities of the European Community on sport: 3rd edition.* Brussels, DGX of the European Commission.

Defrance, J. & Pociello, C. (1993) 'Structure and evolution of the field of sports in France (1960-1990): A "functional", historical and prospective analytical essay', *International Review of the Sociology of Sport*, Vol. 28, No. 1: pp. 1-21.

Donzelot, J. & Estèbe, P. (1994) *L'État Animateur: Essai sur la politique de la ville.* Paris: Éditions Ésprit.

Eisenschitz, A.& Gough, J. (1993) *The politics of local economic policy: The problems and possibilities of local initiatives.* Basingstoke: Macmillan.

Featherstone, M. (1991) *Consumer culture and post-modernism.* London: Sage.

Galès, P. (1995) 'Du Gouvernment des Villes à la Gouvernance Urbaine', *Revue Française de Science Politique*, Vol. 45, No. 1.

Giddens, A. (1990) *The consequences of modernity.* Polity: Cambridge.

Harvey, D. (1987) 'Flexible accumulation through urbanization: Reflections on post-modernism in the American city', *Antipodes*, Vol. 19, No. 3: pp. 260-286.

———— (1989) *The condition of postmodernity.* Oxford: Blackwell.

Heller, A. & Fehér, F. (1991) *The postmodern political condition.* Oxford: Polity.

Henry, I. (1993) *The politics of leisure policy.* Basingstoke: Macmillan.

Houlihan, B. (1994) *Sport and international politics.* Brighton: Harvester Wheatsheaf.

Jessop, B. (1990) *State theory: Putting capitalist states in their place.* Polity: Cambridge.

Keating, M. and Midwinter, E (1994) 'The politics of central-local grants in Britain and France', *Environment and Planning C: Government and Policy*, Vol. 12, No. 3: pp. 177-194.

Lash, S. and Urry, J. (1994) *Economies of signs and spaces.* London: Sage.

Lyon, Ville de (1994) 'Pour Une Politique Sportive de Qualité', *C'est 9 à Lyon: Revue Municipale de Lyon*, No. 55, April.

Mayer, M. (1994) 'Post-Fordist city politics', in Amin, A. (ed) *Post-Fordism: A reader.* Oxford: Blackwell.

Ministère de la Jeunesse et des Sports (1993) *Le Financement du Sports par les Conseils Généraux et Régionaux*. Paris: Report of the Ministère de la Jeunesse et des Sports.

Morel, H. and Racouchot, E. (1993) *Organigramme des Service des Sports des Communes du Rhône et le Recensement des Piscines du Rhône avec leurs M.N.S. (BEESAN), l'UFRAPS, l'Université*. Claude Bernard, Lyon 1.

Pearson, C. (1991) *Beyond the Welfare State?*. Oxford: Polity.

Rhodes, R. (1994) 'The hollowing out of the State: The changing nature of the public service in Britain', *The Political Quarterly*: pp. 138-151.

Rojek, C. (1995) *Decentring leisure: Rethinking leisure theory*. London: Sage.

Schmidt, V. A. (1990) *Democratising France*. Cambridge: Cambridge University Press.

Stoker, G. & Mossberger, K. (1994) 'Urban régime theory in comparative perspective', *Government and Policy*, Vol. 12: pp. 195-212.

Tomaney, J. (1994) 'A new paradigm of work organization and technology?', in A. Amin (ed) *Post-Fordism: A reader*. Oxford: Blackwell.

Vénissieux, Ville de (1993) *Tableaux de Bord. Service du Sport*, unpublished document.

Villeurbanne, Ville de (1994) *Bilan sur le Sport 1989-1995; Service Des Sports*, unpublished document.

Chapter 6

SPORT MEGA-EVENTS, URBAN POLICY AND YOUTH IDENTITY: ISSUES OF CITIZENSHIP AND EXCLUSION IN SHEFFIELD[1]

Alan France

Warwick University

Maurice Roche

Sheffield University

Introduction

Throughout the late 1980s and 1990s the urban policy problem of how to 'regenerate' declining cities, particularly old industrial cities hit by 'de-industrialization' processes, has had a high priority on national political agendas in all major Western societies. The achievement of economic restructuring and growth has been seen as the essential ingredient and the ultimate test for any regeneration policy worthy of the name. However urban regeneration has typically been seen as requiring more than the purely economic. It has increasingly come to be connected with cultural and political development in addition to economic change (Bianchini and Parkinson, 1993). On the one hand urban leaders have attempted to promote renewed and positive city images and 'place identities' to the outside world of potential investors and tourists. On the other hand they have attempted to raise local morale and renew the civic community and its collective identity. Thus they have claimed to be concerned with the promotion of such things as social inclusion, citizen empowerment and active citizenship as well as economic growth. For local politicians and citizens the overriding goal of job-creation, with its joint economic and cultural-political benefits, provides a practical link between these various aims, connecting urban policy strongly with the sphere of production. But comparable linkages and joint benefits are also claimed to exist for policies related to the sphere of consumption, and participation in consumer markets, the sphere of images and symbols, of which more later.

Urban leaderships often attempt, both implicitly and explicitly, to kill the two birds of economic and socio-political regeneration with one stone by prioritising one particular local economic sector and by using one particular kind of strategy to develop this sector. The local economic sector is that of the 'popular cultural' consumer economy, broadly understood to include such 'industries' as sport, tourism, leisure entertainment and retailing. And the strategy involves the use of what we refer to here as 'mega-projects', namely major projects such as large-scale sporting and cultural events, and the construction of large-scale visitor attractions like major sports facilities and regional shopping centres.

In this chapter we focus on one important component of such urban policy, namely sport mega-events. We ask an apparently simple general question, namely, do these sorts of urban regeneration developments tend to promote positive civic identity understood in terms of 'social inclusion' and 'active citizenship' or not? For the purposes of our account we outline a provisional and arguably over-simplified but clearly negative answer to this question. As a contribution to debate in this area we take a critical view of the aspirations implicit and often explicit in the 'booster' rhetoric which often surrounds the policy-making processes connected with urban regeneration in general and mega-projects in particular.

Mega-projects like sport mega-events may appear to bring (and sometimes might actually succeed in delivering) net economic benefits. However we consider the possibility that, even if they do sometimes produce such effects, they can also often be shown to promote the opposites of social inclusion and active citizenship they promise, namely new forms of social exclusion and of dis-empowered and passive (or here 're-active') citizenship.

To illustrate and focus our discussion we will look at the views on these issues of one particular social category, namely young people, and one particular British city's experience with mega-projects, namely Sheffield's production of the World Student Games multi-sport mega-event in 1991 and its attendant sport facilities in the 1988-91 period. In the late 19th century Sheffield was the world's leading iron and steel city. However in the late 20th century it seems to be embarked on changing its image and identity from being a 'steel city' to becoming a 'sport city'. Having invested heavily in major sport facilities to support the 1991 mega-event the city now has no alternative but to seek to maximise their usage and their revenue flows by committing itself to the treadmill of securing popular and/or prestigious sport events with which to programme them. This in turn implies that — whether it would have ideally chosen to promote itself this way or not, (and the city's leadership chooses to) — the city's identity and image have inevitably become connected with the marketing of its new generation of sports venues and events, and thus with the re-imaging of the city itself as a importantly a sports venue.

Our analysis of the event which inaugurated the city's new career carries strong implications for the analysis of subsequent similar events in the city and in cities like this. We recognize that the negative findings and critical overall assessment of Sheffield's experience in the 1988-91 period which we outline in this chapter do not explicitly relate to the post-event period and the broader post-event re-imaging strategy of promoting Sheffield as a 'City of Sport' (see, for instance, Henry and Paramio-Salcines, 1996; Gratton, 1997 and Williams, 1997). Nonetheless they address a necessary context and, in our view, provide a useful critical perspective for understanding these more recent aspects of Sheffield's civic identity and urban development. Beyond that, the case study illustrates the broader theoretical and conceptual aims of our analysis in relation to sport mega-events on the one hand and local urban identities, particularly working class youth identities, on the other.

Citizenship, social exclusion and youth

'Social exclusion' is normally taken to refer to poverty and low income and, related to this, unemployment. But it should also be taken to include a range of problems stemming from other social divisions and inequalities in modern society such as those associated with gender, ethnicity, culture, age and physical and mental health status. Social exclusion, at base, is best understood in relation to the core social statuses defining membership and participation in modern societies; and, besides employment, the core social status is that of being a citizen (Roche and van Berkel, 1997).

'Citizenship' refers to membership and identity within a modern society and to possession of rights within that society (Roche, 1992). It provides individuals with collective identity and it enables active participation in civil society and communal life. The notion of collective membership and identity typically refers to nationality, and thus to the nation-state. But in the contemporary world it must also be understood to be multi-level and multi-dimensional. That is, it must be understood to encompass sub- and trans-national social formations, such as cities and regions on the one hand (Hill, 1994), and world-regions (e.g. Europe) and the world (human rights, UN institutions, etc.) on the other[2]. It refers to obligations as well as rights and to informal and substantive rights as well as formal/legal rights. It is multi-level and multi-dimensional as a system of rights referring to the complex of civil, political and social (Marshall, 1964) and cultural (Turner, 1993) rights, obligations and forms of participation which exists in modern society at local, national and EU levels.

Social exclusion, then, includes such things as social isolation in relation to local social networks and communities, non-participation in political life (e.g. non-voting etc.), racial discrimination, exclusion from naturalization processes and national citizenship rights. In a European context it also includes exclusion from EU citizen status and associated rights (Meehan, 1993; Close, 1994; Roche and van Berkel, 1997). It refers to the deprivation or disempowerment of citizen-based membership and identity and citizens' rights in modern society. Social exclusion in modern societies is thus best understood as the deprivation or disempowerment of the core social status of citizenship, together with the benefits, rights and responsibilities typically associated with it (Hill, 1994).

This issue is especially relevant for young people. Although the status and rights of citizenship have been more fully developed in the advanced industrial societies of North America and Western Europe than in other world regions in the modern period nonetheless, even in these societies young people tend to be denied many of the rights and much of the status that comes with full member-ship of society. They tend to be denied many citizenship rights such as the right to vote (over 18 years old only in the UK), and the right to welfare benefits (e.g. unemployment benefit is only available over 18 years old in the UK). Although they may carry many adult responsibilities they tend to be denied full adult citizen status (Jones and Wallace, 1992; France, 1996). 'Youth' is typically understood as being a state of transition between childhood and adulthood, in which people are neither 'grown up' autonomous adults nor dependent children. It is thus by definition an ambivalent and ambiguous status, significantly disempowered vis-a-vis the status and rights of full citizenship and significantly excluded from them.

Urban regeneration, mega-projects and citizenship

It is an increasingly common practice for urban leaderships and elites in contemporary Western societies, in the course of urban regeneration stra-tegies[3] to attempt to 're-imagine' and 're-image' 'their' cities[4]. This process (interestingly following the usage of the Disney Corporation) can also be refered to as urban 'imagineering' (Rutheiser, 1996). The reasons urban leaderships usually give for this process are typically economic as well as politically self-aggrandizing. That is re-imaging is assumed to be strategically necessary to cities in the contemporary world in order to counter economic decline and to regenerate them by making them attractive to international capital and consumer markets (mainly markets for investment, industrial relocations and tourism)[5].

Favourite instruments and vehicles of re-imaging policies are the creation of a critical mass of tourist attractions usually including new local 'heritage' sites and museums and, (where possible), sequences and cycles of major cultural and/or sporting events (Roche, 1992a, 1998; Hall, 1992). In order to progress their major event cycle strategies, urban elites have to explore and address three sorts of contemporary national and (more importantly) international cultural industry, namely (i) tourism, (ii) the mass media (particularly television), and (iii) large event 'franchising' organisations (for instance, leadership of the Olympic 'movement'). Urban leaderships, through their agents and representatives, have to forsake the temptations of parochialism and have to become known to and closely involved with leading organisations, companies and controlling elites in each of these fields nationally and world-wide.

Urban heritage attractions aim to construct an image of the past life of the city as uniquely memorable and valuable, while the mega-event attraction aim to present an image of the present and future life of the city, and participation in it, as uniquely interesting and rewarding. Besides the 'boost' these developments are intended to provide externally to the city's image and identity to outsiders and foreigners, they are also intended, internally, to boost local citizens' 'civic pride' and sense of civic identity. Externally, urban events and related urban images are typically projected and promoted actively by various marketing and media processes to national and international markets and audiences.

In pursuing urban regeneration policies involving 'civic boosterism' and the promotion of urban tourism, contemporary civic leaders and elites typically have to address and resolve two main types of problem: (i) the problem of elite coherence and coordination; and (ii) the problem of citizen support and mobilisation. In respect of each of these problems they have to form new types of alliances and coalitions. Firstly, they have to form what are commonly refered to in the USA and the UK as 'urban partnership leaderships' or 'growth coalitions'[6]. These are effectively neo-corporatist arrangements. Typically they involve the local state and the local private sector, the latter drawn from both the traditional (e.g. industrial) and the newly emerging (e.g. service and cultural) industries. These are the major partners in what is often institutionalised in some sort of legal or quasi-legal partnership organisation. Often partnerships can also involve, at least nominally, some attempt to substitute citizens for labour in the (third and junior) place usually reserved for it in traditonal corporatist arrangements. Incorporated citizens are usually addressed either as 'active citizens' (namely as altruistic volunteers) or as consumers (in the spirit of the British Conservative government's "Citizens' Charter" initiatives in the 1980s).

Secondly, also in order to develop and legitimate their event strategies, urban leadership and urban elites typically attempt to develop and communicate a 'vision' of the city's possibilities and future to the city's citizens, together with an understanding of how particular tourist attractions, heritage sites and major events contribute to and symbolise that vision[7]. Major events take a number of years to prepare and often require the building of expensive specialist facilities. In this case the urban leadership has to influence significant proportions of, and groupings within, the citizenry to support the event in a number of ways: firstly, by acting as good hosts to the international participants and tourists it will attract; secondly, by being prepared to support taxes to finance it; and thirdly, in the case of volunteers and spectators, to spend money, time and effort in active involvement with it.

Mega-events, urban citizen empowerment and citizenship

In this section we will briefly suggest some ways in which mega-events in particular, as a relatively artificial and elite-inspired form of urban popular mobilisation, tend to promote reactive forms of urban citizenship which are only apparently inclusionary and empowering and which are often on balance effectively disempowering and exclusionary.

Citizenship in modern Western capitalist democracies[8] is usually understood to involve state organised policies and systems to provide civil and political rights to all on an equal basis, together with equal access to some agreed optimal or minimal 'welfare state' packages of social rights (to such things as health, education,employment, social services,leisure etc.). Mega-event policy-makers and researchers have tended to assume that such events are beneficial to local citizens in terms of some of their social rights (i.e.employment and leisure services, and also social integration and community identity), and also in terms of some of their political rights (i.e. to democratic control and character of government via such things as community participation in planning, openness and accountability) and to rational (non-arbitrary/comprehensible, competent and efficient) government.

This view of the potentially beneficial social and political rights effects of mega-events may be summed up by saying that they are assumed to be 'empowering' for citizens[9]. Where traditional cultural events (e.g. rural, folk, and early urban festivals) remain popular in modern society, the 'empowerment' view finds its family relative in the understanding, at once commonsensical and anthropological[10], that such events must be largely beneficial and functional in a variety of ways for the communities which produce them.

Elements of the 'citizen empowerment' thesis are to be found expressed or implied in the early local tourism and events 'economic impact' research literature. In its characteristically methodologically flawed manner[11] this research tended to stress the economic benefits of tourism and/or events while making little or no attempt to calculate net benefit[12]. More recently the optimistic benefits/empowerment theme is also to be found in the much more sophisticated analyses provided by advocates of 'community-based' approaches to local tourism and event planning and management[13]. However the 'citizen empowerment' thesis tends to underplay two important aspects of real-life urban mega-events. These are concerned with the roles of (i) urban citizens and (ii) urban leaders and power elites in the planning and production of mega-events.

On the one hand urban citizens tend to be disempowered by the various practical and financial responsibilities placed upon them by being cast in the role of 'host community'. We will illustrate this issue in particular in our consideration of the Sheffield case later. On the other hand urban leaderships, who on any calculation need it least, tend to be empowered by the production of (successful) mega-events and mega-projects. In addition to the timeworn tendency for the powerful to seek to celebrate and mythologise their power there are specific motivating conditions influencing contemporary urban leaderships to compete for the prestige of having 'their' city stage large events. These conditions are structural and political and this is not the place to explore them in detail[14]. Suffice it to say that, whether or not there is much of a democratic character to urban elites' preoccupations with mega-projects, they are comprehensible in terms of an economically-driven 'situational logic' requiring the regenerating of cities as market-places (for capital investment and consumption) and as marketable places (for tourism, professional/skilled/service class labour etc.).

In recent years a number of notable voices in the tourism management literature have argued strongly for community participation and a community-based approach to the development of tourism in rural and urban communities[15]. And similar calls have been made in the literature on urban cultural and leisure policy[16]. However the dominant approach to urban tourism and cultural policy from the 1970s to the present, both in theory and in practice has tended to be autocratic rather than democratic[17]. In terms of Arnstein's well-known criteria for citizen participation in planning[18], the typical mega-event production process is 'manipulative' or minimally participatory.

Urban regeneration and mega-projects: Britain and Sheffield

Mega-projects and British urban regeneration policy in the 1980s and 1990s

In Britain throughout the 1980s a New Right national government confronted various types of Left local government in Britain's major cities[19]. At the national level the Thatcher government's urban and macro-economic policies restricted local governments' capacity to finance economic development and regeneration from central and local taxation. It stressed service sector growth as a response to de-industrialisation, and eschewed any industrial policy or re-industrialisation policy. These policies imposed a highly controversial and untried enterpreneurial culture and financial environment upon local authorities, encouraging them to see themselves as corporate organisations modelled on private sector corporations rather than as public service institutions, and to market themselves as such, both internally to their own service users and externally[20]. In addition, in series of gestures towards tackling the inner city social problems associated with unemployment in de-industrialising cities, it encouraged them to develop tourism (HMSO, 1985,1990; ETB, 1987) and in some cases large events[21].

At the local level Left urban leaderships attempted various types of economic growth policy, from traditional (trade unionist, 'labourist', welfarist approaches) local state-led housing and infrastructure construction and re-industrialisation programmes on the one hand (e.g. Liverpool), to more pragmatic ('new realist', modernising) investment in high technology, new skills training and service sectors such as 'cultural industries' (arts, media etc.) on the other[22]. The need to be both reactive and proactive — i.e. the need on the one hand to realistically respond to the stimuli and constraints of national policy frameworks, and on the other to experiment with new Left approaches to economic restructuring, growth and employment policies — provided fertile ground and a motivational context in many British cities for private-public sector partnership leaderships and for re-imaging and modernising policies focused around mega-events and urban tourism.

To summarise, then, a number of factors combined to influence contemporary mega-event planning and production in Britain and in countries like it. Firstly, and more indirectly, there has been the influence of structural change and national policy and the general socio-economic problems they produce and exacerbate. Secondly, and more directly, there is the influence of the attempt by local leaderships to develop proactive regeneration and growth strategies to tackle these general problems. The case of Sheffield and its event illustrate the main points of this analysis (Darke, 1994; Roche, 1992, 1994).

Urban regeneration and mega-projects in Sheffield in the 1980s and 1990s

In the mid-1980s Sheffield's economy and its political leadership were both in crisis, and these crises provided the causal and motivational conditions for the city's mega-event project. Throughout this period major job losses occurred in Sheffield's traditional economic base (i.e. iron and steel, heavy engineering, coal mining and some manufacturing, notably cutlery) (Gibbon, 1989; Lawless and Ramsden, 1989; Watts (*et al.*), 1989). This process of de-industrialisation, and its associated structural unemployment disaster, was felt most keenly in the poorer and ethnic minority areas of the city (Westergaard (*et al.*), 1989; DEED, 1991). The process was accompanied by a post-industrial shift in the local economy towards the service sector of a kind widely experienced in this period in the major cities and industrial regions of the advanced Western societies.

Sheffield's modern origins as a city of the Industrial Revolution produced a political culture characterised by strong and longstanding support for the Labour Party and the trade union movement and representing the strength of the city's manual industrial working class. However, since the late 1970s the urban leadership supplied by the Labour Party has gone through two distinct ideological revolutions. The first, in the late 1970s, coincided with the advent of

Margaret Thatcher and 'Thatcherism' to national power. As against the traditional character of Sheffield Labourism (i.e.welfare statist but pragmatic and social democratic), this change involved a younger generation of Labour leaders, 'the new urban Left' who attempted to promote a relatively self-contained 'municipal socialist' programme of economic development.

Against the tides of de-industrialisation and structural unemployment flowing in the local and national economy this programme had next to no impact, and by the mid-1980s it had run out of steam and credibility. From 1986 onwards the Labour leadership took a very different and more pragmatic line in joining with the private sector to create the Sheffield Economic Regeneration Committee (SERC) and 'partnership' form of leadership referred to be some commentators as 'civic entrepreneurialism'[23]. The Council now sought to collaborate with the private sector on a general regeneration and re-imaging strategy, and on major projects contributing to and symbolising this new partnership. It was in the context of these causal and motivating conditions that plans emerged in 1986/7 for Sheffield's two main 'flagship' projects or mega-projects of the late 1980s/ early 1990s. On the one hand, financed and organized from the public sector, there was the production of World Student Games multi-sport mega-event, together with the construction of its attendant world class sports facilities. On the other hand, financed and organized from the private sector, there was the construction of the £400 million Meadowhall Shopping Centre, one of Europe's largest shopping malls, which has turned out to be very successful as a visitor attraction, attracting more daily visitors than, for instance, Paris Disneyland. In this chapter we focus our discussion on the sport project.

In the mid-1980s, then, Sheffield faced a number of major problems including structural unemployment and a minimal or negative image to potential investors and tourists. In addition, in terms of its retailing sector Sheffield and the region was relatively underprovided for, and in terms of its leisure sector the city's stock of 19th century public swimming baths urgently needed major renewal or complete replacement if a core element of the city's longstanding commitment to leisure services was to be maintained.

The possibility of the city staging the World Student Games was originally identified within the city's Leisure Services Committee as a way of providing a *raison d'être* for major capital expenditure on modernisation of the city's swimming pools and other public leisure facilities. However the project was quickly taken over by the new partnership civic leadership (SERC) and used as the key vehicle and symbol of its urban regeneration strategy. For a period (1987 — 1989), within both private and public sector wings of Sheffield's leadership and policy community, faith in this project became the touchstone for judging the seriousness of people's commitment to tackling the city's unemployment, image and other major problems[24].

Youth, citizenship and the city: perspectives on Sheffield's mega-event

Throughout the build-up 1987-91 to the World Student Games 1991 mega-event (hereafter WSG91) Sheffield's leadership attempted to reimage the city from a city of industrial decline to being, among other things, a city of sport and leisure. It was assumed that such a strategy, with its echoes of post-war British sport policy's 'Sport for All' campaigns (Roche, 1993), was something that would be seen as culturally inclusive and positive. The 'flagship project' of this strategy was WSG91 with its tailor-made, new world-class and appropriately costly sport and leisure facilities (including a swimming-diving complex, an athletics stadium and a 10,000 seat indoor arena)[25]. It was assumed that this would be something that 'the people' would welcome and would be willing to support and participate in. Supporters of the strategy claimed that WSG91, and the cycle of major sporting events to which it would lead, would 'benefit all', 'put Sheffield on the map' in terms of sport and tourism, and that the citizens would be empowered by their economic and social impacts, both in terms of job-creation, social integration and feelings of city pride, collective morale and cultural inclusion.

We suggest that these perspectives failed to acknowledge two major difficulties. Firstly, Sheffield like all other contemporary cities contains a diverse and divided citizenry, divided in terms of gender, age and, spatially, in terms of class and ethnicity. While to a certain extent this problem had been long registered in Sheffield's traditional leisure and other social and economic strategies, it tended to be lost in the 'new wave' of urban regeneration-oriented mega-projects the city embarked on in the late 1980s. Populist cultural inclusion strategies such as the WSG91 mega-event — or more recently the 1996 Atlanta Olympics (Rutheiser, 1996: ch 5) — claim to appeal to 'all' and to some homogenous 'city community' and typically invite citizens to feel culturally included by 'sharing the vision, sharing the dream' of the future of the city. However they inevitably tend to deny the real and ongoing complexity, diversity and inequality of city life. Not all groups and categories of people can feel equally addressed and included.

Inevitably some are likely to feel excluded, and some sections of Sheffield's working class youth registered this sense of cultural exclusion as we will see in a moment.

Secondly, as we argued earlier, there is the problem that such strategies are typically created by leadership groups in cities, and tend to be imposed on citizens. This was the case in Sheffield. The City Council and the public-private sector partnership leadership took decisions in a paternalistic, intuitive and at times demonstrably incompetent fashion, 'on behalf of' the citizens rather than in full and open consultation with them. Prior to deciding on the event there was no serious 'options analysis' of alternatives to the strategy, no professional economic impact analysis to justify job-creation hopes, no serious 'cost-benefit' analysis to quantify the real long-term financial costs and to estimate the net benefits (if any), and there was no serious public debate when the key and committing decisions were being taken in 1986/7[26]. Most sections of the citizens of Sheffield were, in effect, excluded from the decision-making process on WSG91 and on the 'sport city strategy'. This is illustrated by the experience of political exclusion registered by the working class Sheffield youth we consider here.

The city of Sheffield is the centre of the industrial region of South Yorkshire, and its distinctive local economy of iron and steel production, drawing on the South Yorkshire coal industry, was largely a creation of Britain's 19th century industrial revolution. As with other Northern British industrial cities, Sheffield has had a long history in the 19th century and 20th century of being a 'working class city' (Taylor, *et al.*, 1996), and this identity still tends to overarch the various social divisions noted above which characterise the contemporary city. From the mid/late-19th century the ordinary people of Sheffield were closely involved in the development of British working- class institutions and movements — from the political, such as those of trade unions and the Labour Party, to the popular cultural, such as mass spectator football and mass tourist excursioning to the expanding Northern resorts of Blackpool and Scarborough. An important part of the story, later told by social historians such as E.P. Thompson (1984), of 'the making of the English working-class', was originally told in Sheffield and in cities like it. Local working-class communities grew around and alongside the expanding iron and steel foundries and mills.

A sense of 'community', both class community and local community, has always been important in British working-class life, not least in Sheffield. As Thompson has argued, class is embedded in the traditions, values, ideas and institutional forms of a community; the history of what has gone before remains a central feature of how life is lived in the present (Thompson, 1989). Related to this perspective, in his accounts of British culture Raymond Williams develops the sense in which being working-class is also, and importantly, a cultural experience, in which everyday practices and familiar meanings shape the present (e.g. Williams, 1989). Such a perspective is relevant to the lives of many young people in the city of Sheffield and the surrounding industrial region of South Yorkshire. It is in this context of local working-class community that they gain their experience of personal and collective identity and feelings of belonging. It is in this context that they develop and 'live' their citizenship as a 'day to day' experience.

It is in their families and also, importantly, in their local communities that working- class young people engage in social, economic and cultural transitions into the adult world. This continues to be the case even though family and community structures have been changed and undermined in the 1980s and 90s by persistent patterns of unemployment, underemployment and low income employment. Living in a working class community continues to give the young a sense of belonging, while providing a site where they can gain a sense of status for their achievements. Being treated and respected as an adult is an essential requirement if young people are to feel 'grown up': in this way communities aid the process of moving into adulthood (Hutson and Jenkins 1989). Not only is it a major site of transition, but also, in spite of rising neighbourhood crime rates, it remains a relatively safe environment in which young people can feel secure about being among friends and family. One example of this is the social life around the local pub. Going into a public house for the first few times to participate as an adult drinker in legal alcoholic consumption, in most Western societies, remains, for many young people, a challenging experience of identity-change, a 'rite of passage'. But within their local community there are greater opportunities than elsewhere for this experience to be managed in a way which enhances rather than threatens their personal identity because of the social support available from friends and family. Living in a community in this way, and in many others, gives working-class youth a sense of security in that they are able to use the support of peers and adults in making the steps into adulthood. Urban neighbourhood 'community life', however changed and changing it may be in the contemporary period, continues to play a key role in the forming of working-class young people's identities in Britain.

In the build-up to Sheffield's WSG91 event, and during it, one of us undertook research on the attitudes and experiences of predominantly white Sheffield working-class youth, living in a traditional working-class locality in the city, to various dimensions of citizenship and various aspects of their city (France, 1995, and Note 1). This study showed that in spite of all of the changes in the economy, culture and politics of the city in recent decades, the city and the local community remained of central importance to working class young people and to their sense of identity and belonging. This is illustrated in the comments (quoted in France, 1995: p.132) of the following young men on the meaning of citizenship and community:

Brian: "It would be more for me like saying your roots and everything. I'm a citizen of Westhill really. It's where I'm from. If I go and live in London for three years or if I go away for two weeks, I'd always see this as my home. This is where my friends and family live, where my roots are."

John: "I could go and live in London for ten years, but I still would be a citizen of Westhill — or travel abroad, but I would always tell people that I am from Westhill in Sheffield."

Brian: I think one thing you do find is that living in Westhill makes you feel safe and secure. In Westhill we know every nook and cranny, and we feel safe and secure in around Westhill. It's like a village where everyone knows everybody and that makes you feel safe."

For Brian and John 'community' is a localised notion related to the geographical location and social networks of where they live on a day-to-day basis. In their view the notion of being a 'citizen of Sheffield' is only likely to become important when they leave the area and have to explain to others where they come from. The attempts by local political elites to create a new image of Sheffield which attempts to avoid and effectively dispense with working class and industrial identity familiar to the majority of Sheffielders fails to recognise the enduring importance of this identity and this work, class and locality-based perspective on citizenship, not least among contemporary young Sheffielders.

The new supposedly inclusive image of the city, 'the city of sport', is an optimistic vision of 'sport for all' inclusiveness, apparently based largely on participating in sport and spectating at major sport events, and extending to the inclusion of tourists. This image is based on the consumption of non-local 'declassed' or middle-class cultural forms and it implies an image of citizenship as cultural consumerism in cultural industry markets. This new discourse is either at odds with, irrelevant to, or excludes much of the city's traditional discourse of collective identification and self-understanding. Given this, it is understandable that the response of some young people in this study to the WSG91 event and its role in the Sheffield's regeneration was dismissive (quoted in France, 1995: p.132):

> *John*:   "I don't give a shit about the World Student Games. I think it stinks when I can't get a job. All they care about is building stupid stadiums."

We will now explore the attitudes of these young people in a little more detail.

"Nobody asked me": Sheffield's mega-event and young people's feelings of exclusion

Sheffield's leadership saw WSG91 as an opportunity for the people of the city to come together as a 'city community' by participating in the event. In 'winning' a mega-event for cities, city leaderships thereby necessarily place their citizens, whether they like it or not, in the position of being the 'host community' for the event. This 'host' role is assumed (e.g. in national and international political and media circles) to carry tangible reponsibility for the success of the event, and hosts are expected to support it and participate in it in various important ways. Citizens are expected to participate in the mega-event staged in 'their' city in two main ways, namely by supporting the event *en masse* as spectators (and thus providing it with finance, spectacle and dramatic occasion) and by supporting it as volunteer workers. In order to achieve this level of popular participation city leaders and event producers need not only to literally 'sell the event' to the paying public through marketing campaigns at the time of the event, but also, more metaphorically to 'sell the event' to the citizens, to 'bring them on board', 'to give them a sense of ownership' of it, through political campaigns years before the event, in the decision-making and the build-up to it. The WSG91 event was fairly well attended and was enjoyed at the time by the paying public. However the recruitment of volunteers, while ultimately sufficient, was not as successful as had been expected (McColl, 1992); and, apart from the short event period itself, the citizens of Sheffield as a whole never felt 'ownership' of the event or gave it whole-hearted support (Friel, 1991, 1994).

Sheffield's young people were involved in WSG91, other than as paying spectators, mainly through the school system and through the volunteer programme. As regards the former, the main sport event was flanked by various simultaneous cultural events including a colourful Children's Festival, organised through Sheffield schools and involving many hundreds of schoolchildren, in the streets and squares of the centre of the city. This festival, unlike the main event, was relatively inexpensive, reached out to the public, was popular and successful and has been retained as an annual event. The volunteer programme was less well received (McColl, 1992), particularly by the young people interviewed in the research we draw on here.

In the build-up to WSG91 organizers attempted to encourage the participation of young people as volunteer workers for the two weeks of the event. This was seen, by the young people in the study we draw on here, not as a form of participation but rather as an exploitative method of saving money on the event (quoted in France, 1995: p.136):

Interviewer: "Are any of you going to volunteer in the Games?"

Kevin: "The World Student Games? It's a lot of crap. What the fuck will we get out of it? All they want us to do is volunteer so that they can get it done on the cheap. I'm not going, it means nothing to me."

There was some basis for this suspicious and dismissive attitude. Throughout the pre-event 1989-91 period, WSG91 organizers certainly needed to keep costs down and to pull in as much free labour and other free goods and services as they could get. Notwithstanding their frequent public disclaimers to the contrary, they suspected that their failure to interest TV companies in broadcasting rights, and their consequent failure to attract relevant commercial sponsorship, would sink their plans for a 'break-even' event financing. Throughout the period national press and TV had periodically carried negative assessments of Sheffield's financial management of the event and also of the facility-build for it, and this had been amplified virtually on a weekly basis in the local media (France, 1991). Two successive event Directors were pressured to resign for reasons of financial mismanagement or incompetence. The event in 1991 did indeed turn out to make a substantial and unplanned loss. In the post-event period the facilities have run at a loss and require continuing revenue subsidy, and the long-term cost of the loan repayments for the facilities crippled the city's budget in the mid 1990s and will continue to constrain its public expenditures into the 21stC. The event and its aftermath were the subject of criticism by a number of official bodies[27].

The volunteer programme survived mainly on the basis of support from university students, usually from middle class backgrounds, who are temporary residents in the city with little cultural connection with it (McColl, 1992). The city leadership's view of the programme as a way to get the people of Sheffield, particularly the young, involved in the regeneration effort, and the creation of 'the city of sport', was perceived by many working-class youth as 'cheap labour', an exploitation of their good will, and irrelevant to their needs and interests. In the following discussion (quoted in France, 1995: p.137), young people suggest what for them is important, and how the city council could have put its finances to better use:

Interviewer: "What do you think about the World Student Games?"

Brian: "I'm really mad. It's going to cost Sheffield millions of pounds and what do we get out of it? It's not going to create any jobs is it? Nobody asked me if I wanted it. I think we've got enough sports facilities in Sheffield. What we need is jobs."

John: "I don't give a fuck about the World Student Games. I helped build it you know. Two years I worked on it as a labourer. But I'm back on the dole now 'cause there aren't any jobs now. They laid us all off once the main buildings were up. it really pisses me off, because half of these facilities are on our doorstep — you know, where Brown Bailey's were. Me dad worked there, and I guess if it was still there that's where I would be working."

This discussion raises a number of issues. Firstly, as Brian suggested 'nobody asked me'. These young people clearly felt a lack of commitment to a project they saw as planned by others without consultation with them concerning their views and interests. Their response to this lack of consultation resulted not so much in disinterest as in outright rejection and condemnation. Secondly there is the issue of jobs. The fact that the city council was spending 'millions' on projects which did not appear as if they were going to generate many long-term job opportunities far outweighed any gain the young men may have been willing to associate with the building of a new generation of sports and leisure facilities. In particular John pointed out that the facilities were built on sites, which, in former years, would have provided long-term employment prospects for young people like him. The Brown Bailey plant, at its peak of output, was a major Sheffield employer and one of the largest steel producers in the world. To John the demise of this plant, and its replacement by the Don Valley athletic stadium, an element in Sheffield's 'culture industries' service sector, seemed to promise limited job opportunities and little future for him. John felt simultaneously dispossessed of both his heritage and his future by Sheffield's WSG91-led regeneration effort, leaving him with feelings of frustration and anger. Ironically what aimed to be a socially inclusive project resulted in him and others in the interview group feeling excluded.

For these young people the World Student Games appeared to have the very opposite effect from what was officially intended. While Sheffield's leadership and the elite groups which circle it attempted to unite and mobilise the city around the mega-event and to promote a perspective of active citizenship through participation in the Games, young working-class people felt anger and frustration at not being involved in the decision-making process and not having their needs addressed through the provision of long-term job opportunities. Young people's perspectives on the city leadership's lack of investment in their future increased their feelings of alienation and marginalisation. The event promised inclusion in a renewed civic image and identity. But instead of feeling empowered and included by the 'great event' the young people whose views have been summarised in this chapter felt mainly dis-empowered and excluded by the whole process (France, 1995; Note 1 below; also McColl, 1992).

Conclusion

In this chapter we considered the relationship between urban regeneration strategies led by sport mega-events and in general by popular cultural mega-projects on the one hand, and on the other issues of local identity expressed in terms of citizenship and social exclusion. We illustrated these relationships through a discussion of the notable case of Sheffield's urban regeneration, its mega-project policies and the responses of working class youth to the 'flagship' World Student games project.

No doubt there have been some slowly emerging positive developments in terms of city image and employment in the local sports and popular cultural economy in Sheffield since the major investment in this project (Henry and Paramio-Salcines, 1996; Gratton, 1997). No doubt also, given the persistently high nation-wide demand for admissions to the two city universities which is based in part on the attractions of the city's popular cultural facilities and opportunities, the re-imaging effort has been relatively successful, at least for temporarily resident middle class youth. But we have suggested that the situation was perceived differently by resident working class youth around the time of the mega-event. Given the continuing vulnerability of the local economy and local employment since the event, not to mention the cuts in local authority leisure services needed to help with debt repayments for event facilities, it is unlikely that the attitudes of indifference and antipathy to the project expressed by these young people in our study will have mellowed significantly in the post-event period.

In general then, our analysis suggests that elite-driven urban re-imaging mega-projects in the contemporary period produce at best 'reactive' forms of citizen-ship which are only apparently 'inclusive' and at worst can all too easily have citizen-disempowering characteristics and consequences for local communities and social groups. Sport mega-events, in particular, can have these consequences for two main reasons. Firstly there are the problems for the citizens of playing the host role, together with its attendant taxation and other obligations and costs. These are rarely fully explored and agreed by citizens during the period when a city is committing itself to a major event. Secondly there is the way in which urban leaderships are constituted and exercise their power through the planning and organisational processes involved both in events as such and also in the general urban strategies (e.g. regeneration, economic growth etc.) with which they tend to be linked.

It has commonly been assumed in the mega-event research literature, and perhaps in the tourism literature more broadly, that the impacts of large scale events are variously beneficial and thus empowering for their host communities, being opportunities to renew and promote city image and civic identity. There is, no doubt, some degree of substance in this view. However our analysis suggests that the weight of the evidence on the relationship between mega-events and citizenship would seem rather to support a 'disempowerment'/'reactive citizen-ship' rather than an 'empowerment'/positive citizenship view of mega-events and their implications for local identities.

Firstly, as we have already seen, there is the leadership power issue; mega-event planning and production has been observed to be often autocratic and non-rational in character[28]. This is arguably disempowering for citizens in terms of their political rights. Secondly there are the (related) rights/duties and benefits/costs issues. The 'economic rights' case for mega-events in terms of their net economic benefits (e.g. local jobs and income) is unclear and unproven because of both the costs to citizens of event-related obligations (e.g. increased taxation, volunteer labour time, ticket costs, opportunity costs) and the general lack of sound data and lack of use of sound methods in research in this field (e.g. Roche, 1992a). The 'welfare rights' case in terms of mega-events' net social benefits (e.g. community after-use of 'event heritage' leisure facilities) is unclear and unproven for the same sort of reasons, and in addition, because 'event heritage' facility marketing and pricing is often targeted at non-citizens (i.e. tourists) rather than at community users. On the basis of the analysis and the case study we conclude that, in the current debate about the nature, planning and effects of mega-events, the 'citizen disempowerment' view would appear to be more grounded in the realities of contemporary urban life and politics than the 'citizen empowerment' view.

Staging sport mega-events can appear to present tempting opportunities for the 'booster' policy cultures around city leaderships in societies across the world in the contemporary period. But the positive balance between the costs and benefits of these events, which may appear so clear and achievable in pre-event analysis, planning and promotion, is always difficult to achieve in practice. The events themselves usually, eventually, turn out to be 'alright on the night'. But whether the citizens of the cities which host them will be left with positive long-term 'event heritages' or equally long-term 'event hang-overs' in financial and city image terms, 'after the party is over', remains, in every case, a matter of speculation, to be decided in practice and not in theory. On the basis of our discussion in this chapter we conclude that, whatever the 'boosters' may say about their allegedly positive economic and city image impacts, sporting mega-events remain intrinsically controversial and risky methods of attempting to promote social inclusion and the renewal of local civic identity.

Notes

[1] An early version of this chapter was presented as a paper at an international seminar on 'Sport and the Urban Context in Britain and France' at Loughborough University, June 1995. We would like to record our thanks for Ian Henry's invitation and his encouragement. The interviews we draw on were part of a research project conducted by Alan France which is fully reported in France, 1995. Also we should note here that in these interviews names have been altered to ensure the anonymity of respondents.

[2] See for instance Falk, 1993; Meehan, 1993; Close, 1994; Roche, 1995, 1997.

3   Fox-Przeworski (*et al.*) (eds), 1991; Feagin and Smith (eds), 1991; Jacobs 1992.

4   Harvey, 1990; Bianchini and Schwengel, 1991; Watson, 1991; Roche, 1992a; Law, 1993; Bianchini and Parkinson, 1993; Kearns and Philo, 1993; Williams, 1997 ch.5, 6 and 9; and Hall and Hodges, Chapter 4 in this book.

5   There are, of course, theoretical stories to be told and debates to be engaged in concerning the (post-Fordist, global, post-modern etc.) structural changes lying behind and providing motivating conditions for these urban policy developments. However to discuss them here would be a diversion given the concerns of this chapter. For some further discussion see Harvey, 1990; Cook, 1990; Featherstone, 1990; Bagguley, 1991; Crook (*et al.*) 1992; Roche, 1992a; Lash and Urry, 1994.

6   See Logan and Molotch, 1987; Cummings, 1988; Judd and Parkinson, 1990; Stone, 1991; Jacob, 1991; Harding, 1991, 1992; Henry and Paramio-Salcines, 1996.

7   On the urban policy discourse or rhetoric of 'visions' in these processes see ETB, 1987, and in relation to the case of Sheffield see ETB, 1988 and Price, 1988. On the urban policy rhetoric of 'dreams' see Rutheiser, 1996 ch. 5.

8   See Marshall, 1963; Turner, 1986; Roche, 1992c, 1997.

9   On UK and USA urban policy in general and the theme of empowerment see Jacobs, 1992.

10   See Duvignaud, 1976; Falassi, 1986; Worpole, 1992.

11   See Schaffer and Davidson, 1980; Della Bitta and Loudon, 1975; Reichert, 1978.

12   For instance by measuring and deducting their economic, ecological and social impacts and costs generally. On net benefit analysis in general see Burns and Mules, 1986; Travis and Croize, 1987; Syme *et al.*, 1989; Roche, 1992a; Mules and Faulkner, 1996.

13   See for instance Murphy, 1985; Haywood, 1988; Getz, 1991.

14   The new structural conditions are connected with major processes of restructuring in contemporary industrial capitalism towards post-industrial, post-Fordist and post-national formations, see for instance Roche, 1992, 1998; also Lash and Urry, 1994; and Note 5 above. The new political conditions are connected with the post-communist ascendancy of pro-market politics and New Right influences on western governments, see for instance Roche, 1992.

[15] See Getz, 1991; Haywood, 1988; Murphy, 1985; Law, 1993.

[16] See Worpole, 1992; Henry, 1990; Bianchini and Parkinson, 1993; Bianchini and Schwengel, 1992.

[17] This has been clearly demonstrated by Armstrong's authoritative but little known international and comparative research into the policy-making approaches involved in over 20 major urban prestige projects and events world-wide. His findings (Armstrong, 1984) were as follows:

> Eighteen of the 23 publicly funded projects came about through the efforts and influence of individuals who were powerful politicians.... (p. 13)

> ...prestige projects are usually the product of an influential elite or a particularly powerful individual .... (p. 291)

> Contemporary prestige projects, even private ones, are highly political. (p. 302)

Armstrong's report was produced in 1984, but a number of studies of mega-event production since that time, (e.g. Butler and Grigg, 1989; Thorn and Munro Clark, 1989; Hall, 1992, 1994; Hiller, 1989; Ley and Olds, 1988, Rutheiser, 1996), have confirmed the persistence of autocratic patterns and processes in this field.

[18] See Arnstein, 1969 (adapted for tourism planning, Haywood, 1988).

[19] See Robson, 1988; Stewart and Stoker (eds), 1989; Stewart, 1990; Jacobs, 1992.

[20] See Gyford, 1990; Corner & Harvey, 1991; McColl, 1992.

[21] For instance the cycle of biennial Garden Festivals inaugurated in Liverpool in 1984, and subsequently held in Stoke, Glasgow, Tyneside and Ebbw Vale.

[22] For instance the Greater London Council, Sheffield, Leeds; on Leeds see Henry *et al.,* 1990.

[23] Seyd, 1990; Lawless, 1990; Judd and Parkinson, 1990; Henry and Paramio-Salcines, 1996.

[24] For instance Labour Councillor (now MP) Helen Jackson's views, cited in Roche, 1992b.

[25] The capital costs were £150 million excluding interest charges on the loan from foreign banks. The loan is repayable over 10 years, and the city's annual repayments and interest payments vary within the range of £20-£30million p.a.

26 See Roche, 1992b, 1994; Darke, 1991; also see District Audit Service, 1992 and HMSO, 1995.

27 Sheffield City Council, 1992; District Audit Service, 1992; HMSO, 1995.

28 See for instance Armstrong, 1984; Hall and also Thorne and Munro-Clark, both in Syme *et al.,* 1989; Hall, 1992, 1994; Roche, 1994.

Bibliography

Armstrong, J. L. (1984) 'Contemporary prestige centres for art, culture, exhibitions, sports and conferences: An international survey' (unpublished Ph.D.), University of Birmingham, Birmingham, UK.

Arnstein, S. (1969) 'A ladder of citizen participation', *Journal of the American Institute of Planners* Vol. 35: pp. 216-224.

Bagguley, P. (1991) 'Post-fordism and enterprise culture', in Keat, R. and Abercrombie, N. (eds) *Enterprise culture.* Routledge: London.

Bianchini, F. and Schwengel, H. (1991) 'Re-imagining the city', in Corner, J. and Harvey, S. (eds) *Enterprise and heritage: Crosscurrents of national culture.* London: Routledge.

Bianchini, F. and Parkinson, M. (eds) (1993) *Cultural policy and urban regeneration: The Western European experience.* Manchester: Manchester University Press.

Burns, J. and Mules, T. (1986) 'A framework for the analysis of major special events', in Burns, J. *et al., The Adelaide Grand Prix: The impact of a special event.* Adelaide: Centre for South Australian Economic Studies.

Butler, R. and Grigg, J. (1989) 'The hallmark event that got away: The case of the Pan-American Games and London Ontario', in Syme *et al., op. cit.*

Close, P. (1994) *Citizenship, Europe and change.* London: Macmillan.

Cooke, P. (1990) *Back to the future: Modernity, post-modernity and locality.* London: Unwin Hyman.

Corner, J. and Harvey, S. (eds) (1991) *Enterprise and heritage.* London: Routledge.

Crook, S. *et al.* (1992) *Postmodernization: Change in advanced society.* London: Sage.

Cummings, S. (ed) (1988) *Business elites and urban development.* Albany: SUNY Press.

Darke, R. (1991) *Gambling on sport: Sheffield's regeneration strategy for the 90s.* Department of Town and Regional Planning, Sheffield University, Sheffield.

DEED, (1990) *World Student Games economic impact study*, Vol.I. DEED (Department of Employment and Economic Development), Sheffield City Council, Sheffield.

Della Bitta, A.J. and Loudon, D. (1975) 'Assessing the economic impact of short duration tourist events', *New England Journal of Business and Economics*, Spring, pp. 37-45.

District Audit Service (1992) *The World Student Games: Report of the District Auditor*. Audit Commission: Sheffield.

Duvignaud, J. (1976) 'Festivals: A sociological approach', *Cultures* Vol. III, No. 1: pp. 13-25.

ETB (English Tourist Board) (1987) *A vision for England*. London: English Tourist Board.

——— (1988) *A vision for Sheffield*. London: English Tourist Board.

Falassi, A. (ed) (1987) *Time out of time: Essays on the festival*. Albuquerque: University of New Mexico Press.

Falk, R. (1993) 'The making of global citizenship', in Turner (1993) *op. cit.*

Feagin, J. and Smith, M. (1991) 'Cities and the new international division of labor: An overview', in Smith and Feagin (eds) (1991) *op.cit.*

Featherstone, M. (1990) *Consumer culture and post-modernism*. London: Sage.

Fox-Przeworski, J., Goddard, J., and de Jong, M. (eds) (1991) *Urban regeneration in a changing economy*. Oxford: Clarendon.

France, A. (1991) 'Building an Image of the future: Sheffield and the World Student Games', Sociology Department Working Paper, Sheffield University, Sheffield.

——— (1995) 'Youth and citizenship: A study of young people in Sheffield'. Unpublished Ph.D. thesis, Main Library, Sheffield University, Sheffield.

——— (1996) 'Youth and citizenship in the 1990s', *Youth and Social Policy*, No. 53: pp. 28-44.

Friel, E. (1991) 'Keeping the spirit alive: Sheffield after the Games', BBC2 TV, BBC North TV Centre, Leeds.

Friel, E. (1994) 'The Friel report', Sheffield City Council, Sheffield.

Getz, D. (1991) *Festivals, special events and tourism*. New York: Van Nostrand Reinhold.

Gibbon, P. (1990) 'Employment in Sheffield in the 1980s', Centre for Regional Economic and Social Research, Sheffield Polytechnic, Sheffield.

Gratton, C. (1997) 'The economic and social significance of sport in society', unpublished paper, Leisure Industries Research Centre, Sheffield Hallam University, Sheffield.

Gyford, J. (1990) *Citizens, consumers and councils: Local government and the public.* London: Macmillan.

Hall, C. M. (1992) *Hallmark tourist events: Impacts, management and planning.* London, Bellhaven Press.

Harding, A. (1991) 'The rise of urban growth coalitions, UK-style?', *Environment and Planning C: Government and Policy* Vol. 9: pp. 295-317.

———— (1992) 'Urban regimes and growth machines: Towards a cross-national agenda', European Institute for Urban Affairs, Liverpool University, Liverpool.

Harvey, D. (1990) *The condition of postmodernity.* Oxford: Blackwell.

Haywood,K. (1988) 'Responsible and responsive tourism planning in the community', *Tourism Management* Vol. 9: pp. 105-118.

Henry, I. *et al.* (1990) 'Leisure, culture and the political economy of the city: A case study of Leeds', conference paper, XIIth World Congress of Sociology, Complutense University, Madrid.

Henry, I. and Paramio-Salcines, J. (1996) 'Sport, urban regeneration and urban regimes: The case of Sheffield', unpublished paper, Department of Physical Education, Sport Science and Recreation Management, Loughborough University, Loughborough.

Hill, D. (1994) *Citizens and cities.* Brighton: Harvester/Wheatsheaf.

Hiller, H. (1989) 'Impact and image; urban factors in 1988 Calgary Winter Olympics', in Syme *et al.* (1989) *op. cit.*

HMSO (1985) *Leisure, pleasure and jobs: The business of tourism.* London: HMSO.

———— (1990) *Tourism and the inner city.* London: Department of the Environment.

———— (1995) *Bids to stage international sports events, 5th Report.* London: National Heritage Committee, House of Commons.

Hutson, S. and Jenkins, R. (1989) *Taking the strain.* Milton Keynes: Open University Press.

Jacobs, B. (1992) *Fractured cities: Capitalism, community and empowerment in Britain and America.* London: Routledge.

Jones, G. and Wallace, C. (1992) *Youth, family and citizenship.* Milton Keynes: Open University Press.

Judd, D. and Parkinson, M. (1990) 'Urban leadership and regeneration', in Judd, D. and Parkinson, M. (eds) *Leadership and urban regeneration.* London: Sage.

Kearns, G. and Philo, C. (eds) (1993) *Selling places: The city as cultural capital, past and present.* Oxford:Pergamon Press.

Lash, S. and Urry, J. (1994) *Economies of signs and spaces.* London: Sage.

Law, C. 1993 *Urban tourism*. Poole: Mansell/Cassell.

Lawless, P. (1990) 'Regeneration in Sheffield: From radical intervention to partnership', in Judd and Parkinson (eds) (1990) *op. cit.*

Lawless, P. and Ramsden, P. (1989) 'Sheffield into the 1990s: Urban regeneration and the economic context', Centre for Regional Economic and Social Research, Sheffield Polytechnic, Sheffield.

Ley, D. and Olds, K. (1988) 'Landscape as spectacle: World's Fairs and the culture of heroic consumption', *Environment and Planning D: Society and Space*, Vol. 6: pp. 191-212.

Logan, J. and Molotch, H. (1986) *Urban fortunes: The political economy of place.* Berkeley: University of California Press.

Marshall,T.H. (1963) 'Citizenship and social class', in his *Sociology at the cross-roads*. London: Heinemann.

Meehan, E. (1993) *Citizenship and the European Community.* London: Sage.

McColl, J. (1992) 'From stainless steel to spotless service: Civic leaders and the production of urban tourism in Sheffield 1988-1991', unpublished Ph.D. thesis, Main Library, Sheffield University, Sheffield.

Mules, T. and Faulkner, B. (1996) 'An economic perspective on special events', *Tourism Economics* Vol. 2, No. 2: pp. 107-117.

Murphy, P. (1985) *Tourism: a community approach.* London: Methuen.

Price, P. (1988) 'The Games — A "visionary's" view', unpublished paper, Sheffield District Labour Party, Sheffield City Council, Sheffield.

Reichert, A. (1978) 'The Three Rivers Festival: Economic impact study', *Indiana Business Review* Vol. 53, No. 1: pp. 5-9.

Ritchie, B. and Aitken, C. (1984) 'Assessing the impacts of the 1988 Winter Olympic Games', *Journal of Travel Research* Vol. 22, No. 3: pp. 17-25.

Ritchie, B. and Lyons, M. (1987) 'Olympulse IV: A mid-term report on resident attitudes concerning the XV Olympic Winter Games', *Journal of Travel Research*, Vol. 14, No. 1: pp. 18-26.

Robson, B. (1988) *Those inner cities: Reconciling the social and economic aims of urban policy.* Oxford: Clarendon.

Roche, M. (1992a) 'Mega-events and micro-modernization: On the sociology of the new urban tourism', *British Journal of Sociology* Vol. 43, No. 4: pp. 563-600.

——— (1992b) 'Problems of rationality and democracy in mega-event planning', *Proceedings of VIIIth European Leisure Research Congress* (ELRA). Bilbao: ELRA.

——— (1992c) *Rethinking citizenship: Welfare, ideology and social change.* (reprinted 1996) Oxford: Polity.

——— (1993) 'Sport and community: Rhetoric and reality in the development of British sport policy', in C. Binfield and J. Stevenson (eds) *Sport, culture and politics.* Sheffield: Sheffield Academic Press, pp. 73-114.

——— (1994) 'Mega-events and urban policy', *Annals of Tourism Research*, Vol.21, No. 1: pp. 1-19.

——— (1995) 'Citizenship and modernity', *British Journal of Sociology*, Vol. 46, No.4: pp. 715-733.

——— (1998) (forthcoming) *Mega-events and modernity: Olympics, expos and the construction of public culture.* London: Routledge.

Roche, M. and van Berkel, R. (eds) (1997) *European citizenship and social exclusion.* Aldershot: Avebury Press.

Rutheiser, C. (1996) *Imagineering Atlanta.* London: Verso.

Rydell, R. (1984) *All the World's a Fair: Visions of empire at American international expositions 1876-1916. Chicago.* University of Chicago Press.

Schaffer, W. and Davidson, L. (1980) 'A discussion of methods employed in analysing the impact of short-term entertainment events', *Journal of Travel Research*, Winter: pp. 12-16.

SERC (1988) 'Sheffield vision', Sheffield Economic Regeneration Committee (SERC), Sheffield City Council, Sheffield.

Seyd, P. (1990) 'Radical Sheffield: from socialism to entrepreneurialism', *Political Studies* Vol. XXXVIII: pp. 335-344 .

Sheffield City Council (1987a) 'World Student Games 1991' (Bid document), World Student Games Bid Team, Sheffield City Council, Sheffield.

——— (1987b) 'Going places: Sheffield's strategy for tourism', Tourism Joint Officers Group, Sheffield City Council, Sheffield.

——— (1992) 'XVI Universiade financial out-turn enquiries: Report of the Chief Executive to the Policy Committee', Sheffield City Council, Sheffield.

Smith, M. and Feagin, J. (eds) (1991) *The capitalist city: Global restructuring and community politics.* Cambridge MA: Blackwell.

Southar, I. (1991) 'World Student Games', *Sheffield Telegraph*, 26th July.

Stewart, M. (1990) 'Urban policy in Thatcher's England', School for Advanced Urban Studies, Bristol University, Bristol.

Stewart, J. and Stoker, G. (eds) (1989) *The future of local government.* London: Macmillan.

Stone, C. *et al.* (1991) 'The reshaping of urban leadership in US cities: A regime Analysis', in Gottdeiner, M. and Pickvance, C. (eds) *Urban life in transition.* London: Sage.

Syme, G. *et al.*, (eds) (1989) *The planning and evaluation of hallmark events.* Aldershot, Avebury Press.

Taylor, I., Evans, K. and Fraser, P. (1996) *A tale of two cities: Global change, local feeling and everyday life in Manchester and Sheffield.* London: Routledge.

Thompson, E. P. (1984) *The making of the English working class.* London: Penguin Books.

Thorne, R. and Munro-Clark, M. (1989) 'Hallmark events as an excuse for autocracy in urban planning', in Syme *et al.,*(1989) *op. cit.*

Travis, A. and Croize, J. (1987) 'The role and impact of mega-events and attractions on tourism development in Europe: A micro-perspective', in AIEST, *The role and impact of mega-events and attractions on regional and national tourism development.* AIEST, St.Gall, Switzerland.

Turner, B. (1986) *Citizenship and capitalism.* London: Allen & Unwin.

Turner, B. (ed) (1993) *The condition of citizenship.* London: Sage.

Watson, S. (1991) 'Gilding the smokestacks: The new symbolic representations of deindustrialising regions', *Environment and Planning D, Society & Space* Vol. 9: pp. 59-70.

Watts, D. *et al.* (1989) *Sheffield today.* Sheffield, Department of Geography, Sheffield University, Sheffield.

Westergaard, J. *et al.* (1989) *After redundancy: The experience of insecurity.* Cambridge: Polity Press.

Williams, C. C. (1997) *Consumer services and economic development.* London: Routledge.

Williams, R. (1989) 'The importance of community', in his *Resources of hope.* London, Verso.

Worpole, K. (1992) *Towns for people: Transforming urban life.* Buckingham: Open University Press.

III.

PERSPECTIVES IN SPORT
AND THE POLITICS OF IDENTITY

Chapter 7

SPORT, POLITICS AND IDENTITIES: FOOTBALL CULTURES IN COMPARATIVE PERSPECTIVE

John Sugden and Alan Tomlinson

University of Brighton

Football cultures and identity

In May 1997 500 million people from 202 countries were reported to have watched the television coverage of the final match of the European Football Federation's (UEFA's) Champions' League. The Italian side, Juventus, was a hot favourite to retain its title, and crown a season of achievement in which it had retained its Italian Serie A league title, comprehensively defeated the French side Paris St. Germain in the European Super Cup, and won what was effectively seen as the world club title by defeating River Plate of Argentina. Juventus' opponent, Borussia Dortmund of Germany, was widely considered to have little chance against a side described by the Ajax defender Frank de Boer as "a team from another planet". The legendary Dutch player Johann Cruyff, who swept his Ajax club side to three successive championships from 1971–73, was quoted as saying of Juventus that "they can't fail". The Italian side's record in the progress to the final had been imperious, including brilliant victories combining tactical acumen, team discipline and creative individual style. For almost the first half hour of the final Juventus swarmed all over an outclassed-looking Dortmund side, the latter's ageing squad appearing to be out-run, out-thought and out-expressed. Then the German side overturned all the pundits' pre-match projections, scoring twice in a few minutes with their first two attempts on goal, both emanating from corner kicks, and clinically executed by Riedle, the first with his left foot, the second with his head. The German hero had told his team-mates that he had dreamt that he would score twice, once with his left foot, once with a header. After the first strike, he recalled when the game was over, he told himself just to keep on dreaming. An impudently brilliant goal by the prima donna Juventus substitute,

169

Del Piero, threatened to open up the game in the second half of play, but a stunningly executed lobbed goal by the German substitute Ricken clinched the game for the Germans. Ricken had been on the pitch for just 15 seconds, and the shot was his first touch of the ball. Juventus' French star Zidane had struck the post of the Dortmund goal just before half-time, and Vieri had drilled the ball into the German net soon after, only to have the strike disallowed for a handballing infringement. It is one of the great dramatic qualities of football that territorial domination does not translate directly into scores or points, that superior creativity counts for nothing unless translated into goals. The players and the managers know this. As the Juventus coach Lippi said after the game, 'We're not unbeatable, we have never said we were"[1]. In football, as Bromberger has argued, can be found:

> ...the worth and allegorical depth of a great piece of theatre ... a profoundly significant game is being played out on the field which intensifies and enacts the fundamental values of life. (1994: p. 281)

Bromberger speaks against any interpretation of a football match as a "seductive fiction" or a "pernicious mirage", for it has the capacity to "mobilise and display loyalties"; and he recognises that, at a variety of levels, football is expressive of deep and complex meanings:

> Football in its current organisational format — from local and regional leagues to a world championship — provides a forum for the expression of affirmed collective identities and local or regional antagonisms. (Bromberger, 1994: p. 283)

Thus on the night of the Dortmund-Juventus game, fans in the stadium could unite around the colours, costumes, chants and insignia of their respective teams. And the media pundits and commentators could set up a classic clash of national character: phlegmatic, disciplined Northern European German forces marshalled against the flawed genius of the Southern European Latin artists. Of course this was in one sense absurd: four of the Dortmund side — three Germans and a Portuguese — were former Juventus players, and the side also included a Scot and a Swiss; and the Juventus team included two Frenchmen, two players from the Balkans and a Uruguayan. But this was not enough to hold back the English television commentary team, and as the game progressed the "mental strength" of the German team, and the wastefulness of the Latin side, emerged as the prevailing interpretive themes. In domestic lounges, public bars and sports clubs worldwide the same interpretations of the collective symbolism of the game would have been read into the evening. For, "like a caricatural drama", football:

> ...lays bare the major symbolic axes of our societies. Its deep structure (the laws of the genre rather than the rules of the game) represents the uncertain fate of man in the world of today. (Bromberger, 1994: p. 284)

Within that deep structure, Bromberger also reminds us, "uncertainty and chance" can play a great part. Juventus personnel would testify to this. Sport, then, and football in particular, can embody the polarities of hope and despair, generating simultaneously both a certainty of commitment and an uncertainty of outcome and emotions. With this expressive capacity, football has become a significant source for the expression of identities — at local, regional, and national levels; and in personal, social and cultural forms.

In this chapter, we draw upon some of our own fieldwork and comparative studies on sports cultures and politics, and especially upon examples of football in comparative cultural settings, in order to address some of these central themes in contemporary social and cultural theory. We see sport, and particularly football — the world's most popular game — as critical sites of and sources for the expression of forms of collective belonging, affiliation, and identity. Yet sport itself has a surprisingly low profile in some of the wider debates around these themes — paradoxically, its high profile within prominent public sites of contemporary cultural life and the private spaces of media consumption is not matched by its prominence in academic analysis and theorisation of the popular. We will, when looking at selected examples of local, regional, national, and global football cultures, be concerned primarily with the lived dimensions of those cultures, whilst simultaneously recognising that the semiotics of everyday life rest upon a constant reworking or absorption of the textual within the lived. Before the sports fan — or indeed any traveller — arrives in a new city or country, interpretations, anticipations and expectations are well-established, from media-based rather than first-hand sources. Lived cultures are themselves in great part mediated by and negotiated through textual sources and discourses, though never — and especially so in the cases which we have chosen to consider in this chapter — necessarily or exclusively determined by them. They must also be observed, as appropriate participated in, and documented. It is observed lived football cultures, and the politics of the popular inscribed within them, with which we are primarily concerned in this chapter[2]. Observation and interpretation of the complex and changing nature of football cultures in an increasingly interrelated and interconnected world can contribute to an understanding of the politics of the popular, and its relation to issues of cultural, collective and social identity.

Football cultures in the modern period have been sources of cultural creativity in a variety of ways. The reformed football codes of the nineteenth century public schools in Britain created an enormously influential model of team games which was used as a basis for moral reform and the training of a male elite — athleticism and the amateurist code became major expressions of elite male identity in the dominant culture of a transforming society (Mangan, 1981). In new industrial communities in later nineteenth century England and Scotland, the professional code provided vital sources for the expression of local identity — it is in the heartlands of the industrial communities of central Scotland, the English Midlands and the North-West of England that the roots of the professional game were most fully established (Holt, 1989; Tomlinson, 1991). Social and oral historians — as well as novelists and other storytellers — have testified to the impact and significance of the game at informal and amateur levels as well as in the professional mode (Davies, 1992). Football historians have demonstrated the spread of the game across the world, and the appropriation of the game of colonial and commercial elites by the indigenous populations of third-world and underdeveloped countries (Mason, 1980 and 1986; Murray, 1994). With the expansion of the international dimensions of the game, football has become a major source for the expression of national identity. As the European Championships of 1996 showed, this has been as true in a world of post-Cold War revivalist nationalism as it was in a post- Second World War period of the dissolution of Empires. Through football, East European states in the 1990s expressed aspirations and tensions comparable with those of African and Asian nations, which expressed their autonomy and world significance, through football, from the 1960s onwards (Sugden and Tomlinson, 1996b; 1997; 1998, chs. 6–8). Some boundaries of affiliation have become more blurred than previously in an age in which Paris St. Germain vs Manchester United could be watched by someone in Santa Cruz or Sydney, wearing the replica shirt and cheering on players from all over the world. But — as attendance at major events such as the World Cup, Euro '96 or the African Cup of Nations illustrates — the dominance of globalized media industries has not eroded the capacity of football

The biggest flaw in placing at the centre of the interpretive stage such a conceptualisation, and elevating it to the status of a general theoretical framework, is the lack of detailed and sustained research into the everyday realities of creating, acting out and reproducing cultural identities; and of any adequate recognition of the social and structural contexts of and constraints upon identity-formation. Theoretically, Larrain is surely right in his observation that any formation of cultural identities "presupposes the notion of the 'other'; the definition of the cultural self always involves a distinction from the values, characteristics and ways of life of others" (Larrain, 1994: p. 142) — in fact, this was the fundamental insight of classical interpretive approaches of a micro-sociological kind. In the perspective of symbolic interactionism, for instance, in George Herbert Mead's or Charles Cooley's terms, there is no self without the interacting other. Cooley's "looking-glass self" identifies three elements: "the imagination of our appearance to the other person; the imagination of his judgment of our appearance, and some sort of self-feeling ..." (Cooley, 1969: p. 217). Mead, in *Mind, Self and Society* as cited by Coser, posited categories of the "I" and the "me" which are inherently related to social experience, but are distinct in the following way:

> [the 'I' is] ... the response of the organism to the attitudes of the others; the 'me' is the organized set of attitudes of others which one assumes. The attitudes of the others constitute the organized 'me', and then one reacts toward that as an 'I'. (Coser, 1971: p. 338)

From such perspectives there simply is no meaningful self without the other: the individual self is an assemblage of responses to social contexts and situations. Such a premise is illustrated brilliantly, of course, in the interactionist sociology of Erving Goffman, whose work is so firmly rooted in chosen institutional and anthropological settings (Goffman, 1959 and 1968). Yet the minutely articulated ways in which the play of appearances, and the dynamics and distinctions of the 'I' and the 'me' are expressed, reaffirmed, at times challenged and resisted, rarely feature in the broader theoretical syntheses which have made the notion of *identity* such a prominent and pervasive one. Let us consider an example from a major theorist in the sociological field — Anthony Giddens, for whom the notion of identity features in *Modernity and Self-Identity* (Giddens, 1991).

In his concern with identity, Giddens' offers no reductionist rejection of the structural realities of modern societies to the experiential realities of the interpersonal relations of social actors. On the contrary, his concern with self is justified as a type of holistic theorisation of a complex world of interrelated structurising macro-forces and lived micro-realities. In "high modernity", he believes, "for the first time in human history, 'self' and 'society' are interrelated in a global milieu" (1991: p. 32). High levels of "time-space distanciation" contribute to this, and to "the relation between self-identity and modern institutions" (*ibid.*). In such circumstances, "the self becomes a *reflexive project*" (1991: p. 32). What does this mean for sociological analysis and for an understanding of the cultural forms through which certain kinds of meaning are conveyed and transmitted, and categories of identity expressed? We will consider this question in the light of Giddens' discussion of "the body".

For Giddens, through his analysis of Janette Rainwater's *Self-Therapy*, a how-to manual for self-realization, the contemporary body can be seen as itself (as Giddens puts it, consistent with his understanding of Rainwater) "part of an action system rather than a merely passive object". Body awareness is a means of:

> ... constructing a differentiated self, not as one of the dissolution of the ego. Experiencing the body is a way of cohering the self as an integrated whole, whereby the individual says 'this is where I live'. (Giddens, 1991: pp. 77-78)

Although Giddens recognises that there are questions that can be asked about the ideological context of Rainwater's conceptions, he argues that "they signal something real about self and self-identity in the contemporary world — the world of late modernity" (*ibid.*). Here Giddens starts from a text and textual discourse and moves towards the contexts about which that text is claimed to speak. Analysis of what may be an arbitrarily chosen instance proceeds to theorisation of the wider socio-cultural condition. Giddens prioritizes self-identity over social identity, the analysis of the individual body over consideration of contexts in which bodies might express cultural identity or collective identity. Reading Giddens, it is as if to talk of collective identities is to talk of some past romantic age. He recognizes, in a discussion of dress and social identity, that group pressures and factors such as socioeconomic resources and advertising have influences upon dress, and can "promote standardisation rather than individual difference" (Giddens, 1991: p. 99). But appearance still, for Giddens, "becomes a central element of the reflexive project of the self" (Giddens, 1991: p. 100).

Giddens (1991) has also recognized the increasing importance of the relationship between the local and the global, in his reflections upon self-identity, self and society in the late modern age. For him, the *"dialectic of the local and the global* is a basic emphasis of the arguments" (Giddens, 1991: p. 22) developed within those reflections. Globalization, Giddens implies, is nothing more nor less than the growth and spread of the modern across the contemporary world, involving "an ongoing relation between distanciation and the chronic mutability of local circumstances and local engagements" (Giddens, 1991: pp. 21-22). This is a gloomy view of modernity and the conditions of self-identity, in which spheres of locality are presented as uncontrollably fickle, and those of the supra-local as remote and beyond one's control. Indeed, Giddens describes the "late modern world" as "apocalyptic ... because it introduces risks which previous generations have not had to face" (Giddens, 1991: p. 4). Giddens identifies the dynamic at the heart of modernity between the existential angst of wondering who one is, and the supra-individual forces which situate one precariously and catch one up, perturbingly, in "massive waves of global transformation" (Giddens, 1991: p. 184). Sporting events — in terms of their impact upon the self-identity of individuals and the profile, pride and identity of nations — capture and articulate such contradictory forces, premised upon an infrastructure of communications and a sophisticated global media system.

There is an enormous body of contemporary writing on the concept of *identity* — social, cultural, personal. For Stuart Hall, identity has become a central concept: he points to "two different ways of thinking about 'cultural identity'" (1990: p. 223). The first way of thinking sees cultural identity as a single, shared culture, reflecting "common cultural experiences and shared cultural codes", providing "stable, unchanging and continuous frames of reference and meaning". Hall's second way of thinking, or position, acknowledges the "deep and significant *difference*" which contributes to "what we really are" (Hall, 1990: p. 225).

> Cultural identity, in this second sense, is a matter of 'becoming' as well as 'being'. It belongs to the future as much as to the past. It is not something which already exists, transcending place, time history and culture. Cultural identities come from somewhere, have histories. But, like everything which is historical, they undergo constant transformation. Far from being eternally fixed in some essentialised past, which is

waiting to be found, and which, when found, will secure our sense of ourselves into eternity, identities are the names we give to the different ways we are positioned by, and position ourselves within, the narratives of the past. (Hall, 1995: p. 225)

Narratives of the past are social products too, and any talk of the "reflexive self" and of the "constant transformation" of identities must never be at the expense of an awareness that self and identities are in part determined and constrained by society and social structure. To talk about identities in any sociologically adequate way it is useful to draw upon Durkheim's analytical categories of mechanical and organic solidarity (Durkheim, 1984). For Durkheim, mechanical solidarity was the cement which bound the individual to the collective social order, so that ascribed aspects of life determined actions, in relatively unreflective ways. In a situation of increased differentiation, a temporarily constructed form of solidarity could establish a sense of unity and connectedness that could accommodate more individual difference: in Coser's words: "...mechanical solidarity was founded upon likeness, organic solidarity arose because of complementarity between actors engaged in different pursuits" (Coser, 1984: p. xvi)[4]. As the scope for the development and negotiation of identities expands, sport has become an important site for the expression of unity within difference, a temporarily constructed mechanical solidarity, at a level of national identity[5]. Multiple identities become possible in a differentiated society, but can also be expressed as one in appropriate collective settings: the Manchester United, Arsenal, Burnley and Everton fans (can) suspend regional identities and rivalries when supporting the English national side.

However, in spheres of popular culture embracing the collective, sub-cultural and individual dimensions, identities are not always there just for the taking or the making. Many collectively experienced and consumed popular cultural forms are far from a matter of individual choice. Their meanings and impacts can be bound up with the political dynamics within and between societies. The "reflexive project of the self" or the "constant transformation" of cultural identity is not an easy, or even available, option to the individual born into the sectarian culture of Northern Ireland, or into the black majority of a South African township; and it may be that very option or prospect that the cosmopolitan World Cup fan is striving to reject. In the following section we look at some particular settings in which football cultures have found their expression, arguing that collective and cultural identities as expressed in football can be seen as elements in a less reflexive project of the self, in which is sought a meaningful cultural identity and collective affiliation, and in which fewer choices of identity are available than some orthodoxies would recognize.

Comparative football cultures: Issues of cultural and political identity

Northern Ireland '95: peeping through the peace process

In the Summer of 1995, from a distance, and through the mist and the drizzle, Belfast looked like any other Northern European seaport. It is only when you get down to the streets that the city's pronounced sectarian geography was revealed. Even in the political optimism of talk of the peace process, the urban iconography of sectarianism dominated the public culture of the streets. Kerbstones painted red, white and blue marked the fixed territoriality of space. Orange Halls and commemorative archways in Protestant North Belfast flew the Union Jack, the flag of St George and the orange lodge flag, testifying to the significance of flags and emblems in the expression of identity. In this community your religious affiliation and your political persona, and any involvement in public or popular culture, were not for negotiation. Bunting across the Shankill Road professes an assertive politics of identity. Woven in with the flag of the Union, and the red white and blue decorations, are political statements about the status of loyalist 'prisoners of war'. Loyalist paramilitary murals are prominent in the shadow of the Shankill Leisure Centre. One features deceased city councillor George Seawright, famous for the speech in Belfast City Hall council chambers in which he proclaimed that "all Catholics should be incinerated along with their priests". He was also famous for climbing onto the rooves of leisure centres in nationalist areas and waving his (legally held) pistol to keep the mob at bay as he hauled down the Irish tricolour. Ironically, his head was blown off by the Provisional IRA while waiting in his car in the car park of the Shankill Leisure Centre, fifty feet from this mural.

In another part of town, more painted kerbstones mark the boundaries of sectarian territories. Green, white and gold kerbstones off the Falls Road mark the territory of Catholic nationalism and Republicanism. The Gaelic game of football is played at Casement Park, home ground to County Antrim Gaelic Athletic Association. Gaelic spelling — Páirc Mhic Áismaint — makes a culturally specific statement, as do the Gaelic game's distinctive goalposts, at the end of a playing area surrounded by barbed wire. An empty sports ground can be a desolate, apparently soulless place, innocent or meaningless. But cultural spaces have narrative histories and cultural identities too. Casement Park is named after Sir Roger Casement, hanged by the British for treason for negotiating with the Germans to supply arms to the IRA around the time of the Great War. In more recent years, the two army corporals who were dragged from their car and beaten before being shot were 'executed' inside Casement Park. The ground was occupied by the British forces for a while in the 1970s. Given the symbolic and ceremonial significance of the site, this incensed local nationalists. Next door is Andersonstown Leisure Centre, symbolically claimed by the Irish flag. Fifty yards up the street from the Leisure Centre is the head-quarters of Sinn Fein.

Less than a mile from Sinn Fein HQ is loyalist South Belfast — known locally as 'the village', and replete with the insignia and the iconography of its inhabitants' identity — a warren of streets and terraces looking like so many inner-industrial communities at a time of celebration or festival, until the cultural and political specificities of the red, white and blue, and orange, alter the everyday landscape of the gable-end, the ice-cream salesman's patch, and the sport and leisure facil-ities. Inside these sectarian stockades this atmosphere of the 'village' is a felt and lived reality. It is also an appropriate metaphor for the cultivation of forms of mech-anical solidarity: such forms of solidarity constrain and inhibit the possibility of breaking free and selecting alternative identities. In the centre of the village is Windsor Park, home to Linfield FC, and also the 'national' stadium. Named after the House of Windsor (the British Royal Family), it is replete with loyalist symbol-ism, reinforcement of a separate and persisting identity. It is a hostile environ-ment for Catholics, despite their sporting preferences and passions, for they are seen as having pledged their football/soccer alliances to the Republic of Ireland.

What do we learn from these images of sporting sites and cultures in Northern Ireland?

- Affiliations in sport and football are far from malleable and flexible — they are marked by culturally and politically specific and entrenched meanings;

- Football in its public form is a site for symbolic reaffirmation of cultural affiliation and identity;

- Football spaces, with their legacy of cultural and political meanings, can inhibit or block potential forms of cultural transformation;

- Cultural identity in and through sport is not a matter of personal choice; cultural identity is fixed and constrained by the weight of history and supra-individual influences.

To summarise the case, we quote from an earlier article:

> ... it is difficult to ignore the proximity of sport to politics when during a Gaelic football match a heavily armed helicopter hovers deafeningly just above the heads of the players before disappearing into the confines of a corrugated-iron fortress built by the British army on an adjoining field, an area of land which was, before the 'Troubles', part of the playing area — or when a number of expensive new municipal sport and leisure facilities are constructed, at taxpayers' expense, alongside military and police stockades in the most troubled areas of Belfast" (Sugden and Bairner, 1992: p. 155).

The British government has a statutory duty to provide public sport and leisure in Northern Ireland, and an overriding responsibility for maintenance of public order and, ultimately, union with the United Kingdom. However, the 'ownership' of the facilities which it provides in the furtherance of these goals is contested. As one civil servant put it: "A lot of community centres are being virtually run by paramilitaries, and the decent citizen is just not welcome" (Sugden and Bairner, 1992: p. 160). Thus, in these ways, sport and leisure, often hailed as matters for individual choice, are, in such a context, the suppliers of prescribed and non-negotiable cultural identities.

South Africa '96: scenes from Soccer City

At the FNB (First National Bank) Stadium (more popularly known as Soccer City) on the edge of Soweto, Johannesburg, on Saturday 3 February 1996, Nelson Mandela donned a replica shirt of the South Africa national football side and presented the African Nations Cup to the team captain in front of an ecstatic home crowd and, as ever, the lenses, cameras and eyes of the world media. South Africa had defeated Tunisia to win the trophy, and it seemed that sport was tailored by some spiritual or supernatural force for the President and his Rainbow Nation. Before its victory against Ghana the previous week, Mandela had exhorted the team with a pledge of faith: "My children, I'm leaving the country and its people in your hands" (Block, 1996: p. S12).

In winning the Rugby World Cup in 1995, humiliating England in cricketing matches in 1995-96, winning the continent's football championship, and producing the country's first black African Olympic gold medallist at the Atlanta Olympics in August, 1996 (marathon runner Josia Thugwane), South Africa has presented, through sport, an image of cross-cultural unity and harmony resonant of the political rhetoric around claims concerning its transformation into the Rainbow Nation. The scenes in Soccer City were unforgettable ones of collective celebration. Mandela — "the cheerleader as sport unites all South Africans" (van Niekerk, 1996: p. 19) — led the celebrations, hailing the ecstatic crowd from the pitch, escorted out there and protected by an elaborate choreography of heavily armed militia. Beneath the surface of such an integrated expression of collective affiliation, the tensions of a society reared in conflict — with different elements in the society endemically mistrusting of the other elements — were still there: in the stadium, heavily armed white paramilitary police patrolled the concrete moat between the crowd and the pitch.

Football had the power, with its extensive base in black culture, to bind the different ethnic elements of the society together in unprecedented, symbolic ways. Elaborate costumes and face-painting captured the carnival atmosphere of the occasion. Men and women stood together on the terraces where there was a genuine mingling of black and white — a multi-cultural fandom, uniting around star players like Mark Fish. This was a genuine expression of cultural commonality and national unity. The witty puns of Soweto's tabloid, *The Sowetan*, were transformed into banners of support for the South Africa side, 'Bafana, Bafana', (Boys, Boys) throughout the tournament. 'Pharoahs go home to mummy', mocked one directed at the Egyptian side. Inside the stadium, just before the final, the South African cricket team — all white, but for one Asian — paraded on the pitch, fuelling the collective spirit.

But the cultural harmony of the moment did not erode a cultural politics for which large-scale sport has always provided an opportunity. A figure of revilement for the crowd was the Nigerian dictator Abacha, responsible for the hanging of Ken Saro Wiwa, the dissident poet, and in alliance with the Shell company in environment-threatening industrial developments in Nigeria. "Shell and Abacha must go to hell", proclaimed one poster, carrying the picture of Saro Wiwa on the other side. Meanwhile, overhead, and in full view of Nelson Mandela, a light aircraft circled Soccer City, trailing a banner with the slogan "Go well Bafana Bafana, Go Shell". Sponsored in their celebrations by such a representative of global domination, the ecstatic South African fans were unlikely to sustain the collective euphoria and symbolic solidarity of the moment into a troubled future.

We are reminded by these images of and moments in South Africa's remarkable sporting renaissance that, in particular sets of circumstances:

- Football can create a cultural identity over and above deeply-rooted cleavages and difference;
- Collective identity can be expressed in highly distinctive ways by forms of sport and popular culture;
- Within collective expressions of identity there are complex intra-layers of meaning;
- Expressions of cultural and collective identity in sport are dramatic but often transient, reflecting the frailty of cultural and political alliances.

For in South African sport, as expressed to us by the country's most expert football journalist, white South African Mark Gleeson, football remains the "Mafia sport ... the sport of thugs", at least in the administrative sphere, with a succession of corruption scandals that have robbed the game of finances and facilities. And no national victory can change such a profile overnight[6]. Beneath the worldwide profile of the continental victory, long-established divisions were likely to reassert themselves in the world of sport, across the country and in the regions. As Tommy Ballantine, veteran white sports journalist, in Durban, put it to us: "Can you ever see a Zulu playing Rugby?"[7]. For Rugby was still the sport *par excellence* of the Afrikaan male elite. Comparably, football in South Africa remained an essentially black working-class sport, with its own history of off-field maladministration and financial scandals, as well as a history of considerable achievement on the playing side. One high-profile tournament and success would not miraculously transform its historical, social, political and cultural base[8]. Indeed, the rainbow metaphor was soon to lose its gloss, as the residues of apartheid recurrently resurfaced within South African sports cultures (Guelke and Sugden, 1997). In early 1997, the coach of the Springbok rugby team, André Markgraaff, was dismissed after making racist remarks; and soon after the historic football victory in the Africa Cup of Nations, white footballer Sean Dundee accepted German citizenship, claiming that he had been discriminated against, as a white, within South Africa's football culture.

World Cup USA '94: football, commodity and spectacle

As any student of media reception and the process of consumption confirms, cultural products are open to a variety of interpretations. The World Cup final, for instance, is both a global spectacle and a local cultural event. This multi-faceted nature of the single football match was captured in a television documentary coordinated by Andreas Rogenhagen (1995), drawing on footage shot by directors from forty countries during the broadcasting of the final[9]. Production lines were stopped in a Teheran car factory, workers moving to a space where a screening had been set up. In Cameroon, Mongo Faya's harem was feasting, dancing and celebrating with him throughout the event. In Argentina, fans chanted their support for the Italian side, allies in their arch rivalry with Brazil. The vodka and orange was out for the game for the remote couple in Lapland. The street party in jubilant Rio moved into the ecstasy and the hysteria of triumph when Italian Roberto Baggio failed to score in the penalty shoot-out half a continent away in Pasadena, California, whilst the despondent Italian fans in Turin were speechless and drained. Monks in their monastery in Prague, myriad groups of people from Belorussia to Costa Rica, gathered around televisions, from giant public screenings in Beijing to smaller-scale viewings of black and white portable sets. Choosing to let the global culture of football speak for itself, director Rogenhagen offered no commentary, no sub-titles, just name-labels for countries and cities, and for the players who featured most tellingly in the dramatic finale of the shoot-out. The global reach of sport and television was vividly captured and conveyed in this documentary. Differences of age, status, gender, ethnicity and culture seemed, however fleetingly, superseded by a shared passion for and response to the event and its outcome. It is cultural phenomena such as the Olympics and the football World Cup that have the capacity to engage audiences across the world, whatever the various modes of reception and cultures of consuming expressed in the process and the act of viewing. Such sports events have claimed a hugely prominent place in the world media's calendar. Because competitive events such as these are staged regularly, and in planned sequence without overlapping, they can provide a source for continual review and anticipation, a context in which histories can be developed, soap operatic narratives fostered, and the intensifying symbiosis of top-level performance sport and television reaffirmed. As live events, they provide opportunity for the expression of cultural and national identity, as well as a cosmopolitan consumerism that is a prerequisite for participation. As it has grown in scale, the World Cup has offered the opportunity — to those privileged and resourced enough to be able to get there — for the simultaneous expression of their local identity and their cosmopolitan self.

The USA World Cup was a huge success as spectacle and investment (Sugden and Tomlinson, 1996a). To the watching billions around the world, the blue-shirted followers of (the *Azzurra*) and the yellow-shirted followers of Brazil would have blended into anonymous homogeneous hordes. But at the entrance turnstiles and on the bleachers, it was clear that this was far from the case, and that spectator's motivations and identities were varied and complex. We had acquired tickets from the Irish Football Association, and two pugnacious and pinkish Irish Protestants were in the same row. For them, the appeal and qualities of the game were of little interest. Regularly, throughout the event, they unfurled their own flag, a red cross on a white background, and brandished it proudly and defiantly: for them, if they had been football fans, there would have been a problem, for both the finalists were from predominantly Catholic countries. For these two 'fans', the game was an opportunity to make propaganda in a nation known for its Republican sympathies on the Irish question — so living out a complex mix of organic and mechanical solidarity. The more carnivalesque and celebratory dimension of the event could be seen in a female fan for whom the Brazil side was 'her' team. Even though she was Colombian, not Brazilian, her affiliation was straightforward enough on the basis of continent, history and tradition.

For some Brazilian fans themselves, the final was an opportunity to engage in a politics of protest, to demonstrate against the effects of the FIFA President Havelange's influence upon domestic football in his home country. 'Brasil Si, Havelange No' screeched one prominent banner. A form of reductive individualism could retell the World Cup Final event as a series of unique individual narratives, mini-dramas of choice and life-chances. That this would be at all possible is indicative of the organic solidarity which is characteristic of the international sports event. For the moment of the event at least, a unity-in-difference is accomplished: all those at the Pasadena Rose Bowl had at least one thing in common. They were there, sharing in the staging of a major event of globalized consumer culture, their presence supporting some of the world's largest companies, 'exploiting the world's most popular game for what in advertising parlance is known as 'global mileage'" (Sinha, 1994: p. 1996).

Concluding comment

We have taken three examples in which football has expressed, respectively, constraining forms of inherited cultural-political identity, emergent and spectacular (yet frail) forms of collective and politically progressive identity, and cosmopolitan forms of consumerism within a globalized political economy. They show how, in sport, cultural identity and particular forms of social solidarity can be given expressive form, in some cases (involving sufficient complementarity of interests in collective contexts) counterbalancing the alienating and anomic dimensions of contemporary life. In examples such as the three considered, identities are theoretically open to negotiation and renewal, and might provide the possibilities of effective contestation, but they remain practically constrained by the contexts of their initial production, and the flexibility or rigidity of the social setting[10].

Football cultures contribute in myriad ways to forms of personal, cultural social and national identity, but never regardless of the social structure and relations of the society. Identity is contingent upon the ascribed dimensions of a society in which mechanical solidarity prevails in the Northern Irish case. It is a modified mechanical solidarity which is expressed in football in the South African post-apartheid context. On the world level, the World Cup mobilizes a much more fluid set of identities, on the basis of a football culture whose collective expression represents the quintessentially organic solidarity of a supranational world order and globalized consumer economy and culture, which nonetheless co-exists with the mechanical solidarity of separate nationalisms.

Global sporting events can express the paradox of a condition in which individual angst can blend with collective constraint:

... the exhilaration of following events of worldwide interest, of involving oneself in matters of cosmopolitan modernity, sits alongside a recurrent sense of unease concerning who one really is. Rooting for the nation, in a context of a global discourse of competitive sport, is both an expression and a resolution of this paradox. (Sugden and Tomlinson, 1994: pp. 10-11)

As a cultural phenomenon in which fate plays such an important part, football retains a capacity to confound expectations. One could hardly imagine that Juventus could fail against Dortmund, Patrick Urbini of *L'Équipe* commented to the Italian side's French star, Didier Deschamps, before the 1997 European Champions League final. Deschamps replied:

> That's what a lot of people are thinking, yes. But we, we know that we'll be facing an experienced and high-quality opponent, capable of being very good in the final. In a match such as this, there's no margin of security. Thus, one can lose.
>
> [Urbini: With Dortmund, where are the dangers?]
>
> In all ways, with the Germans, the matches are always battles. It is in their mentality ... they never let go.[11]

Football is a game of fate, but protagonists in the varying theatres of the game cannot reinvent themselves totally, and historical traditions persist: Deschamps was to be proved right about the major strength of the Germans. The fates meet history in the realm of sport and international sporting exchange; and cannot escape the politics of a particular time and place. If cultural identity is a zone of possibility, in Hall's optimistic conceptualisation, sport space in Northern Ireland, in its zonal reaffirmation of exclusion, erodes such possibilities. Football cultures have histories, and are framed by the realities of politics, the politics of the popular, and political economy. The football fan might switch replica jerseys as some fluctuating meanings of time and space are negotiated. But such switches of affiliation and identity are not equally available or open, and in societies in which a sporting cultural identity is an element of that society's mechanical solidarity, the collective chant of the terrace culture can veil — as the popular speaks for the political — an agonized inner scream of the suppressed self.

Acknowledgements

This chapter draws upon presentations made at: 'Culture and Identity: City Nation World', the 2nd *Theory, Culture & Society* Conference, 10-14 August 1995, Berlin Hilton Hotel, Berlin; and 'Popular Culture and Collective Identity', a workshop held at the Fondation Nationale des Sciences Politiques, University of Paris, 4 July 1996. We are grateful to participants in those events for critical and suppportive responses; and especially to Maurice Roche, organizer of the Paris event and editor of this volume, for a stimulating response to our initial oral presentation and our written submission.

Notes

1   Quotes are taken from match reports in *The Mirror* ('Double Spice Karlheinz stuns Euro kings Juve', p.33), *The Independent* (David Milne, 'Juventus wrecked by German bite', p. 32), and *The Guardian* (Richard Williams, 'Riedle double sinks Juve', p. 26): all on Thursday 29 May 1997.

2   No doubt we run the risk of being perceived as crudely empiricist in this intent; and we are certainly making claims that any understanding of sport and popular culture should involve observation of concrete socio-cultural realities with complex historical legacies. In this we are guided by C. Wright Mills and his warnings against Grand Theory. For Mills, Grand Theory is "the associating and dissociating of concepts"; Grand Theory's basic cause is "the initial choice of a level of thinking so general that its practitioners cannot logically get down to observation. They never, as grand theorists, get down from the higher generalities to problems in their historical and structural contexts" (Mills, 1970: pp. 34 and 42). For Mills, Grand Theorists are also guilty of fetishizing the Concept.

3   We would argue that both the concepts illuminate the central dilemma for modern societies — how to generate coherence out of diversity, to promote forms of collectivity in an age of individualism? For Marx, the answer was economic and political transformation. For Durkheim, the modern work organization — the corporation — provided the potential to fill the moral vacuum of which anomie was the symptom, and suicide the tragic exemplar (Durkheim, 1952). Although it may seem to be an unfashionable, unorthodox and perhaps even controversial view, we see both alienation and anomie as indices of the disintegration of a more collective human experience. Widespread concern with questions of identity is an echo of this classical sociological issue.

4   Durkheim himself was not entirely consistent in his discussion of the different forms that mechanical and organic solidarity take, implying in one case that there might be weaker social ties in the former than in the latter. For the purposes of the analysis in this chapter, we are most concerned with the general importance of grasping the persisting relevance of the conceptual category of social solidarity for any adequately sociological understanding of cultural identity. We are indebted to Maurice Roche for pointing out the ambiguity in Durkheim's analysis.

5   It is interesting to compare Victor Turner's notions of *liminality* and *communitas* here (Turner, 1967; 1969; 1974; 1982). Liminality refers to a

phase — often transitional — 'betwixt and between' positions or states: "...the liminal group is a community or comity of comrades and not a structure of hierarchically arranged positions" (1967: p. 100). Communitas is "a perception of shared emotional states" (1982: p. 21), linked to a de-emphasis upon the "logical, linear, and classifying functions associated with social structuring..." (*ibid.*). Communitas — along with *sacra* (sacred things) and *ludic recombination* (the element of play) — is one of the major components of the liminal process: "a direct, spontaneous, and egalitarian mode of social relationship..." (1992: p. 202). For Turner, liminal states of communitas are potentially transformative, processual and constitute a kind of cultural time-out potentially threatening to social structure itself.

A full sociological and cultural application of Turner's ideas to sport spectacle and sports cultures would be an important contribution to understanding the sources of identity and symbolic meaning in popular culture. MacAloon, for instance, has drawn upon the notions of liminality and marginality in his brilliant work on de Coubertin and the birth of 'olympism' (1981).

6   Interview with authors, Johannesburg, January 1996.

7   Interview with authors, Durban, January 1996.

8   Although the reported views are those of white journalists, black activist sports writers also recognise the problem of deep-rooted corruption in African football administration, as well as its progressive potential. See Sugden and Tomlinson, 1998 (ch. 6); Quansha, 1996; and Maradas, 1996.

9   This summary of the documentary is taken from Tomlinson, 1996.

10   To fail to recognise this is to support the fallacy of the fetishization of the Concept, to analytically privilege a notion of identity within modernity which is too often read from reaffirming textual sources, rather than observed in the complex and confusing contexts of cultural and social settings.

11   Interview in *L'Équipe*, Tuesday 27 May 1997, No. 15879, p. 8 (our translation).

References

Block, R. (1996) 'Team that truly represents a nation', *The Independent Sport*, Monday 5 February: p. S12.

Bromberger, C. (1994) 'Football passion and the World Cup', in J. Sugden and A. Tomlinson (eds) *Hosts and champions — Soccer cultures, national identities and the USA World Cup*. Aldershot: Arena/Ashgate Publishing Ltd., pp. 281-290.

Chaney, D. (1994) *The cultural turn: Scene-setting essays on contemporary cultural history*. London and New York. Routledge.

Cooley, C. H. (1969) 'Looking-glass self', in J. G. Manis and B. N. Meltzer (eds) *Symbolic interaction — A reader in social psychology*. Boston: Allyn and Bacon, pp. 217-219.

Coser, L. A. (1971) *Masters of sociological thought: Ideas in historical and social context*. New York. Harcourt Brace Jovanovich, Inc.

Coser, L. (1984) 'Introduction', in E. Durkheim *The Division of Labour in Society* [translated by W.D. Halls]. London: Macmillan, pp. ix-xxiv.

Davies, A. (1992) *Leisure, gender and poverty: Working-class culture in Salford and Manchester, 1900-1939*. Buckingham: Open University Press.

Durkheim, E. (1952) *Suicide*. London: Routledge and Kegan Paul.

———— (1984) *The division of labour in society*. London: Macmillan [translated by W.D. Halls].

Giddens, A. (1991) *Modernity and self-identity: Self and society in the late modern age*. Cambridge: Polity Press.

Goffman, E. (1959) *The presentation of self in everyday life*. New York: Doubleday Anchor.

———— (1968) *Asylums*. Harmondsworth: Pelican.

Guelke, A. and Sugden, J. (1997) 'South Africa', in A. Bairner and J. Sugden (eds) *Sport in divided societies*. Aachen: Meyer & Meyer [forthcoming].

Hall, S. (1990) 'Cultural identity and diaspora', in J. Rutherford (ed) *Identity: Community, culture, difference*. London: Lawrence and Wishart, pp. 222-237.

Holt, R. (1989) *Sport and the British: A social history*. Oxford: Oxford University Press.

Larrain, J. (1994) *Ideology & cultural identity: Modernity and the Third World presence*. Cambridge. Polity Press.

MacAloon, J. J. (1981) *This great symbol: Pierre de Coubertin and the origins of the modern Olympic Games*. Chicago: University of Chicago Press.

Mandel, E. and Novack, G. (1970) *The marxist theory of alienation*. New York: Pathfinder Press.

Mangan, J. A. (1981) *Athleticism in the Victorian and Edwardian public school: The emergence and consolidation of an educational ideology*. Cambridge: Cambridge University Press.

Maradas, E. (1996) 'The long road to South Africa', *African Soccer Souvenir* (January): pp. 16-17.

Mason, T. (1980) *Association Football and English society 1863-1915*. Sussex: The Harvester Press.

—— (1986) 'Some Englishmen and Scotsmen Abroad: the spread of world football', in A. Tomlinson and G. Whannel (eds) *Off the ball: The football World Cup*. London: Pluto Press, pp. 67–82.

Mills, C. W. (1970) *The sociological imagination*. Harmondsworth: Penguin.

Murray, B. (1994) *Football: A history of the world game*. Aldershot: Scolar Press.

Quansha, E. (1996) 'The cup to surpass all cups', *Africa Today* Vol. 2, No. 1: p. 27.

Rogenhagen, A. (1995) *The Final Kick*. Directed by Andreas Rogenhagen and Directors from 40 countries, Litchblick Production in coproduction with Last Border, in cooperation with arte: broadcast in BBC 2 "TX" Series (25 November), Series editor John Wyver.

Sinha, D. (1994) 'World Cup USA: A different perspective', *Economic and Political Weekly* Vol. 29, No. 31 (July 30): pp. 1,996-97.

Sugden, J. and Bairner, A. (1992) '"Ma, there's a helicopter on the pitch!": Sport, leisure and the State in Northern Ireland', *Sociology of Sport Journal* Vol. 9, No. 2 (June): pp. 154-166.

Sugden, J. and Tomlinson, A. (1994) 'Soccer culture, national identity and the World Cup', in J. Sugden and A. Tomlinson (eds) *Hosts and champions: Soccer cultures, national identities and the USA World Cup*. Aldershot: Arena/Ashgate Publishing Limited, pp. 3-12.

—— (1996a) 'What's left when the circus leaves town? An evaluation of World Cup USA '94', *Sociology of Sport Journal* Vol.13, No. 3 (September): pp. 236-254.

—— (1996b) 'The price of fame', *When Saturday Comes* No. 109 (March): p. 39.

—— (1997) 'A Gulf in class?', *When Saturday Comes* No. 120 (February): pp. 36-37.

—— (1998, forthcoming) *Who rules the people's game? FIFA and the contest for world football*. Cambridge: Polity Press.

Tomlinson, A. (1991) 'North and South: The rivalry of the Football League and the Football Association', in J. Williams and S. Wagg (eds) *British football and social change: Getting into Europe.* Leicester: Leicester University Press, pp. 25-47.

———— (1996) 'Olympic spectacle: Opening ceremonies and some paradoxes of globalization', *Media Culture & Society* Vol. 18, No. 4 (November): pp. 583-602.

Turner, V. (1967) *The forest of symbols: Aspects of Ndembu ritual.* Ithaca: Cornell University Press.

———— (1969) *The ritual process.* Chicago: Aldine.

———— (1974) *Dramas, fields and metaphors: Symbolic action in human society.* Ithaca: Cornell University Press.

———— (ed) (1982) *Celebration: Studies in festivity and ritual.* Washington D.C.: Smithsonian Institution Press.

van Niekerk, P. (1996) 'Mandela is the cheerleader as sport unites all South Africans', *The Observer*, Sunday 4 February: p. 19.

Chapter 8

THE LEGAL REGULATION
OF FOOTBALL AND CRICKET:
'ENGLAND'S DREAMING'

Steve Greenfield and Guy Osborn

University of Westminster

Introduction

British football's reinvention in the 1990s has been startling. The report which followed the Hillsborough disaster in 1989 (Taylor, 1990) surveyed not only the blighted history of 'the national game' but more importantly what steps needed to be taken to restore its ailing health. One of the most obvious changes has been to the physical environment in which football at the highest professional level is played. The need to radically alter this aspect has led to a number of clubs, such as Middlesborough, Millwall, Northampton Town and Walsall, relocating to new stadia away from their traditional homes[1]. The move of Sunderland Football Club had long been forecast, but the mooted plans to resettle by 'neighbours' Newcastle United is perhaps more surprising given that St James Park has only recently been fully completed at a cost since Taylor of £23.5m (Inglis, 1996). Clubs remaining at their existing sites have been forced into a major update of facilities, removing terraces and building new all-seater 'stands'. This in itself has caused disquiet amongst some fan groups which has included demonstrations about such changes, although the developments have found approval in many quarters. Inglis notes for example the following incident on the day that the impressive North Bank at Arsenal's Highbury Stadium opened[2]:

> ...tattooed and apparently menacing, the fan told Dein [Arsenal vice-chairman] in no uncertain manner that he had been one of the 5,000 who protested on the final day of the North Bank. He then hugged Dein and declared, "But if I have to sit down, then this stand is the business. It's the dog's bollocks!". (1996: p. 29)

193

Changes have not been confined to purely the geographical and physical; football has witnessed alteration to the economic and legal status of some of the clubs. As the stadia have developed so has the body corporate; this has largely manifested itself in a switch from private finance towards the model of the Public Limited Company. The two moves are inextricably linked: the money for ground improvements needs to be raised and the club is an asset that can be floated to obtain the necessary capital. It seems likely that as clubs require greater income this trend will continue[3].

Whilst football has been apparently successful in adapting to such external pressures, cricket has also had to consider a changing geographical and economic landscape. At the highest level the game has been suffering a crisis induced by the continual failings of the national side; the most recent response to which has been the formation of a single controlling body, the English Cricket Board. As with the formation of the Premier League by the Football Association, it has been persuasively argued that the primary need is to resurrect the position of the national side even if this requires a radical restructuring of the professional game[4]. Geographical issues are also of great significance within cricket. Recently, a dispute between a homeowner and his neighbouring cricket club found itself reported in the broadsheets as a debate about private and public rights was played out through the courts. The upshot of a victory for the aggrieved home owner would have seen the club having to relocate to a new site in a completely different part of the village.

Indeed fear of change, of discontinuity, the unknown, 'the other', are central to many of the doubts and fears that are expressed when a place of often great romantic and nostalgic importance is threatened with closure, demolition, or the effects of undue legal regulation. The issue of sporting 'topophilia' (and the related issue of topophobia) is admirably and exhaustively tackled by Bale (1991, 1993, 1994) and we do not intend for the purposes of this chapter to retread ground that Bale has ploughed so thoroughly to show that sporting grounds are capable of becoming imbued with a sense of place rather than merely 'space'[5]. Our analysis will consider how the law has been utilised within the spheres of football and cricket and the effects that this operation of law has had upon the consumption of these sports.

There are two distinct parts to the question of legal intervention. Firstly, there may be external regulation through Government action or the (re)application of existing legal principles to the sport. This largely addresses the external construction of sport, how and where it is played and who 'consumes' it. Within football the primary issues, in this sphere, are the changing physical dimensions of the grounds inspired by the Taylor Report, the increased control of spectator behaviour and the increasing criminalisation of events on and just off (as in the Cantona incident) the field. In cricket the major issue has been attempts to regulate the very existence of the village green as a site for the game through applying the civil law of nuisance and negligence, although as we have explored elsewhere, recent criminal legislation may also have implications for cricket supporters (Greenfield and Osborn, 1997).

Secondly, law may become involved to regulate the internal relationships within the sports themselves. This alteration of the terms and conditions under which participants play will inevitably effect the external construction of the game; for example, football's internal revolution has also affected the spectacle through the quality of overseas players that have been drawn into the English game. In football the two key areas are the changing legal and economic structures (the shift from private to public) and the increasing freedom for players to avoid the stricture of a previously harsh contractual regime, coupled with massive increases in television income. This issue, of free(er) movement, appeared at a European level through the Jean-Marc Bosman case, the ramifications of which for the English game are still not clear. Cricket has also had to face up to this changing contractual landscape in the form of 'Packerisation' in the late 1970s (Greenfield and Osborn, 1996a) and recent successful attempts by players such as Martin Speight to move more freely between County Clubs. The whole question of a transfer market within professional cricket is a subject that has yet to be satisfactorily resolved.

In terms of ownership, football clubs have historically been dominated by wealthy families often with local business connections. Whilst costs remained relatively low this was an appropriate economic model of club ownership that could deliver or at least maintain the institution itself. Taylor's recommendations on the construction of stadia had enormous cost implications and different models of economic organisation have now emerged partially in response to this. Premier League football clubs are now the domain of the very wealthy or an entirely different corporate beast: the Public Limited Company. Fans fear that as the primary loyalty is now to shareholders, priorities may change. An alternative view of the changing corporate construction of football is that it can allow fans to purchase an interest in the club itself, although this is largely irrelevant when compared to the power of professional investors. Share-holding fans can however attend the relevant Annual General Meeting, ask awkward questions and highlight the problems that they have experienced. The clear perspective from the boardroom[6] is that the 'Company' needs an attractive (in all ways) and successful football side to act as the focus for other parts of the enterprise. In short, Ryan Giggs' bedspreads sell if the football side are performing on the pitch and in the home, via satellite. Accompanying this change has been a desire to sell a suitable 'family based' product which doesn't offend and this in turn may have an effect upon traditional notions of fandom and identity:

> Old Trafford is being Americanised, swabbed with the antiseptic of family values, deproletarianised, stuffed with the slick, plastic fast food of the stadium rock gig ... replace Fred the Red with Ronald and rename it all Old McTrafford. You can stop this by standing up, shouting fuck a lot and singing your hearts out for the lads forever! (Kurt, 1994: p. 112-13)

Within cricket too, some of the traditional aspects of supporters' behaviour and what might be termed 'cricket culture' have been affected. At some grounds fans have been prohibited from bringing musical instruments and restrictions have been placed upon alcohol consumption. The method of ticket allocation has also made it more difficult for groups of fans to gather together. Parts of this approach have mirrored moves in football which have linked unruly behaviour to excessive drinking and sought to tightly control ticket sales. This chapter explores the implications for supporters that increasing legal regulation has and argues that such interventions may have profound effects upon identity and future practice of fandom.

The external regulation of sporting space (i)—Football

An interesting perspective on the changing nature of football consumption, and the evolution of the football stadium itself, can be found in the four stage model that excavates the shift from folk-football to football's increasingly commodified state (Bale, 1993). Bale makes the point that initially the places upon which football was played were plains or fields and that there was no sense of finite fixed territory on which the game was played. Indeed the 'game' was remarkable for its fluidity and permeability with the line between spectator and player blurred[7]. However, during the rise of capitalism in the nineteenth century there was a marked move towards territoriality exacerbated by a need for a standardisation of footballing rules as inter-regional games began to become more prevalent:

> There was a time for work and a time for play; there were also to be specific places where various activities, previously found in streets and commons, could now be undertaken in the 'carceral city'. (Bale, 1993: p. 15)

Football's trajectory was firmly set by the formation of the Football Association and later by the formal demarcation between players and spectators made in 1882 with the introduction of the touchline. With the separation thus made, the move towards football as spectacle was firmly entrenched with the concomitant opportunity for selling the game. Perhaps the then most famous blurring of the lines of demarcation between players and spectators occurred at the 'White Horse' FA Cup Final at Wembley in 1923. Much in the way that Hillsborough provided the impetus for the Taylor Report over sixty years later, the events of this match provided the catalyst for a review of crowd control and safety in the form of the Shortt Report (1924). So many people attended the game that the police were forced to try to clear the pitch as many fans were forced to seek sanctuary on the pitch itself, the bifurcation of players and spectators became less marked once more:

> Of course, touch lines were the human one. The ball bounced off them and went on. If it went over the top it was a throw in, but otherwise, the referee got the game through. (Harry Beattie in Taylor and Ward, 1995: p. 22)

> Even corners, when taken, had to be accommodated by forming a small corridor for the kicker to take a run outside the pitch in order to swing the ball inwards. (Dr Sydney Woodhouse in Taylor and Ward, 1995: p. 22)

Shortt perceived these large crowds to be a problem, and one that was made worse by the fact that especially at games of this nature supporters were not in their natural habitat. Further to this football was in the most serious position due to the passionate nature of the game itself and to the problems inherent in allowing a great number of people to congregate quickly in a confined space and to be dispersed even quicker (Shortt, 1924, Para 2a)[8]. The construction of the ground, and in particular the future construction, was deemed to be crucial, and the Committee put forward a number of proposals based on the overriding principle of public safety.

Since Shortt, there has been a depressing line of official reports that have considered football regulation — often in the wake of sporting disasters[9]. However, the crucial phase for the contemporary organisation and administration of professional football took place in the 1980s with a series of disasters that culminated with the tragedy at the FA Cup Semi Final match at Hillsborough on 15 April 1989 where 96 fans were crushed to death.

These tragic events were the very public (the subject of widespread, often live television coverage) manifestation of the deep problems within the game. Throughout the 1980s hooliganism, whether following local sides or the national team abroad, had become a political embarrassment. The disturbance at Luton Town caused by Millwall supporters brought direct interference from the Prime Minister through the Department of the Environment. In the first Chapter of his report on Hillsborough, Lord Justice Taylor outlined the problems facing football as he saw them:

> Football is our national game. We gave it to the world. But its image in our country has been much tarnished. In my Interim Report I concentrated on overcrowding because it was the cause of the Hillsborough disaster. But wider and deeper enquiry shows that overcrowding is only one feature amongst a number causing danger or marring football as a spectator sport. The picture revealed is of a general malaise or blight over the game due to a number of factors. Principally these are: old grounds, poor facilities, hooliganism, excessive drinking and poor leadership. Crowd safety and crowd behaviour with which I am concerned are closely related to the quality of the accommodation and facilities offered and to the standards which are encouraged and enforced. [Para 26, p. 5]

Legislation was the tool used by the Government to tackle these issues both before and after Hillsborough — a prominent feature of this legislative reaction to the various incidents was the undue haste with which the Bills were drafted and presented to Parliament for approval. Given the parliamentary majority enjoyed by the Government approval was guaranteed and football is not the only example of a panic law solution to a perceived problem during this period. There are pieces of both, football specific and other (football affecting) legislation to be considered.

The Sporting Events (Control of Alcohol etc.) Act 1985

> There is widespread agreement that alcohol is a major contributory factor in violent and disorderly behaviour in football grounds and it is this aspect of the problem that the Bill deals with. [Hansard, 3 July 1985, Col. 333]

The introduction of this piece of legislation preempted even Popplewell's Interim Report; as Popplewell (1986) pointed out, there wasn't even any drink available to the general public at the Birmingham ground for the Leeds game. Similarly at Kenilworth Road (Luton's ground), the scene of the disorder in March, alcohol had not generally been available since 1979. The Act sought to prohibit the supply and consumption of alcohol in a number of areas. For fans it creates specific offences relating to travel to games, entry and drinking within the ground. For example simple possession of alcohol inside the ground at a point where the pitch may be viewed or at the point of entry to the ground is an offence carrying a term of imprisonment of up to three months on conviction. It also has serious implications for the licensing for the consumption of alcohol by the clubs. It was subject to amendment by the *Public Order Act 1986* which sought to address the point raised by Popplewell (1986); that the provisions of the Act should be reviewed with respect to executive boxes. He did point out that there was some considerable disagreement as to whether a total alcohol ban was a positive measure. Not only was there the issue of those supporters in private boxes, but more importantly the problem that fans may congregate in local public houses until the last possible minute — not only causing congestion when they arrive at the ground but also having consumed more alcohol than they would have done inside the ground.

The Football Spectators Act 1989

The Football Spectators Act 1989 (FSA) straddled the two influential reports of Popplewell and Taylor (1986) and sought to tackle the problem of hooliganism. The decision to proceed with the legislation whilst awaiting the outcome of the Hillsborough inquiry itself caused considerable consternation.

> To seek to progress this Bill in the midst of such awful, horrific and unbearable tragedy for the bereaved, the injured, the emotionally damaged, the clubs, the players and the cities of Liverpool and Sheffield seems to me to be an act of unspeakable obscenity. [Lord Graham, Hansard (HL) 16 June 1989, Col. 1647]

The Act was duly passed despite unease on the opposition benches and amongst some Tory members. It contains not only the regime of the licensing of grounds but also the issue of a national membership scheme. However following Taylor's criticisms the provisions relating to the membership scheme have never been enacted:

> ...I have grave doubts about the feasibility of the national membership scheme and serious misgivings about its likely impact on safety. I also have grave doubts about the chances of its achieving its purposes and are very anxious about its potential impact on police commitments and control of spectators. For these reasons, I cannot support the implementation of Part I of the Act. [1990: para 424, p. 75]

Since the failure of this aspect of the *Football Spectators Act 1989* there have followed a number of provisions that have a fundamental effect upon how football is consumed; most notably the *Football (Offences) Act 1991* and the *Criminal Justice and Public Order Act 1994*.

The Football (Offences) Act 1991

The *Football (Offences) Act 1991* (FOA) has three main objectives; to outlaw racist chanting, prohibit incursion onto the pitch and proscribe missile throwing. A crucial aspect of the Act is that it is football *specific* and adds weight to the view that football truly was a folk devil worthy of 'personal' policing. The Act was based firmly upon the recommendations of Taylor (1990). Section 2 prohibits the throwing of missiles and Section 4 makes it an offence to invade the playing area without lawful authority or excuse; both of these could theoretically have been covered by existing criminal and common law provisions but it was felt necessary to enact legislation to cover their occurrence *at football games*. It is however Section 3 that has been subject to most critical debate (Greenfield and Osborn, 1996d) due to fundamental flaws in both drafting and policing that hamper its operation. Whilst the actual provisions of the Act are broadly designed to prevent anti-social behaviour or public disorder, Section 4 of the Act makes it clear that the football pitch is a private place and not within the supporters' domain. In addition, whilst few would argue with the rationale for a section on racist chanting (although many would take issue with its effectiveness), chanting and singing are, or at least have been, an integral part of supporting and fandom. New regulations under the *Criminal Justice Act 1994.* may effect this traditional part of the game.

The Criminal Justice and Public Order Act 1994

Whilst the *Criminal Justice and Public Order Act 1994* (CJA) is not a piece of purely football specific legislation in the manner of FOA 1991 and FSA 1989, there are a number of provisions contained within the legislation that have potential implications for football fans. These have been outlined in detail elsewhere (Greenfield and Osborn, 1996c) but certain sections are worthy of exploration in terms of the effects that they may have on the issue of identity. There is however one section of the CJA that does at present only apply to football fans: the provisions regarding ticket touting contained in Section 166. The CJA 1994 selected football as the one area in which it should be a criminal offence to offer a ticket for resale if not authorised to do so. The impetus for the measure was essentially to prevent fans from different clubs being able to circumvent strict ticket segregation rather than any attack on the principle of 'ticket touting'. However in practice this measure has had a harsh effect upon fans with spare tickets who have sought to resell them even to supporters from the same club.

There is a further relevant public order provision within the CJA (S154) which creates a new S4A of the *Public Order Act 1986*. The original provisions were considered by Taylor (1990) who considered that they were insufficient to deal with the problems that he had identified — hence the three specific offences contained in the *Football (Offences) Act 1991*. Popplewell (1986) had earlier taken a view that one specific offence of disorderly conduct at a sports ground should be considered. This new provision is widely drawn and may cover any kind of threatening or disorderly behaviour or abusive or threatening written words:

> A person is guilty of an offence if, with intent to cause a person harassment, alarm or distress, he —
> (a) uses threatening, abusive or insulting words or behaviour, or disorderly behaviour, or
> (b) displays any writing, sign or other visible representation which is threatening, abusive or insulting
> thereby causing that or another person harassment, alarm or distress.

It might also refer to a single incident as the clause does not specify repetitive behaviour. As Turner has pointed out, commenting on the Taylor recommendations and a mooted ban on swearing (that could conceivably now be covered by the CJA amendment):

> I would not argue with the Taylor Report's recommendation that racist chanting ought to be outlawed as it raises tensions and makes grounds unfriendly places. However, the proposed ban on swearing smacks of authoritarianism and the inevitable conclusion of this would be to ban chanting completely (there are a few cases of this happening already, with the police arresting people just for chanting the club's name). No chanting would mean that a part of the traditional atmosphere of the terraces would be lost. Of course, the language is coarse, soccer fans are ordinary people who, when excited, are bound to come out with a few choice expletives. (Turner, 1995: p. 30)

The shift towards all-seater stadia has a significant effect for vocal supporters; it is now far more difficult, because a ticket now refers to a specific numbered seat, to congregate in numbers in a part of the ground, traditionally the home end behind one of the goals. Indeed the concomitant loss of atmosphere that has been noted at many grounds has led to calls for action to recreate an 'authentic' football atmosphere, not least for the benefit of the broadcasters who sell football on the basis of its spectacle. This could conceivably lead to a lowering of prices for unpopular games as the spectacle requires a reasonably sized crowd to avoid the barren scenes created by a lack of supporters. The change in atmosphere at Highbury has caused one marketing manager to dub it 'Highbury the Library' and has proved a contentious enough issue for the club to create a 'singing section' in the previously vociferous North Bank[10]. The creation of a 'singing section' has been seen in some quarters as an admission of defeat (Inglis, 1996); that football has changed forever and that whilst many of the developments are to be applauded, not all change has been positive in nature.

Since the first piece of legislation in 1985, football supporters have found themselves the subject of numerous legislative provisions that have sought to regulate their participation and behaviour. A long-standing cultural tradition has been altered in numerous ways beyond mere attendance at the ground. The whole process from ticket purchase through socialising before and during the game to conduct inside the ground has irrevocably changed. It should be stressed that some of these provisions have had a more significant effect on the highest level of the professional game though the specific criminal offences apply more widely. It is apparent that some modifications may be necessary: the 1985 Act was quickly subject to amendment to rectify some of its faults, though it is unlikely that the major legislative planks will be altered.

The external regulation of sporting space (ii)—Cricket

The new, the foreign, the materialistic, all these nefarious elements threaten truth and community. They threaten the community like a virus for like a virus they are foreign. Unlike even a virus, however, the newcomer is not *natural* — he threatens cricket. (Fraser, 1993: p. 22)

Cricket has certainly not been regulated to the same degree as football. Indeed, where law has intervened within the sphere of (certainly grassroots) cricket, its treatment has tended to be benevolent — in particular the game has fostered judicial support in a number of cases that have dealt with the relationship between the village team (and by implication the village culture) and the outsider, the threat to village life[11]. In *Bolton v Stone* [1951], the first of these cases to come before the courts, cricket had been played on the ground since 1864, whilst the house that formed the focus for the case was constructed in 1910. Here a young lady was struck by a cricket ball whilst standing in the road outside her house. An action was brought against the club for the damage she had suffered using the tort of negligence. However, Stone had little luck in her claim. Her argument that the pitch should have been moved so as to be equidistant between north and south boundaries found little support. Lord Oaksey, having noted that cricket had been played on the ground for ninety years with little complaint, was firmly of the view that no further precautions ought to have been taken to protect Mrs Stone notwithstanding the fact that she was actually hit by the cricket ball:

> The ordinarily prudent owner of a dog does not keep his dog always on a lead on a country highway for fear it may cause injury to a passing motor cyclist, nor does the ordinarily prudent pedestrian avoid the use of the highway for fear of skidding motor cars. [*Bolton*, p. 1084]

The risk of injury was held by the House of Lords to be negligible, and in legal terms the club had not breached any duty of care that was owed to members of the public and adjoining householders. Underscoring the case is the perception that cricket is essentially *a good thing*, and that a decision against the club might be detrimental to both the playing of cricket and the life of the village itself indeed judicial approaches have been to support the playing of cricket wherever possible. Consider the following comments by Lord Denning from a further 'cricket case':

In summer time village cricket is the delight of everyone. Nearly every village has its own cricket field where the young men play and the old men watch. In the village of Lintz in County Durham they have their own ground, where they have played these last 70 years. They tend it well. The wicket area is well rolled and mown. The outfield is kept short. It has a good club-house for the players and seats for the onlookers. The village team play there on Saturdays and Sundays. They belong to a league, competing with the neighbouring villages. On other evenings after work they practice while the light lasts. Yet now after these 70 years a judge of the High Court has ordered them that they must not play there any more. He has issued an injunction to stop them. He has done it at the instance of a newcomer who is no lover of cricket. This newcomer has built, or has had built for him, a house on the edge of the cricket ground which four years ago was a field where cattle grazed. The animals did not mind the cricket. But now this adjoining field has been turned into a housing estate. The newcomer bought one of the houses on the edge of the cricket ground. No doubt the open space was a selling point. Now he complains that, when a batsman hits a six, the ball has been known to land in his garden or on or near his house. His wife has got so upset about it that they always go out at weekends. They do not go into the garden when cricket is being played. They say that this is intolerable. So they asked the judge to stop the cricket being played. And the judge, much against his will, has felt that he must order the cricket to be stopped; with the consequences, I suppose, that the Lintz Cricket Club will disappear. The cricket ground will be turned to some other use. I expect for more houses or a factory. The young men will turn to other things instead of cricket. The whole village will be much the poorer. And all this because of a newcomer who has just bought a house there next to the cricket ground. [*Miller v Jackson* (1977), pp. 340–341]

Explicit within Denning's analysis is that it is the 'outsider', the newcomer, the threat to village life who is in fact the most culpable party. Indeed, were he to succeed in his case the life of the village would be far poorer with the spectre of the once green pastoral site becoming a bleak factory belching smoke into the country air whilst the young men who once would have spent an evening at net practice would turn instead to the pub or some less wholesome pursuit. Indeed as we have previously argued, "… whilst the dispute in *Miller* masqueraded as a legal dispute it was in fact a cultural and social dispute that had as its nexus a public/private dichotomy — when should the private interest (of the house owner) outweigh the public interest of society (the village)?" (Greenfield and Osborn, 1996b: p. 278)[12]. Cumming-Bruce LJ in *Miller* felt that such a task involved balancing conflicting interests:

> ... the right of the plaintiffs to have quiet enjoyment of their house and garden without exposure to cricket balls occasionally falling like thunderbolts from the heavens, and the opportunity of the inhabitants of the village in which they live to continue to enjoy the manly sport which constitutes the summer recreation for adults and young persons, including one would hope and expect, the plaintiffs' son. *[Miller, p. 350]*

Remarkably, not only is the Judge here noting that cricket is a character building and in his words a manly sport, but also that although the plaintiff is bringing an action against the Club, he would expect his son to play for them!

The judiciary do indeed appear keen to allow cricket to flourish — in *Miller* Lord Denning even questions the soundness of the relevant planning authority's decision to allow the builders to erect houses so near to the cricket ground feeling that "[t]he houses ought to have been sited so as not to interfere with the cricket" *[Miller: p. 341]*. Most recently this public/private dispute has arisen in *Lacey v Parker and Bingle* [1994]. The case once again concerned similar issues — attempting to balance the rights of homeowners with the rights of a cricket club. Again, the judge placed his analysis firmly within the context that cricket should be preserved and continued if at all possible. In this case the land had been transferred from a group of Quakers who bought 102 acres of land in 1920 to Jordans Village Ltd who issued a statement in 1921 that "The layout provides for a village green of three acres which will be laid out for sports and pastimes of various kinds" *[Lacey: p. 2]*. At the time of the case, cricket had been played in the village for well over 60 years. When 'the newcomer' came to buy the house the Judge posited that "...they must have realised that the village green was the village cricket ground and that cricket balls would from time to time be hit into their front garden and occasionally against the house itself. If they did not realise that, in my judgement they certainly should have done" *[Lacey, p. 7]*. In addition the Judge was at pains to outline how the club and its members had acted incredibly reasonably and responsibly; having instructed their team and visitors to try to not play shots in the direction of the house, tried to place fielders to stop such shots and even introduced a local rule that clean hits over that portion of the boundary would count as four runs rather than six. Further to this they were even prepared to extend such a rule so as to denote that the batsman would be out if he hit the ball into the offending area. A petition supporting the club was circulated that garnered over 200 signatures. One of the signatories also gave evidence to the effect that "I regard any trivial inconvenience of these occurrences as more than compensated by the amenity afforded to players and spectators …to participate in a traditional English village sport" [*Lacey*: p. 32], a view reiterated by the judge who felt that the granting of an injunction in this case would be "…highly damaging, not only to the members of the Cricket club, but to the interests of the village as a whole" [*Lacey*, p. 38].

As with the playing restrictions employed by some amateur leagues (Greenfield and Osborn, 1996b) the undercurrent of the arguments in this trilogy of cricket cases is firmly on inclusion — inclusion within village life and inclusion within society itself. Persons not operating within such parameters were dangerous, threatening or, in Fraser's words, 'Other'. Contemporaneously to these moves to protect village cricket and cricketers, the professional game is subject to considerable turmoil and the external regulation of supporters is starting to resemble that of football. Efforts by the cricketing authorities to restrict the behaviour of supporters have a parallel with the legislative control exerted over football fans. An interesting phenomena has been the rise of the 'barmy army', a very vocal group of younger cricket fans who have followed England on their recent winter tours. Their presence has not always been welcomed by the more conservative elements within the game and have heightened the argument that cricket crowds are becoming increasingly 'footballised'.

Conclusion

The use of legal regulation in these areas reveals some interesting dichotomies in how the two sports are perceived and dealt with. Football, as noted above, has long been subject to regulation in many forms and certainly in the 1970s and 1980s, its intersection with hooliganism made it easy to create an aura of moral panic; the legal reaction to which has been termed by Redhead (1995) as 'panic law'. Cricket has been perceived in a different way and dealt with in a much more supportive way in terms of legal regulation. The differing approaches could perhaps historically have been justified on a crude determinist class basis model of response. Certainly cricket's own internal battle for a long time rested on the division in so far as it manifested itself in the gentleman and player categorisation (Greenfield and Osborn, 1996a).

What has become apparent is that it is more difficult to delineate between elements of football and cricket spectating as football becomes more embourgeoisified and cricket begins to exhibit some of the characteristics more usually associated with football. Indeed, for many years much was made of the issue of MCC membership and issues of inclusion and exclusion in relation to its spiritual heart: The Long Room at Lords. Currently British football seems to be moving towards exclusiveness, setting up tiers of supporters in executive boxes with their own dress codes and etiquette, and discriminating against supporters who don't posses a season ticket or credit card. In contrast, cricket appears to be taking a more inclusionary line, allowing women for the first time to use some of the facilities previously open only to men and developing responses that will allow greater access to a number of cricket matches. It is clear that law has in the past been used as a tool to *include* in terms of cricket and *exclude* (or highly regulate inclusion) in terms of football. These divisions are no longer so easy to make, given the changing natures of both sports. Nevertheless the importance of law in terms of allowing or confronting fandom and identity is not to be disregarded.

Notes

1   The end of the 1996/7 Football season saw a number of clubs leaving grounds with which they have had a long-standing association such as Bolton Wanderers (Burnden Park 1895), Stoke City (Victoria Ground 1878), Brighton and Hove Albion (Goldstone Ground 1902).

2   Interestingly, Arsenal FC is also considering moving because of the difficulty in developing their Highbury ground which is within a built up residential area. It would offer the club the chance to return to its original 'home' Woolwich, which had formed part of the name and from where it had moved in 1913.

3   English Premier League clubs that have already been floated include Manchester United, Newcastle United and Tottenham Hotspur. It has however not been confined to the top flight, with Preston North End and Millwall also listed though the latter has been experiencing considerable financial problems.

4   Since 1968 professional cricket had been the responsibility of the Test and County Cricket Board whilst the recreational game was under the auspices of the National Cricket Association — although both were theoretically under the overall direction of the Cricket Council. The English Cricket Board which came into force on January 1, 1997 has already hinted that a major change to County Cricket may be required.

5   Bale (1991) shows that football grounds may exhibit some or all of the following characteristics: a) The Stadium as sacred place; b) The Stadium as scenic place; c) The Stadium as home; d) The Stadium as tourist place; e) Forum of place pride/local patriotism.

6   Interview with Martin Edwards, Chief Executive, Manchester United Football Club.

7   Eric Cantona's infamous attempt to restore this close relationship with Mr Matthew Simmons at Selhurst Park has perhaps both historical and political justification.

8   Interestingly, in a prescient and pragmatic response to the suggestion that many of the problems could be ameliorated by selling or booking tickets beforehand, the Committee felt "that any such arrangement would be in itself impracticable and open to objection on the ground that it would provide undue opportunities for profiteering in tickets…" (Shortt, 1924, Para 29).

9   The Moelwyn Hughes Report (1946) followed 33 deaths at Bolton Wanderers' ground; the Chester Report (1966) on the 'State of Association Football'; the Harrington Report (1968); the Lang Report (1969); the Wheatley Report (1972) followed 66 deaths at Ibrox; the McElhone Report (1977); the Popplewell Report(s) (1985, 1986) followed the Bradford fire and the riot at Birmingham and extended to include the events at Heysel; and the Taylor Report(s) (1989, 1990).

10   Thanks to John Williams for passing on this anecdote.

11   It was clear in the 'Packer' case *Greig v Insole* [1978] that the judge, despite his finding for the plaintiffs, had some sympathy for the cricket authorities.

12   A traditional legal analysis (which we use here) would consider the landowner had the private right to enjoy his property whilst the public interest element lay with the club. This approach is clearly adopted by Denning in *Miller v Jackson* [1977]. It is however to adopt a different reading with a closed parochial cricket club seeking to defend a private historical right against a public right to enjoy privacy.

References

Bale, J. (1991) 'Playing at home: British football and a sense of place', in John Williams and Stephen Wagg (eds) *British football and social change: Getting into Europe*. Leicester: Leicester University Press, pp. 130–144.

———(1993) *Sport, space and the city*. London: Routledge.

————(1994) *Landscapes of modern sport*. Leicester: Leicester University Press.

Fraser, D. (1993) *Cricket and the law*. Sydney: Institute of Criminology, University of Sydney.

Greenfield, S. and Osborn, G. (1996a) 'Culture, change, commodity and crisis: Cricket's timeless Test', *International Journal of the Sociology of Law*, Vol. 24, No. 2: pp. 189–209.

————(1996b) 'Oh to be in England? Mythology and identity in English cricket', *Social Identities, Journal for the Study of Race, Nation and Culture*, Vol. 2, No. 2: pp. 271-291.

————(1996c) 'After the Act? The reconstruction and regulation of football fandom', *Journal of Civil Liberties*, Vol. 1: pp. 7-28.

————(1996d) 'When the whites go marching in? Racism and resistance in English football', *Marquette Sports Law Journal*, Vol. 6, No. 2: pp. 315-335.

————(1997) 'Enough is enough. Race, cricket and protest in the UK', *Sociological Focus*, forthcoming.

Inglis, S. (1996) *Football grounds of Britain*. London: Collins Willow.

Kurt, R. (1994) *United we stood*. Cheshire: Sigma Leisure.

Popplewell (1985): *Committee of Inquiry into Crowd Safety and Control at Sports Grounds. Interim Report*, Cmnd. 9585

————(1986) *Committee of Inquiry into Crowd Safety and Control at Sports Grounds. Final Report*, Cmnd. 9710.

Redhead, S. (1995) *Unpopular cultures: The birth of law and popular culture*. Manchester: Manchester University Press.

Shortt (1924) *Report of the Departmental Committee on Crowds*, Cmd 2088.

Taylor (1990) *The Hillsborough Stadium Disaster, Final Report*, Cmnd. 962.

Taylor, R. and Ward, A. (1995) *Kicking and screaming*. Robson Books: London.

Turner, R (1995) *In your blood: Football culture in the late 1980s and early 1990s*. London: Working Press.

Cases

Bolton v Stone [1951] 1 All ER 1078.

Greig v Insole [1978] 3 All ER 449.

Miller v Jackson [1977] 3 All ER 338.

Lacey v Parker and Bingle [1994] Slough County Court, 12 May.

Chapter 9

THE HISTORICAL DEVELOPMENT OF RUGBY IN SOUTH-EAST FRANCE: EN MARGE de l'OVALIE?

Philip Dine

Loughborough University

Introduction

Rugby, which combines the popular features of the ball-game and a battle involving the body itself and allowing a — partially regulated — expression of physical violence and an immediate use of 'natural' physical qualities (strength, speed, etc.), has affinities with the most typically popular dispositions, the cult of manliness and the taste for a fight, toughness in 'contact' and resistance to tiredness and pain, and a sense of solidarity ('the mates') and revelry ('the third half') and so forth. This does not prevent members of the dominant fractions of the dominant class (or some intellectuals, who consciously or unconsciously express their values) from making an aesthetico-ethical investment in the game and even sometimes playing it. The pursuit of toughness and the cult of male values, sometimes mingled with an aestheticism of violence and man-to-man combat, bring the deep dispositions of first-degree practitioners to the level of discourse. The latter, being little inclined to verbalize and theorize, find themselves relegated by the managerial discourse (that of trainers, team managers and some journalists) to the rôle of docile, submissive, brute force ('gentle giant', etc.), working-class strength in its approved form (self-sacrifice, 'team spirit' and so forth). But the aristocratic reinterpretation which traditionally hinged on the 'heroic' virtues associated with the three-quarter game encounters its limits in the reality of modern rugby, which, under the combined effects of modernized tactics and training, a change in the social recruitment of the players and a wider audience, gives priority to the 'forward game', which is increasingly discussed in metaphors of the meanest industrial labour ('attacking the coal-face') or trench warfare (the infantryman who 'dutifully' runs headlong into enemy fire). (Bourdieu, 1984: p. 213)

We might wish to take issue with various aspects of Pierre Bourdieu's characterization of the habitus of French rugby football, that is to say its existence as a structured and structuring system of practices and values. We could, for instance, highlight its reductive aspects as part of a broader theoretical critique of Bourdieu's 'barbaric' conception of popular culture. More specifically, we might draw attention to the rather simplistic equation of forwards with popular virtues and three-quarters with aristocratic values. Alternatively, on a technical level, we could draw attention to what is now clearly an outdated analysis of modern rugby in terms of a seemingly inevitable movement towards ever greater emphasis on forward power at the expense of artistry among the backs. (Although, in fairness, such a view of French rugby was understandable when Bourdieu wrote in 1979, given the near total dominance of the domestic game by the AS Béziers club playing precisely along these lines.)

However, there is much in Bourdieu's analysis to recommend it to the foreign observer of French sport, including the very fact of its being made by such a distinguished social analyst. Indeed, as a major site for the construction of masculine, class-based, regional, and national identities, French rugby football has attracted the attention of a wide range of academic commentators: social historians; sociologists, from sports specialists like Christian Pociello (1983) to Bourdieu, that most eminent of *généralistes*; political scientists; ethnographers and anthropologists; and even a distinguished philosopher, in the case of Raymond Abellio (1983). These and other such contributors to the debate have together demonstrated this particular sport's value as a mirror of major structural changes — such as industrialization and urbanization; the commodification and privatization of leisure; the mediatization and globalization of economic and cultural exchanges — and its consequent attraction for the student of French social development over the last century and a quarter. It is as a modest contribution to this continuing discussion of historical transformations in patterns of work and leisure, and of the evolution in mentalities which such changes imply, that the present chapter is conceived. In what follows, therefore, I shall be endeavouring to cast light on French rugby's existence as a socio-economic, political, and cultural nexus; and thereby to hint at the complex reality and even more complex symbolism of this particular sport in contemporary French society.

The 'mystery' of French rugby

Both the historical expansion and the geographical implantation of French rugby football present difficulties for the foreign observer. Indeed, so unusual is the pattern of the game's development since its introduction into France in the later 19th century that it genuinely retains an element of mystery. Why, after all, should rugby ever have been adopted as a national game in France, Britain's foremost imperial rival, when its expansion elsewhere has largely been limited to the British Isles and the major centres for British colonial emigration (notably Australia, New Zealand, and South Africa, the sport's contemporary international power-base)? Why should rugby have become durably established as a popular rather than a socially exclusive sport in France? Why should French rugby have become both so attractive to spectators at home and abroad (the much lauded *rugby-champagne*) and so regularly brutal (the less easily avowed *jeu dur*)? Why should this sport have flourished not, as did so many other sporting imports, in the industrial population centres of the north and east, but rather in the cities, towns, and, especially, villages of the still predominantly rural South-West? Why, above all, should rugby have been elevated to a position of central significance in the construction and reconstruction of local and regional identities throughout its heartland in the *Midi*?

A variety of more or less plausible solutions have been suggested to the enigma of French rugby's highly specific geographical implantation and local cultural assimilation. These include pseudo-anthropological explanations based on preferred models of Basque, Catalan, Gascon, and/or Occitan ethnicity. They also take in political accounts which look to the relative weakness of the (football-promoting) Catholic Church in the radical, republican, and, indeed, actively anticlerical South-West. There are even the grand historical syntheses, which may include everything from the massacres of the Cathars in the 13th century to the phylloxera epidemics in the vineyards of the Languedoc of the 19th century in a list of *méridional* grievances against the rest of France, and especially Paris, and for which the region's success on the rugby field is held to be a symbolic, belated, and partial compensation. To which must be added, of course, such consciously theorized explanations as that put forward by sociologists like Pierre Bourdieu, and which, as we noted above, turn on a belief in this particular sport's peculiar appeal to traditional values of communal solidarity and collective self-defence.

The merits or otherwise of these and competing accounts of French rugby's development of a strongly regional character are beyond the scope of this chapter. However, just as it is certainly the case that French rugby has become synonymous internationally with a cavalier attitude both to regulation ('French indiscipline') and to playing styles ('French flair'), so it is beyond doubt that the game is firmly associated in French minds with the South-West, often mythified as *l'Ovalie*, the land of the oval ball. A critical observer from the South-East of the country has summed up the standard French attitude to the sport in the following terms:

> For them, rugby is something rather quaint which is inextricably mixed up with such familiar aspects of the region's local colour as its famous tourist sites and its gastronomic specialities; rugby is like the Lourdes basilica, the blue sky of Pau, *foie gras*, the volcanic mud of Dax, *cassoulet* from Toulouse, and raw ham from Bayonne, all rolled into one. (Barnoud, n.d.: p. 166; my translation.)

Although this generally unquestioned self-image of the French game does have its roots in a certain historical and sociological reality, it nevertheless remains essentially mythic. By way of a contrast, and in order to begin to draw a coherent synthesis from among the competing narrative strands — academic, journalistic, literary, testimentary, party-political — to which the history of sport, as of so much else, has given rise in contemporary France, it is useful to consider briefly the development of French rugby as a whole, and then to go on to examine the sport's evolution in a region not nowadays generally associated with rugby football: the South-East, and more specifically Lyon, France's second city, and one where rugby has been played, watched, and administered on the margins of the game's geographical and cultural heartland, or in other words *en marge de l'Ovalie*.

The myth and the reality of *l'Ovalie*

Not the least of the many paradoxes displayed by French rugby is its image overseas: a combination of an audacious style of play, habitually characterized as *le panache*, which is generally admired, and a level of violence on the field (and not infrequently off it) which is just as widely deplored. Both of these characterizing features are acknowledged by informed French commentators on the game (Augustin & Bodis, 1994; Augustin & Garrigou, 1985; Bodis, 1987;

Callède, 1987 & 1993), and have their roots in the history of this foreign game's introduction and early development in France. Virtually unknown in France before the 1880s, modern athletic sports were imported from Britain (and specifically the English public schools) by a combination of expatriate business professionals and aristocratic anglophiles as France's belated industrial revolution saw traditional, rural and Church-based, patterns of work and leisure give way to new, urban, modes of sociability, including notably participating in and spectating at sports events.

The first indigenous French sports clubs, such as the Racing Club de France and the Stade Français, were created by pupils and ex-pupils of the most prestigious Parisian *lycées*, in a conscious attempt to emulate the English public school system, with its strong emphasis on the importance of team games. Championed by Baron Pierre de Coubertin, the founder of the modern Olympics, as a means of defending both class and national interests, the new English sports, administered by Coubertin's Union des Sociétés Françaises des Sports Athlétiques (USFSA) and with rugby to the fore, were conceived as the exclusive preserve of the privileged few, who were to be guided by a spirit of élitist amateurism. The first clubs were consequently highly restrictive in their recruitment practices. These socially exclusive, and proportionately prestigious, associations were to be followed by others in the provinces as rugby and the other athletic sports spread across the country in the 1890s. The South-West was to take enthusiastically to the new sports, and particularly rugby, both through the influence of a large colony of affluent expatriate Britons, such as those engaged in the Bordeaux wine trade, and through the local *lycées*, *écoles normales*, and universities.

If Bordeaux was the centre of French rugby's expansion in the period up to World War I, the game's centre of gravity was to shift even further away from Paris in the inter-war years, as the sport took off dramatically in the far South-West, where it would variously be popularized, democratized, commercialized, and municipalized; and as such would become the focus for intense local patriotism. The dramatic increase in this theoretically amateur sport's popularity as both a participant sport and, increasingly, a paying spectacle would bring with it severe problems of administration, including particularly those raised by the related questions of professionalism and violence. So serious were these problems, in fact, that internal schism and international isolation would result in the early 1930s. The decision of twelve of the leading clubs to establish the

Union Française du Rugby Amateur (UFRA) in 1931, in pointed opposition to the laxist Fédération Française de Rugby (FFR, which had taken over the administration of French rugby from the USFSA in 1920), would prompt the British home unions, together with the dominions, to break off relations with the French. France, having started playing international matches in the first decade of the century, would therefore have no official contact with the major rugby-playing nations until after World War II, with the national side reduced to playing increasingly unattractive fixtures against the likes of Nazi Germany and Fascist Italy. The international isolation of French rugby union would in turn prompt the introduction of rugby league (which had split from rugby union as early as 1895 in Great Britain), and the new code was to flourish in several areas which had previously been strongholds of the union game until its administrative suppression by the collaborationist Vichy regime in 1941.

The 1940s (including, paradoxically, the war years themselves) would see French rugby rebuild internally, with its international golden age co-inciding, almost as if according to a Gaullist party script, with the socio-economic and political regeneration of France during *les trente glorieuses*, the thirty years of unprecedented economic expansion and social reconstruction from 1945 to 1975, and particularly after the return to power of General de Gaulle himself in 1958. As has been suggested by Augustin & Garrigou (1985: p. 338), the association in the public mind of these two faces of *la France qui gagne* [triumphant France] may well have been consciously encouraged by de Gaulle, as a famously shrewd manipulator of the mass media. His support for the national side was regularly signalled through his well publicized preparedness to go to extraordinary lengths to watch televized matches, as well as by official receptions for successful French teams. The involvement of former rugby players in his administration — most notably Jacques Chaban-Delmas, mayor of Bordeaux, hero of the Resistance, international tennis player as well as a rugby star, and future prime minister — was also of significance in this establishment of *le XV de France* as the sporting arm of de Gaulle's new Fifth Republic. The process of rugby-based national 'team-building' in a period of rapid and radical social transformation was also significantly encouraged by the development of live outside broadcasting and the advent of affordable television sets, with televised international matches bringing not only Twickenham, Murrayfield, Cardiff Arms Park, and Lansdowne Road to the French provinces for the first time, but also, in very many cases, the first glimpse of the national stadium at Colombes in Paris.

It was, moreover, a particular variety of French rugby, the *rugby-champagne* of Albaladejo, the *frères* Boniface, Gachassin, Jean Prat and the like that was now presented to the whole French nation, via the new medium, as part of its inalienable heritage. How was this possible? Particularly given French rugby's compromised political position before and during the war years and its specifically regional character hitherto? The rhetoric of the game's mediatic representation during this key period awaits detailed analysis, however even the most cursory examination of this discursive field suggests that rugby was fixed upon by a new, national, and television-based audience as a means of reconciling traditional — i.e. rural, regionally specific, and peasant-based — value systems and the post-war drive for economic growth and social regeneration. A star figure like Lucien Mias, captain of the all-conquering French side which was to become the first to defeat the Springboks in a test series in South Africa in 1958, provides a particularly striking image of rugby's symbolic reconciliation of the old and the new in a contemporary documentary film. This shows the national hero going back to his roots in Laprade-Basse in the Aude *département*, described very significantly by the narrator as "un village presque abandonné, mais qui ne veut mourir" [a virtually abandoned village, but one which is determined not to die], and specifically to the *école communale* where he was once the local schoolmaster: a particularly potent symbol of French republican virtues. Although he has now gone on to a thoroughly modern career as a general practitioner with a professional interest in sports medicine, and despite the all too apparent signs of rural decline and depopulation displayed by the village, the viewer is reassured that "rien n'a changé" [nothing has changed] (Driès, 1988). In a period when France was required to recover from the physical and psychological damage of the war years, to undergo the painful and belated decolonization of its overseas territories, to commit itself to the project of Europeanization, to experience a major flight from the land, and to come to terms with the rise of an urbanized, nationally unified, and televisually mediated culture of mass consumption, this and other such appeals to the apparent certainties of the past were hardly surprising. Rooted in the popular culture of the South-West, where it had for long been a primary repository of regional specificity, rugby was now subject to a symbolic reappropriation which saw it presented henceforth as a symbol of national continuity in the midst of often traumatic change.

Rugby in South-East France

Where, then, does the South-East fit into the broader picture? In order to understand the implications of this question, we need to make a distinction between the on-the-field performances of the leading South-Eastern clubs (as reflected by their record in the national championship), the influence of these same clubs at the national level (as suppliers of international players and federal administrators), and, most difficult to assess but perhaps most significant, the place of rugby in the popular culture of the South-East. For the post-WWI hegemony of South-Western rugby is a composite of these three elements: the domination of both the national championship and the national side by famous clubs like Toulouse (in the 1920s, the 1940s, and at the present time), Lourdes (in the 1950s and 1960s), and Béziers (in the 1970s and 1980s); the stranglehold of the South-West on the Paris-based national federation, as exemplified by the quasi-dictatorial presidency of Albert Ferrasse from his Agen powerbase from the late 1960s to the early 1990s; and the leading role of rugby, frequently in a municipalized form, in the imaginative life, and especially the collective festivities, of cities, towns, and villages from the Gironde to the Pyrenees, and from the Atlantic to the Mediterranean; a popular culture, that is to say, which brings together Basques, Catalans, Gascons, Occitans, and other ethnically or linguistically determined groups in a conscious (and not infrequently self-conscious) celebration of regional specificity.

The South-East, in comparison, is very much a poor relation, with periodic success on the field, but little representation of players and administrators at the national level, and only isolated pockets of *culture rugbystique* to compare with the game's preeminence as *the* local sport, and *the* privileged point of reference for the construction of local identities, in the South-West (this last as reflected by such standard indicators of the game's hold on the popular imagination as the number of established clubs and licensed players per *département*: Pociello, 1983; Augustin, 1987). So various South-Eastern clubs have done well in the national championship over the years, and an authentically local rugby culture may be seen to have grown up in consequence in pockets along the Rhône valley (Bourgoin, La Voulte, Romans, Valence, Vienne), on the South-East's Mediterranean littoral (Nice, Toulon), and in the Alps (Grenoble). However, the very limited federal and international influence of the South-East underlines its operation on the margins of French rugby's real heartland, the South-West. An examination of the development of rugby in the Lyon conurbation, France's second city, will help to contextualize and thus to explain this situation.

Rugby in Lyon: the early days, 1893-1914

As elsewhere, rugby in Lyon had its origins in the recreational activities of *lycéens* and expatriates: in this case the students of the *lycée* Ampère and British businessmen involved in the city's silk trade. Together they constituted the backbone of the Football Club de Lyon (FCL), the first athletic sports club to be established in the South-East, in 1893, and still in existence today as a genuine multi-sports association. However, it was as a rugby club that the FCL was to have its finest hour, being crowned French champions in 1910 and regularly playing against the top South-Western and Parisian sides over the next two decades. The FCL's great local rival, the Lyon Olympique Universitaire club (or LOU) was set up just three years later in 1896, and was to go on to become champions of France in 1932 and 1933. Indeed, it was at this time of internal schism and international isolation that the South-East was to have its strongest influence on the French national championship: RC Toulon defeated the LOU in the 1931 final; Lyon were champions for the following two seasons; and CS Vienne, just a few miles further down the Rhône, were champions in 1937, under the inspired leadership of an 'imported' international star from the 1920s, the Basque Jean Etcheberry. However, later South-Eastern successes were to be both fewer and farther between, such as Grenoble in 1954 and La Voulte in 1970.

In essence, the history of Lyon rugby in the period from the 1890s to 1914, by which time the great majority of the leading clubs had been established, mirrors that of rugby in the South-West. The early days of expatriate influence and student enthusiasm were followed by a partial democratization as the game was taken up by the lower middle classes, as often as not adopting the back room of the local café as their headquarters (Holt, 1981: pp. 71-2). Indeed, the prefectural archives regarding the establishment and dissolution of sports associations in the Rhône *département* very clearly show that the cafés, the new 'salons de la démocratie' of the Third Republic, were nearly always, and sometimes exclusively, the focus for associative activity in this intense period of (often ephemeral) sports club creation.

As a sporting spectacle, rugby did not begin to have any meaningful competition from association football in France as a whole until after World War I, and its increasing attraction in the Lyon context is revealed by the FCL's move to a purpose-built stadium in 1907, where the club began to attract large crowds for its matches against the leading teams from Paris, the South-West, and, increasingly, elsewhere in the South-East. The rise of Lyon rugby at this time was also reflected in the FCL's contribution to the first French international sides, including two members of the side which achieved France's first international success, against Scotland in 1911. One of this pair would also, incidentally, play in the 1913 version of this fixture, a humiliating defeat which gave rise to the infamous 'Affaire Baxter', as the outraged French crowd turned on the English referee, who had to be escorted from the pitch under police guard, before going on the rampage through the streets of Paris, finally dispersing only after a police cavalry charge.

The ascension of the FCL reached its zenith in 1910, with a victory in Paris over the mighty Stade Bordelais which made the Lyon club champions of France for the first and last time. However, the club's official historian, Daniel-Guy Gardian, is obliged to talk of 'les rares supporters lyonnais' who actually made the effort to witness this triumph, in marked contrast the 27,000 supporters who would see the Stade Bordelais return to Paris to lift the seventh of its pre-WWI championships just one year later. The very limited attention given to the FCL's triumph by local newspapers such as *Le Progrès* and *Le Nouvelliste* would seem to bear out this impression of a lack of local interest to compare with the already intense investment in the sport of the South-West. By the same token, the apparent lack of an official municipal reaction (such as a formal reception) is an indication of the muted response to the club's victory by the city.

Rugby in Lyon: the reflection of national pressures, 1918-1939

Sport in the dramatically changed social order of post-1918 France would be a focus for new pleasures, but also new conflicts, and rugby in Lyon would reflect these changed national preoccupations. The 1920s saw a massive expansion of the game, with a variety of associated problems. In the South-West, the game undoubtedly entered the mainstream of local culture, but in the South-East too the take-off in the number of clubs, players, and spectators was, although less dramatic, still marked. So, in the specific area covered by the Lyonnais committee, the number of clubs competing in the national championship more than doubled between 1920 and 1922 (from 22 to 51) (Bodis, 1987: p. 200).

Moreover, it was in this period that sport established a more concrete footing in local political terms, when Edouard Herriot, future President of the Republic, and mayor of Lyon, decided to create the Comité Lyonnais des Sports, whose task it was to coordinate the activities of the various regional sporting associations, to distribute a substantial municipal grant (20,000 francs) to these same clubs and committees, and to manage the municipal sports infrastructure, such as the grandiose and classically inspired Stade Municipal de Gerland (which had been built in 1916), and the later Stade Georges-Vuillermet, named after the FCL's most famous son. At this time, in fact, rugby, organized from 1920 onwards not by Coubertin's multisport USFSA but by a specific federation, the new Fédération Française de Rugby (FFR), was easily the country's most watched team sport: for instance, 10,000 would-be spectators were shut out of the 50,000 capacity Colombes stadium for the 1923 France-England match. Moreover, the game saw its popularity reflected in contexts as diverse as the radio, which broadcast its first live match commentary in 1923; the music-hall, where Maurice Chevalier sang 'La Marche du Rugby'; the cinema, in the form of a 1928 film entitled *La Grande Passion*; and even male fashion, with the general adoption across France of the *béret basque*, as popularized by the adventurously attacking players of the Aviron Bayonnais club over the previous decade (Nicaud, 1992: pp. 46-7 *et passim*). The game also significantly featured as an official competition sport in the 1924 Paris Olympic Games.

As suggested above, the later 1920s and the whole of the 1930s represented a period of crisis for French rugby football as a whole, with problems arising as a direct result of the game's dramatic success. In the words of Augustin and Garrigou, the rapid popularization and democratization of rugby in this period constitutes "un cas particulièrement net d'une mutation de signification sociale passant d'une sociabilité aristocratique à une sociabilité communautaire" [a particularly clear case of a shift in social signification away from an aristocratic model of sociability and towards a community-based one] (1985: p. 9). The linked problems of *amateurisme marron* (shamateurism) and the so-called *rugby de muerte* which together came to characterize championship games, particularly in the Languedoc, were dealt with in a 'pragmatic' fashion by the French rugby authorities, up to and including the FFR, which proved unable or unwilling to intervene to restore order.

The violent confrontations between clubs in the South-East at this time may not have achieved the abiding notoriety of such brutal South-Western clashes as Carcassonne-Toulouse 1927, Lézignan-Béziers 1929, Quillan-Perpignan 1929, but there can be little doubt that that they reflected similar pressures within the game. The LOU-FCL derby in the 1929-30 season is a case in point, and was dominated by exchanges of insults and blows between the players. Such was the animosity between the two clubs that the LOU team refused to use the changing rooms at the FCL's Stade de la Plaine, changing instead in a public bathhouse in the city centre and travelling to the ground in a specially hired bus (Nicaud, 1992: p. 74). The newspaper evidence provided by the *Lyon-Sport* newspaper of 22 November 1929 includes a photograph of punches being thrown in what was a charged atmosphere heightened by systematic poaching between the two clubs and the importation of South-Western stars, especially Catalans, who were particularly highly prized on the rugby market, to the FCL.

With the FCL's decision in 1931 to join the Union Française de Rugby Amateur (UFRA) when it split from the FFR in an ultimately futile bid at aristocratic resistance to unstoppable pressures within the newly democratized game, contact between the two clubs was broken off. The LOU remained faithful to the FFR and would be rewarded by becoming the dominant Lyon club after the period of internal schism and international isolation had ended in 1945. Yet rugby union's hitherto pre-eminent position in Lyon as a popular sporting spectacle would increasingly be challenged during the sport's period of national weakness in the 1930s: first by rugby league, which, like basketball in more recent years, was to prove particularly popular in the Villeurbanne municipality of the Lyon conurbation, as well as in neighbouring industrial towns like Roanne; then by association football, in the form of the Olympique Lyonnais professional club. The Vichy administration's ideological opposition to professional sport would see rugby league suppressed and football reduced, while the regional rugby union committee organized 'veillées du rugby' which combined rugby with camping trips and the systematic inculcation of pro-Pétainist sentiments. The fact that the majority of the Lyonnais administrative committee remained untouched by post-war political purges, and this in the city which Jean Moulin had made the centre of the internal French resistance to Nazi occupation, may help to explain the startling decision of the FCL, *le doyen* of Lyon rugby union, to go over lock, stock, and barrel to rugby league in 1946.

Rugby in Lyon: *en marge de l'Ovalie*, 1945-1995

The decline of Lyon rugby in the post-war period may be measured in a number of ways. One of the most revealing is by contrasting the treatment accorded to local newspapers to rugby and football before and after World War II. Compare for instance *Lyon-Sport*'s juxtaposition in 1930 under the headline "Pauvre Football" of an overflowing championship rugby match between the FCL and Bègles-Bordeaux and a virtually deserted encounter between the FCL and Marseille in the French FA Cup, with Jean Nicaud's criticism of the Lyon press's own increasingly favourable treatment of soccer and rugby league (with their more straightforward championship structures) by the later 1940s (Nicaud, 1992: pp. 74-5 & 118).

An alternative indicator is the inability of the LOU, the city's one remaining senior club, in spite of massive recruitment drives within France in the 1940s and 1950s, and the importation of New Zealanders and South Africans like Chris Laidlaw, Bob Burgess and Richard Loe in the 1970s and 1980s, to achieve durable success on the national stage. In the 1949-50 season the LOU had the third highest gate receipts in France, after the Racing Club de France and Toulouse, and in 1982-3 the club were the runners-up in the national championship, defeated only by the unstoppable AS Béziers. However, these real achievements were the high points in a steady decline both on the pitch and off it; the end of an era symbolized by the death in 1977 of Louis Pradel, more familiarly known as "Zizi", who as an ex-FCL player and mayor of Lyon had personally incarnated the Gaullist link with rugby in much the same way that Chaban-Delmas continued to do in Bordeaux. Henceforth, the banner of South-Eastern rugby would have to be borne by such isolated outposts as Grenoble, La Voulte, Toulon, and, most recently, Bourgoin-Jallieu. In Lyon, the game is now simply one of many minority sports competing for players and spectators in the increasingly fragmented leisure market.

Conclusion

The foregoing sketch of the evolution of rugby in the South-East of France, and specifically in the Lyon conurbation, tends to reinforce the initial impression of the sport's 'inessential' role in local popular culture; this in marked contrast to the centrality of the sport in the leisure, imaginative life, and particularly the festive rituals of the South-West. However, this brief survey has also hinted at unresolved tensions within French rugby as a whole which threaten its continued cultural dominance even within its South-Western heartland. In particular, the fragmentation of traditional communities, the collapse of established social hierarchies (including especially those based on gender), and, perhaps above all, the privatization of leisure mean that this privileged site of individual and communal self-definition is currently fraught with conflict. Indeed, the capacity of French rugby durably to reconcile its South-Western regional dynamism, its televisually mediated national image, and its international commercial aspirations in the brave new world of globalized sporting practices and practitioners remains to be seen.

References

Abellio, R. (1983) 'Le rugby et la maîtrise du temps', *Cahiers Raymond Abellio* No. 1 (November): pp. 75-6.

Barnoud, R. (n.d.) *Quel drôle de ballon!* Lyon: A. Rey.

Augustin, J.-P. (1987) 'L'étonnante implantation du rugby dans le Midi', *Midi* No. 4: pp. 3-12.

Augustin, J.-P. and Bodis, J.-P. (1994) *Rugby en Aquitaine: Histoire d'une rencontre.* Bordeaux: Centre Régional des Lettres d'Aquitaine & Eds. Aubéron.

Augustin, J.-P. and Garrigou, A. (1985) *Le Rugby démêlé: Essai sur les Associations Sportives, le Pouvoir et les Notables.* Bordeaux: Le Mascaret.

Bodis, J.-P. (1987) *Histoire mondiale du rugby.* Toulouse: Bibliothèque Historique Privat.

Bourdieu, P. (1984) *Distinction: A social critique of the judgement of taste.* London: Routledge & Kegan Paul. Translated by Richard Nice. Originally published in 1979 as *La Distinction: critique sociale du jugement.* Paris: Minuit.

Callède, J.-P. (1987) *L'Esprit sportif: Essai sur le développement associatif de la culture sportive.* Bordeaux: Presses Universitaires de Bordeaux.

Callède, J.-P. (1993) *Histoire du sport en France: Du Stade Bordelais au SBUC, 1889-1939.* Bordeaux: Eds. de la Maison des Sciences de l'Homme d'Aquitaine.

Driès, R. (1988) *100 ans de rugby en France: Un film à la gloire du sport roi.* (Video)

Holt, R. (1981) *Sport and society in modern France.* London: Macmillan.

Nicaud, J. (1992) *100 ans de rugby régional.* Bourg-en-Bresse: Les Eds. de la Taillanderie.

Pociello, C. (1983) *Le Rugby ou la guerre des styles.* Paris: Métaillé.